Redreaming America

SUNY series in Latin American and Iberian Thought and Culture

Jorge J. E. Gracia and Rosemary Geisdorfer Feal, editors

Redreaming America

Toward a Bilingual American Culture

DEBRA A. CASTILLO

State University of New York Press

Published by
State University of New York Press, Albany

Printed in the United States of America

For information, address State University of New York Press, Albany, NY
www.sunypress.edu

Production by Judith Block
Marketing by Anne M. Valentine

Library of Congress Cataloging-in-Publication Data

Castillo, Debra A.
Redreaming America : toward a bilingual American culture / Debra A. Castillo.
p. cm. — (SUNY series in Latin American and Iberian thought and culture)
Includes bibliographical references (p.) and index.
ISBN 978-0-7914-6297-3 (alk paper)—ISBN 978-0-7914-6298-0 (pb : alk paper)
1. American literature—Hispanic American authors—History and criticism. 2. Hispanic American literature (Spanish)—History and criticism. 3. Hispanic Americans—Intellectual life. 4. Hispanic Americans in literature. 5. Hispanic Americans—Language. 6. Bilingualism—United States. I. Title. II. Series.

PS153.H56C37 2004
810.9'868—dc22 2004042988

10 9 8 7 6 5 4 3 2 1

Para mis hijos, Carlos y Melissa:

brought up entre dos culturas, con un Spanglish impecable.

Contents

chapter one

Introduction: El Boom Latino

HOT SAUCE OVERTOOK CATSUP as the condiment of choice and McDonald's was serving breakfast burritos long before the media hype around Jennifer Lopez, Salma Hayek, Benicio del Toro, and Enrique Iglesias helped the mainstream United States define the "Latin Boom" in popular culture.[1] This salsa is also spicing up mainstream speech patterns. Nowadays, says John Lipski, "all Americans are immersed in a morass of what the anthropologist Jane Hill has called 'junk Spanish'—for example, the menu items at Tex-Mex restaurants . . . that juxtapose real and invented Spanish words with total disregard for grammatical concord and semantic coherence, linguistic niceties implied to be as optional as the little packages of salsa that come with our ready-made tacos" (1249). Nevertheless, the latest census statistics sparked widespread excitement and worry, as even the admitted undercount clearly indicated that the previously projected growth in the Latino/a population in the United States fell far short of the recorded numbers. Whether or not the Latin Boom is a mere marketing ploy, the demographics are real. The first draft of the 2000 census cites 35.3 million Latino/as in the United States, and we need to note that this number does not include the 3.8 million U.S. citizens who are residents of Puerto Rico. Later press releases have revised that figure up to 37 million, and these numbers only partially account for the estimated 7 million undocumented immigrants, who have good reason to evade government scrutiny. Thus, even by the most conservative estimate, there are now over 40 million Latino/as in U.S. territory.[2] These astonishingly high numbers ground arguments like those of Juan Gonzalez when he writes trenchantly, "this demographic shift is so massive it is transforming the ethnic composition of this country and challenging key aspects of its accepted national identity, language, culture, and official history, a seismic social change that caught the power structures and institutions of

U.S. society unprepared" (xi–xii). It is perhaps too easy to merely dismiss popular culture's celebration of *latinidad* with the same reflexive gesture we often use to decry reactionary warnings about the browning of America. Gonzalez's challenge, however, is to think differently—ultimately, to think biculturally.

Rey Chow summarizes the conundrum of cross-cultural dialogue in her elegant reading of Derrida's analogy to Chinese writing in his early book, *Of Grammatology*, which she finds productively symptomatic of many other less subtly argued scholarly positions. Chow notes that "Derrida's move to read across cultures . . . involves a moment in which representation becomes, wittingly or unwittingly, stereotyping, a moment in which the other is transformed into a recycled cliché." What is important to note, however, is that Chow, along with Derrida, not only acknowledges that stereotypes are simplistic—an all-too-obvious conclusion. She argues along with the French philosopher that they are also enabling fictions that allow theoretical formulations to take shape, that these clichés are always and everywhere absolutely essential to group relations and cannot be summarily dismissed: "The point, in other words, is not simply to repudiate stereotypes and pretend that we can get rid of them . . . , but also to recognize in the act of stereotyping . . . a fundamental signifying or representational process with real theoretical and political consequences" (70–71). Reading together Chow and Gonzalez offers us an important warning. The conjunction of these two thinkers suggests that the latter's implicit call for a positioned cultural critique, unless prudently and subtly tended with an eye to unavoidable consequences, could potentially devolve into a collision of each culture's worst stereotypes about the other rather than an encounter among various local knowledges with real transformatory effects in the nation's sense of itself. Along parallel lines, Chow's important caveat about the power and inevitability of stereotype could fall into the kind of simplistic reading she would deplore unless rigorous structures of critical exegesis are vigilantly tended.

Several of the recent discussions about Latino/a cultures in the United States worry about precisely this problem. Javier Campos, for instance, reflects that the so-called Latin Boom in the United States is deeply imbued with such clichéd and frequently erroneous understandings, which from both sides of the U.S./Latin America divide look like exoticized projections of expelled local desires. Campos traces the stereotypes to various sources: on the U.S. side, the 1920s fascination with Caribbean music on the East Coast, the reprocessing of that image in Hollywood films, the invention of the cowboy from disconnected bits of Mexican-Southwest U.S. vaquero culture, the partial knowledge brought back to the United States by artists, writers, and photographers who roamed the exotic South in search of images and texts.[3] From the South he cites a plethora of Mexican movies and the stereotypes that Latin American writers have promulgated about the United States after short stays in this country, generally as a land of abundant resources and absurdly inept inhabitants (81–82). By staying on only one side of the national borders, studies tend to be self-limiting and often misleadingly incomplete. There is certainly something interesting to be said about the relation, for example, among vaquero culture, Hollywood cowboy flicks, and Mexican movies from the 1950s, or Carmen Miranda, the salsa scene in New York, and Caribbean immigration; or alternatively, the United States and Latin American variations on the theme of the Ugly American. Campos's specific worry, however, is that uninflected stereotypes too often pass for complete knowledge about Latino cultures.

He is not alone in his concern; this is a critique raised in other contexts with respect, for example, to John Leguizamo's highly successful, controversial "Mambo Mouth," "Spicorama," and "Freak" performances. Leguizamo is widely recognized as a brilliant comedian by mainstream press, and his work is often celebrated in Latino/a circles as well. Yet, despite the recognition of his talent in alluding to and signifying on a variety of different Latino/a "types," his very use of these familiar figures raises a concern among some Latino/a scholars and journalists as well, one often articulated as a fear that his mordant satire would be misread by uninformed gringos as reflecting eternal verities of Latino culture. As Moya notes, "He clearly intends for his audience to identify him as 'Latino' " (248), yet the question remains of how "Latino" is deployed strategically in both mainstream and Latino/a cultures, and how well the putative audience understands and appreciates humor built upon stigmatized ethnic identities. In a more general sense, the question remains, as many scholars have already intuited, of how to frame a rigorous critique in the absence of ground on which to stand, or when the choice of a particular grounding discourse must always be taken in consciousness of its incompleteness, its flaws, and its unwelcome political and social consequences.

When we turn from popular to literary culture, there is also a long and deep history of looking at the South from a northern perspective and vice versa that might well serve as helpful points of departure to thinking through the further implications of this dilemma. Even ignoring colonial-period writings, there is an impressive corpus of works by recent and contemporary Anglo-American and European authors who have traveled to Latin America to seek objects of knowledge, exotic or mundane, as Paz-Soldán and Fuguet mention in the introduction to their recent volume of U.S.-based voices in Spanish (17). Paz-Soldán and Fuguet state tendentiously that "no se puede hablar de Latinoamérica sin incluir a los Estados Unidos. Y no se puede concebir a los Estados Unidos sin necesariamente pensar en América Latina" [it is not possible to talk about Latin America without including the United States. And it is not possible to conceive of the United States without necessarily thinking about Latin America] (19). Néstor García Canclini agrees. In his *Latinoamericanos buscando lugar en este siglo* he writes, "la condición actual de América latina desborda su territorio. . . . América latina no está completa en América Latina. Su imagen le llega de espejos diseminados en el archipiélago de las migraciones" [The current condition of Latin America overflows its territory. . . . Latin America is not complete in Latin America. Its image arrives back from mirrors disseminated in the archipelago of migration] (12, 19). To take just one instance from another scholarly work that reflects on this cross-fertilization: Dewey Wayne Gunn identifies more than 450 novels, plays, and narrative poems on Mexico published between 1805 and 1973 by British and U.S. writers in his book on that topic. Similarly, Mexican critic José Joaquín Blanco explores the famous obsession with indigenous Mexico in writers like Artaud or Bataille, who with a tourist's Spanish, rudimentary and secondhand anthropological concepts, no knowledge of Mexican history, and no understanding of indigenous languages, imagine and create a Mexico that fits their preconceived notions (26). Likewise, there is a significant body of Latin American work looking at the North with a Southern perspective. Paz-Soldán and Fuguet list some of the most well-known names in their essay, "El monstruo come (y baila) salsa" [The Monster Eats (and Dances) Salsa]: Puig, Fuentes, Valenzuela, Donoso, Allende, Skármeta, and so on (17–18). Along more developed lines of analysis, scholars like Alberto Ledesma and Maria Herrera-Sobek have traced a prolific body of Mexican narratives about life in the United States, falling into at least two well-represented subgenres: the academic narrative (which would include writers like José Agustín and Gustavo Sainz) and the *bracero* novel (Spota, Becerra González, Topete, Oropeza). Such North-South dialogues (or parallel monologues) need to be read together, and read with the work by U.S.-based Latino writers from the many cultures and generations of *latinidad* in this country.

In its most general sense, as Mike Davis argues, "the idea of the Latino is fertile precisely because it is problematic." Here, Davis quite rightly makes a helpful distinction between the too-often essentializing discourse of identity, "the Latino," and the intellectual construct of what he calls an "idea." This "idea of the Latino" signals nodes where the discourse of culture is articulated in ways other than through the traditional dichotomy of center versus periphery, even as some of the most direct effects of the political structuration of nation-states play themselves out on the very material Latino/a body. Davis points out how the crossover effect between nations and cultures works in both directions: "It complicates how Latin Americans think of themselves now that constant migration between American border zones makes it hard to demarcate between Latinos and Latin America. . . . Conversely, the influx of Latin Americans affects historical Latino groups, inching them closer to national roots and requiring greater levels of Spanish competence" (xv–xvi).

Doris Sommer explores a related issue in her lucid analysis of the title of Puerto Rican poet Tato Laviera's collection *AmeRícan,* where the poet's sensibility to the slight variations between what is written and what is heard, in Spanish and in English, opens onto a powerful implicit indictment of narrowly nationalist cultural politics. Laviera, she writes, is an artist who succinctly condenses this impossibility of demarcation in a single word:

> His genius is to skip a beat, to unravel a seamless label by reading the English sign for America with an eye for Spanish. In Spanish this country looks like "Ameríca," because without an accent on the "e" to give the word an irregular stress, a default, unwritten stress falls on the "i." Laviera's hypercorrection displaces the logic of diacritical marks from one language to another and performs a time lag of translation. The alleged omission of an accent mark is an opportunity to read the country in syncopation as AmeRíca, a time-lagged sound whose sign reforms that country's look too. (301)

For Sommer, as for Laviera, these subtle transformations speak to and within a bilingual context, where the stumble of the poet's syncopated language, as well as the accent mark, capitalize on the interplay between the homey and the defamiliarized versions of the word, which in English typically refers to a country and in Spanish a continent. The stumble and catch of the hypercorrected awkwardness, says Sommer, playing between languages in her turn and shifting from homey English to très chic Français, transforms what "is just a word into a *mot juste* in Spanglish" (301). In this manner, the unauthorized mixture also hints at the way language politics submerge the dissonant and strange into a particular kind of valued order: here, the kind of privilege that is accorded alterity in some of the most dominant theoretical commentaries on a globalized, postmodern culture. And yet, of course, by writing English with an eye to Spanish, by writing AmeRíca as a syncopated, Spanglishized nation, Laviera also marks the primacy of the English-speaking dominant culture's perspective that underlies his meaningful distortion of it.

This syncopation, that in the specific sense we can associate with interlingual poets like Laviera, in a broader sense hints at a troubling dislocation, what we might see as an infinitesimal disturbance in the grammaticality of the literary-cultural enterprise as it currently exists. This disturbance, as Sommer hints, also evokes a specific kind of musical form, the measure of an interval between two sounds. "The interval between two simultaneously sounded tones," says Reingard Nethersole, "is perceived within the context of production as dissonance, and hence requires mediation" (53). Laviera's dislocation is so evocative in part because it reminds us of the fractures we see, or hope to create, in the institution's monolithic face, the fault lines that disturb its accepted verities, the institution's dissonances, and the potential for mediation. Indeed, in recent scholarship, metaphors such as "syncopation," "dislocation," "fractures," "dissonance," and "gaps" appear consistently and symptomatically in the discussion of such issues.

Thus, for instance, Samuel Weber too addresses the question of mediation and the problem of a dissonance or dislocation in his recent work on the U.S. culture theory enterprise. He has pointed out that in the U.S. academic system, "global," disturbingly, has become "globular," in the sense of self-containment: not the planet, but a bubble. He discusses the irony in the reduction of foreign language instruction in U.S. universities precisely at the same time as globalization has become the new buzzword in scholarly work. "This suggests," he adds, "that from an American point of view, at least, 'globalization' is equivalent with 'monolingual' " (16). In the area of literary and cultural study, analogously, he argues that "though the glamour names of theory remain French, the mechanisms of mediation have increasingly become American" (5). For Samuel Weber, as for J. Hillis Miller and other scholars who worry about the current state of theoretical work in this country, high theory, those names to reckon with, seems foreign only in its originary dislocation from the United States, in the slight strangeness that still attaints texts by and large read in English, commented upon in English, and treated as part of the U.S. monolingual enterprise. The globular becomes The Blob, reaching out to engulf its neighbors until it reaches a point of self-destruction.[4] Throwing Spanish into this mix, as Laviera does, as Sommer does, reinforces another interval and a different mediation, hiccupping between two languages at home, strange to each other but neither of them foreign.

Scholars over the years have often commented on the very different nature of the privileges of the strong and the strategies of the weak that condition so many of the (non)exchanges between the United States and Latino/a America. Eduardo Mendieta, for example, talks about the often narrow and parochial perspectives of some of this country's most well-known and respected scholars; of one such individual, he notes: "his selection leaves the bitter impression that he only reads his friends, and a small group of critics, or a very narrow spectrum of magazines and journals" (229). In contrast, like Laviera, like Sommer, no scholar or thinker from Latino/a America can ignore the U.S. dominant society or speak about an "Otherness" by way of the highly abstract discursive practice that is all too frequently deployed with respect to Latino/a America. For Latino/as and Latin Americans, their knowledge of the dominant culture's Otherness can be incomplete, but it cannot be blank. In contrast, in the analogous context, U.S. dominant culture has, and feels no compunction about exercising, the privilege of ignorance. As Thomas Foster comments in his study of Gómez Peña, "the Chicano virtual reality machine makes visible the double experience of having a body that is too definitely marked, too easily read, but that for that reason does not register to (Anglo) others as needing any interpretive attention" (63). Curiously enough, and at the same time, as Pratt has noted, Anglo culture has a propensity not only to stereotype the Other's outcast alterity, but to fetishize it as exotic and attractive in contrast with Anglo America's own blankness: "asked to define or describe their culture . . . white American students often react with pain and anger, for they tend to know themselves as a people without culture" ("Daring to Dream" 13).

Between these two easily cast types emerge understandings of a U.S. imaginary seen differently, seen as the heterogeneous grouping of a multiplicity of national origins and ethnicities, of highly diverse peoples and identities. "What is different here (and a possible challenge to traditional American literary historiography)," say Moya and Saldívar in their elaboration of a similar project, "is our proposal to shift the tradition enough that it can respond to a transnational framework . . . that yokes together North and South America instead of New England and England" (2). Like J. Hillis Miller, who sees in the pedagogical challenge of studying U.S. literature and culture in its multilingual complexity a possibility for reinvigorating a moribund theory, Moya and Saldívar too ask us to rethink the national subject as postnational, transnational, as a displaced subject, always in process. Far from a utopian project, however, both Miller and Moya and Saldívar stress that their work aims in precisely the opposite direction: to deconstruct the uncritical and overly celebratory narrative of U.S. history and culture, and "open up the conversation to alternative worldviews and frameworks" (Moya and Saldívar 6). This conversation, it almost goes without saying, has a substantial theoretical as well as political and pedagogical edge. And yet, the question remains, how does one more adequately document the transnational subject in process?

In mainstream social science research, there is a widespread agreement that all identity, including ethnic identity, is instrumental in nature—that is, it is a means to certain ends whether those ends can be defined as state-sponsored or as social-situational (Jones-Correa 110). For Jones-Correa, nevertheless, this instrumental theory of identity, while it serves both political and social purposes, does not fully capture the past constraints and present anxieties of the felt in-betweenness and lack of belonging that often becomes the most salient complaint of new Latino/as caught among multiple and conflicting identities, locked in a kind of double differentiation from whatever the home culture is described to be at a given moment (11). Strategic choices, internalized constraints, and historical and cultural factors all affect the degree to which individuals reinforce or resist identity claims made on their behalf. The result is often a recurrence of simplistic, unreflective stereotypes without a counterbalancing critique of knowledge.

In the case of the new Latino/as, that first-generation immigrant population, the potentiality for misunderstanding multiplies vertiginously. Not only does the new Latino/a have to take into account stereotypes by and about Latino/as in the United States, and stereotypes by and about non-Latino/a U.S. residents, s/he also has to deal with the baggage carried from Latin America, and the implications of that baggage in terms of U.S. cultural politics around issues of ethnicity, race, assimilation, bilingualism, international hemispheric relations, and so on. This is not a trivial problem, nor is it a hidden one. Demographically, just under one half of all Latino/as in the United States are first-generation immigrants (Jones-Correa 2). This fact, numerous social scientists suggest, has deep implications for the study of Latino/as in this country, who have traditionally been seen only from the perspective of a U.S. minoritized population. Equally important, argue scholars like Gonzalez and Jones-Correa, a corrective to traditional U.S. understandings of old and new Latino/as would include a perspective derived from Latin America. Unfortunately, says Gonzalez, too often, recognized Latino/a writers take on the task of explaining their stories and their cultures solely within a U.S. context, and solely to a dominant-culture reader, with the result that these narratives "fall into what I call the safari approach, geared strictly to an Anglo audience, with the author as guide and interpreter to the natives to be encountered along the way. . . . Few attempt to understand our hemisphere *as one New World, north and south*" (xvii–xviii). Gonzalez, like Jones-Correa and other prominent Latino social scientists, argues for a nuanced approach that would provide an important corrective to the exoticized Latino/a image too often promulgated and even self-promoted. This more balanced approach, in their view, has to include a wider hemispheric component.

Literary historian Kirsten Silva Gruesz would agree. In her analysis of Latino/a writers from the nineteenth century, she notes that not only are the authors bicultural, but also their tools of analysis are extranational rather than indigenous. Thus, analyses of their work that derive from a single perspective are not only insufficient but actually distorting. The writers that most interest her are those who move fluidly between cultural systems: "the writers most aware of this paradox, most creative and conscientious in their responses to it, are often those who resist identification by nationality" (15). The critic, she argues, must be similarly fluid. Her observations about the complex relations of Latin American immigrant writers to the U.S. contact zones they inhabit provide one of the most important recent analyses of the continuing contributions of Latino/as to shaping the U.S. national imaginary.

While the specific cultural and geographical sites in the United States' contact zones provide one of the most richly mined areas for study, a second look at these sites would also pay closer attention to the language communities and discourse flows independently of political borders. Influential Mexican culture critic Carlos Monsiváis has for years been tracking the Mexican middle-class phenomenon of what he calls the "Chicanization" of Mexican popular culture under influence from CNN and U.S. movies, U.S. rock and hip-hop musical forms, and the pressures of the English language. In a recent conference presentation, quoted by the online news service Notimex, Monsiváis developed this discussion in what is for him unusually negatively valenced terms. In a panoramic overview of contemporary Mexican letters titled "Cultura y globalización en América del Norte: Desafíos para el siglo XXI," Monsiváis worries that "la introducción del espanglish inevitable y avasallante, obliga a que se desvanezca en las nuevas generaciones el sonido prestigioso y clásico del idioma" [the inevitable and overwhelming introduction of Spanish will cause the wearing away for the younger generations of the prestigious and classic sound of the language], and he expresses his deep concern that "jóvenes incapaces de memorizar un soneto, se saben al detalle la letra de las canciones de los Backstreet Boys, y por supuesto, de los Beatles y The Rolling Stones" [young people are unable to memorize a sonnet but they know by heart the lyrics to songs by the Backstreet Boys, and of course the Beatles and the Rolling Stones] (Notimex, June 10, 2001).

Perhaps the most surprising element in this comment is its source. While *ubi sunt* laments for past literary and linguistic glories are a well-established part of the academic mode, Carlos Monsiváis has more typically been celebrated for his sympathetic and amusing commentaries on the foibles of Mexican popular culture, as a defender of the vitality of cultural mixing rather than its retrograde opponent. This shift in Monsiváis from describing Chicanization to decrying Spanglish seems to me symptomatic of a significant body of commentary from highly educated, polylingual representatives of Latin America's most exclusive cultural circles, often reflecting an unproblematized age and social-class bias that is so obvious as to require no further commentary.

This bias is not worth critiquing on its own grounds, except insofar as it offers a clear point of entry into the procedures of a specific storytelling discourse that has consequences for theoretical elaborations and that offers us insights into institutional practices and investments with respect not only to Backstreet Boys fans in Mexico but also to the young urban writers of the current generation in Latin America, where identity expresses itself in a hyperinternational cosmopolitan awareness, and who often, like the transnational nineteenth-century writers in Gruesz's study, move with intellectual and creative fluidity between the United States and their countries of origin. Perhaps unsurprisingly, a significant number of these up-and-coming writers are rejecting as stale the localized modalities of the Latin Boom, and finding inspiration in U.S./international popular culture, a knowledge anchored in their own first-generation experience in the United States—writers like Jaime Bayly (Peru), Alberto Fuguet (Chile), Ilan Stavans (Mexico), and Mayra Santos-Febres (Puerto Rico), to name just a few.

Culturally, the new Latino/as, suggests Ricardo Armijo in an unpublished manuscript, are currently caught between the expectations arising from the much-hyped Latino boom in the U.S. media on the one hand, and the well-established Latin American literary boom of the 1960s on the other. Armijo considers the key question to be "¿Cómo los escritores hispanoparlantes de los Estados Unidos podemos abordar nuestra realidad estadounidense si no tenemos una limitación nacional? ¿Cómo podemos imaginar la realidad que nos rodea cuando nuestro argumento básico es aquél que dice que venimos de otro lugar, de otra realidad?" [How can Spanish-speaking writers of the United States take account of our U.S. reality if we do not have a national boundary? How can we imagine the reality that surrounds us when our basic narrative is that which tells us that we come from another place, another reality?] (1). In raising this question, Armijo signals the unavoidable crisis arising whenever we put "politics" and "knowledge" together in the same theoretical structure: knowledge claims are inevitably embedded in a complex web of contested meanings and can only be verified through complicity with an exclusionary system that defines an inside and an outside, a really real and an "other" reality that lies outside the established boundaries.

Armijo also points to a more knotty problem, one that is fraught in the United States because of the long-standing historical minefields of social disturbance around ethnic identity issues. Who is a Latino/a? Who or what defines "real" *latinidad*? Or, as Palumbo-Liu perceptively asks with respect to Asian Americans, "what kinds of historical memory enables certain claims and disables others?" (218), and later, "What is the nature of the various 'collectivities' that might vie for primacy in our recollective processes? How does recourse to such collectivities inevitably bracket out other modes of identification? . . . [W]hat is the nature of memory in a transnational or cross-cultural situation?" (298). Variants of these questions have been asked and answered in charged language by scholars and activists of many persuasions, and seem more urgent in certain circles due both to expanding first-generation populations, and, for other reasons, to the extensive mixed-ethnicity second-plus-generation cohort. Such identitarian claims are often expressed in tense exchanges between established Latino/as and newer arrivals, who have sometimes found themselves accused of being usurpers, frauds, not "real." In one of his studies, Bruce-Novoa ponders the provocative question, "At what point can an immigrant Mexican writer be considered a Chicano?" ("Chicano Literary Space" 174), and Hector Calderón asks the similar question, "Are Mexican writers and expatriates traveling through or living in Texas and California to be included as Chicano writers?" (103). Similar questions are frequently posed about every conceivable national-origin individual. Should undocumented workers be included? Cubans who still consider themselves as "in exile" after forty years in the United States? How to resolve the tensions about Puerto Rico? If an *indio* from Guatemala qualifies as Latino, how about a Jew from Argentina?

Code switching and the use of Spanglish is also a hotly debated issue in U.S. Latino/a circles, but I would argue that the perspective goes beyond narrow concerns about the decline of the poetic range of the language in the mouths of undereducated adolescents that exercises Carlos Monsiváis. Rather than bemoaning the impoverishment of fine classical Spanish, many of the new Latino/a writers find in the rhythms of the two languages rubbing against each other an exciting and vital potentiality for new poetic expression. Tato Laviera's poetry provides one such index of vitality. Similarly, the contributors to the recent post-McOndo Alfaguara volume *Se habla español*,[5] while consistently functioning within the South to North view of first-generation Latinos in their encounters with the United States, often punctuate their narratives with loan blends or English words and phrases that more accurately capture the rich in-betweenness of their characters' experiences. Some of the writers in the collection go farther than others: Gustavo Escanlar's entertaining "Pequeño diccionario Spanglish ilustrado" [Brief Illustrated Spanglish Dictionary] in the opening pages of the volume offers perceptive, and often bitterly estranging, insights on the intersection of various new and established Latino communities punctuated by key words in Spanglish: *bacunclínear, chatear, flipar.* The volume closes with the aggressive Spanglish of Giannina Braschi's "Blow-Up," and the jangling discords of her code-switching narrator perfectly match the exasperated exchanges between two people whose dysfunctional relationship is dissolving in a flood of petty accusations: "¿dónde está el tapón de mi botella de agua? Tú no sabes que le entran germs, pierde el fizz, y no me gusta que el agua huela como tu chicken curry sandwich, ésta ya no sirve. . . ." (37).[6]

The push and pull of the interlingual voice is at the very heart of these texts, as, in a more general sense, the punctuation of one language by another serves as a political and poetic device. Such texts defy translation into either of their constituent parts in a particularly strong sense, for to translate such performative utterances into either Spanish or English would be to distort them into meaninglessness, to subject them to a kind of linguistic assimilation and erasure. Such translations could speak to the reader only in a very limited sense, since they would inextricably dislocate the doubleness of the language into an unacceptable version of the monolinguism against which these writers are defining their entire poetics.

This book has opened with reference to some of the familiar myths and stories we tell each other about Others. Of these tales, the story of immigration is itself one of the principal among U.S. national myths (we're all immigrants in this country), but in the most familiar (Anglo) versions of this story, immigration is celebrated in the abstract rather than explored in the particular. Also, of course, it is worth underlining that while—stereotypically—we're all immigrants (except for the Native Americans, it goes without saying, runs the PC footnote), some immigrants are clearly more "American" than others (and, strangely enough, Native Americans seem the most "foreign" of all). Nevertheless, for many Americans of whatever national origin, their relation to the United States, whether it is a story of arrival or a story of conquest, is a traumatic one, certainly not the smooth transition into American Dream narrative that too many elementary school history books still describe as a fundamental sequel to the equally problematic myth of a melting pot initiation.

A few years before his death, Michel de Certeau proposed, for the purpose of debate, that all theory rests inescapably upon a bedrock of story, that, in fact, storytelling necessarily defines the shape of all theoretical work:

> 1. Procedures are not merely the objects of a theory. They organize the very construction of theory itself. . . .
>
> 2. In order to clarify the relationship of theory with those procedures that produce it as well as those that are its

> objects of study, the most relevant way would be a *storytelling discourse*. . . . Stories appear slowly as the work of displacements, relating to a logic of metonomy. Is it not then time to recognize the theoretical legitimacy of narrative, which is then to be looked upon not as some ineradicable remnant (or remnant still to be eradicated) but rather as a necessary form for a theory of practices? (192)

I would like to propose that not only does theory rest upon a body of narrative, but that storytelling offers us a particularly valuable theoretical methodology for exploring some of the dilemmas that have engaged us here. Story and stereotype become, then, my two most important tools, and I deploy them throughout this text gingerly, and I hope respectfully, with full knowledge of their seductive and simplifying potential, trying to parse out the enabling fictions and wrest them from a more unwitting tropic(alized) deployment.[7]

Thus, I have organized this book as something like a story about immigration. It begins with "Origins;" a chapter in which I look at early struggles with how to define an American (as opposed to European) self in two writers who use the conquest of Mexico as a metaphorical scaffolding: Robert Montgomery Bird (the only gringo in this study), and the anonymously published *Jicoténcal,* whose author was one of two Cuban writers living in Philadelphia in the early decades of the nineteenth century. This story continues with an alternative encounter with cultural otherness through the image of "crossing," in a chapter where I explore the stories of coming into contact with the United States in Ana Lydia Vega (Puerto Rico), Eduardo González Viaña (Peru), Carlos Fuentes, and Margarita Oropeza (Mexico). Crossing, of course, is followed by arrival, and in the stories of arrival I focus particularly on the strategic feminization of the Other culture as a way of dealing with cultural dissonance. The authors that help me think through this issue are Ariel Dorfman (Chile), Boris Salazar (Colombia), Gustavo Sainz (Mexico), and Sonia Rivera-Valdés (Cuba). In the final stage of this journey, I focus on the language games played by established Latino/as, exploring their self-conscious appeals to a cultural and linguistic doubleness—Rolando Hinojosa Smith (Texas), Dolores Prida (Cuba), and Giannina Braschi (Puerto Rico)—before closing the book with some thoughts on U.S. curricular practice.

The basic intent of this project is to take pursue an inquiry into the cultural and linguistic dissonances that Spanish in the United States creates. I focus primarily on the first-generation new Latino/as who choose to write in Spanish as a particularly understudied group of authors, in contrast with the more established second-plus-generation cohort, who often choose to write in English and whose literary and theoretical work has been more assimilated into the U.S. academy. My contention is that the new Latino/as serve as important markers to help understand how the topography of literary study has come to its current state of uneasy disruption. In this respect, my project echoes a discussion that has been occurring in U.S. American studies in the United States at the theoretical level for twenty years concerning the shape of what we understand to be U.S. literature, that is: what would U.S. literature look like if we included literature from the United States in languages other than English? The study inevitably also entails a parallel question that is only beginning to be asked in U.S. Spanish departments, and has only nervously been hinted at in Latin America: what would Latin American literature look like if we understood the United States to be a Latin American country and took seriously the work by U.S. Latino/as with respect to what our departments consider the generally accepted hemispheric canon in Spanish? Most important, what are the challenges this shift of perspective poses to our institutional and curricular projects, to our projects of reading and thinking about culture? If we think from the United States as the second largest country in the Hispanic world, we are indeed entering the territory described by Walter Mignolo when he calls for the "reordering of the geopolitics of knowledge" from an unexpected place (93). This meditation seems to me particularly pertinent for those countries with the longest and most intensely intertwined relationship with the United States—Cuba, Puerto Rico, Mexico—and thus writers from these cultural backgrounds are highlighted in this study. I complement these analyses with commentaries on authors from a sampling of other Latin American heritages (Peru, Colombia, Chile), not to be exhaustive, but merely to suggest some of the richnesses of this literary field.

This is the point to take a step forward into this journey, to parse out this conundrum in more detail, focusing particularly on a few aspects in the counterposing discourses that give shape to the theoretical dilemma of the new Latino/a in the United States.

chapter two

Origins: Bird and *Jicoténcal*

IN HIS RECENT and influential book, *Asian/American,* David Palumbo-Liu suggests that one of the most crucial intellectual challenges posed by U.S. minorities to the national self-imagination involves the "substantial and troubling question as to not only their predication into full 'Americanism,' but what, exactly, America is to be" (42). In his further discussions of this conundrum, he admits that he finds it especially helpful to view the hyphenated American's problem "as a vacillating, multidirectional attempt at predication, rather than a teleologically predetermined and irreversible phenomenon" (171). Here Palumbo-Liu exposes a knotty problem that, in the context of this analysis, I will make even more gnarled, so as to take into account both the national (U.S.) and continental reaches of the discussion of "Americanism." I want to look as well at the analogously bifurcated problem of "America's" historical consolidation in both national and continental imaginations and the stigmatized or exalted figure of the minority character in anchoring a critical discursive role in texts both in Spanish and English. To this end, I will focus on three historical novels, two in English, one in Spanish, set in the same time period—that of the conquest of Mexico in 1519—and published within a few years of each other in Philadelphia by a pair of authors who had a high likelihood of having met at least casually in that city in the mid-1820s.

As a first approximation of the problem, we might note that the tacit exclusion of the minority Other from the stereotypical U.S. discourse about itself seemingly solves by skirting many problems about what it is to be "American"; yet, at the same time, this monological view raises another concern. One of the nation's favored constitutive metaphors is that of a democratic and inclusive "melting pot" that welcomes immigrants from all nations in the name of liberty. This imaginary openness to difference immediately falls into conflict with an underlying xenophobia and with a strong contemporary assimilationist ethos. Thus, the United States likes the idea of itself as a gathering place of freedom-loving peoples from many nations, but is deeply concerned when these people's expression of their cultural difference exceeds picturesque folklore. At another level, the erasure of contestatory and polyglot discourse in contemporary U.S. practice infringes deeply upon the nation's preferred ideal image of itself, creating a fundamental dissonance that is seldom addressed with any seriousness.

Furthermore, if the presence of the minority subject in U.S. discourse creates an instability that highlights the inherent contradiction in his/her interpelation into U.S.-America as an "American" citizen, the presence of the Latin American subject, who insists upon an equal claim to a continentally defined "Americanism"—and moreover frequently does so in the context of a U.S.-based and identified Latino/a population's struggles with U.S. dominant culture—reminds us all the more forcefully of the tenuous and contingent nature of such ontological claims. An even further complication, implicitly raised by the novels under analysis in this chapter, concerns the use of idealized indigenous figures to represent the point of origin for discussions of cultural identity that can be variously configured as U.S. dominant culture, U.S. minority, Latin American dominant culture, and Latin American contestatory culture. Finally, in all of these novels one important strand of the conflict hinges upon romantic entanglements between white men and women from another (Moorish, indigenous) ethnicity, implicitly or explicitly placing the hope for future reconciliation in the hands of the mestizo children.

The Philadelphia of the early days of the Republic offers one key site in deciphering this enigma of what America is to be. The early nineteenth century also provides a context for thinking about the ideological stakes in the spatialization of "America" in both national and continental terms, as well as its racialization in narrative structures. With a population of 67,787 according to the 1820 census, Philadelphia was largest city in the still newly consolidating United States.[1] Its fame as a bastion of liberal thought made it, says González Acosta, the "paraíso de conspiradores" in the early part of the nineteenth century (202), and other commentators note the degree to which it was a highly politicized cultural center in a country just recovering from its second war of independence against Great Britain (the War of 1812). With memories of the United States' own wars fresh in the minds of the city's inhabitants, there was a natural and explicit spillover of solidarity with independence fighters in Spanish America whose independence struggles were exactly contemporaneous to their own. Because so many of the United States' important cultural figures were living in

Philadelphia at the time, and took strongly collaborative roles in supporting the nascent Latin American independence movements, the atmosphere of discussion, exchange, and diffusion of information was exceptionally lively.

Philadelphia was well situated for these discussions on other grounds as well. Economic interests were one part of the story; it had the largest Latin American trade of any city in North America at the time. Mexico and Cuba were Philadelphia's top trading partners, so it is not surprising that many Latin Americans followed the shipping routes, cementing social as well as economic ties among these three countries. The city became, understandably, a magnet attracting visitors, scholars, and exiles from many parts of Spanish America, adding a significant and visible immigrant population to the international mix. For example, Mexican emperor Iturbide's widow and children made their home there as of 1824; it was also an attractive location for Caribbean, Mexican, and South American students: among others, José Morelos sent his oldest son and Simón Bolívar his nephew to study in the city.[2]

The physical presence of passionately committed and exciting intellectuals was one important factor; accessibility to printing presses an important second attraction. Edgar Richardson notes that the 1820 U.S. census listed only ten industries in the entire country with annual sales exceeding $100,000. One of these industries was book publishing in Philadelphia (247), and this publishing enterprise by no means limited itself to English imprints. Historians remind us that English was still a minority language in Philadelphia at the time (German was widely spoken in the state of Pennsylvania, for instance, and native son Benjamin Franklin thought French had a good chance of becoming the national language of the United States). Unsurprisingly in such a polyglot setting, books were commonly printed in Spanish, Latin, Italian, Russian, German, Dutch, French, and many other languages (Sollers, *Anthology* 4).

In the early part of the nineteenth century, both the United States and the newly independent republics of Latin America were engaging openly and collaboratively in elaborating theories of continental America's exceptionality with respect to the old colonial powers. These were innovative projects for both North and South America, and writers and thinkers of the time were well aware of living at a historical crux, with important implications for the future. It is, thus, highly revelatory to explore the kinds of philosophical stakes being debated, as well as the explicit or implicit claims to historical originality, and the documents deployed in support of such discussions.

Briefly: for my purposes here, I might identify two main threads of social interest that were coming together in the 1820s and 1830s in the United States. First of all, there was in the United States a deep interest in Latin America that highlighted theorizing a continental alliance on the basis of a historical rupture with the rejected political systems of Europe. In this respect, the United States and the Latin American republics coincided in invention of new, republican selves in contrast with the tired European models they explicitly left behind. Thus, for example, an anonymous pamphlet from 1819 urges, "There may be in many things a common American continental interest, in opposition to a European interest" (the author has been identified as Brackenridge; cited in Helman 344). Similarly, Willard Phillips in *The North American Review* in 1817 comments that "the attention of men has been drawn to South America; and that part of our continent has become the scene of the most important transactions that are now taking place in the world" (cited in Helman 343). These discussions on the U.S. side were undoubtedly fueled by the numerous debates in Congress between 1817 and 1822 about the recognition of these new republics and the later discussions around the adoption of the 1823 Monroe Doctrine. On the Latin American side, Bolívar and other independence leaders saw in the United States a natural ally in this new, Enlightenment-inspired but anti-European political project.

This mutual interest opens directly onto the second thread of discussion in United States cultural circles of the time; the importance of Spanish in the United States and as a project for the U.S. educated individual. Here the writers of the early nineteenth century sound astonishingly contemporary; or more discouragingly, following upon Sollers' suggestion: "perhaps we know less now than did scholars at the beginning of the past century" (1). This retrospective belatedness is due perhaps to what Mary Louise Pratt calls the "workings of the colonized imagination" in the United States. Pratt argues, "Now, the United States is a world imperial power, and it is admittedly difficult to think of it as having a colonized imagination. But . . . when it comes to culture, Europe has continued to possess the American, especially the Euroamerican, imagination, to be its point of reference, regardless of the realities that surround us here. . . . So it was in the 1980s, at many American colleges, the book lists adopted as representing the cultural heritage of American students contained no Americans!" Pratt concludes tendentiously, "much of this, I suggest, is the legacy of European colonialism from which this country has still to emancipate itself" ("Daring" 13).

For early U.S. cultural and political figures, the stakes of intellectual colonialism loomed large and clear, and their response was often to look to their allies on this side of the ocean. Thomas Jefferson, for instance, argued for the importance of learning Spanish on the grounds that "the ancient part of American History is written chiefly in Spanish" (cited in Helman 342). Jared Sparks, a prominent public intellectual and president of Harvard, was throughout his life a strong supporter of learning Spanish for hemispherically significant purposes—though, like most of his contemporaries, he found it perfectly logical for scholars to go to Spain so as to learn about Latin American cultures. He wrote, for example, "Next to our language, the Spanish will be likely at a future day to become the most important in this country," and he noted particularly "the new theatre of enterprise, which is opening up to the whole world the vast extent of the South American republics, and the intimate intercourse, which from proximity of situation, must necessarily grow up between those republics and the United States" (1825, cited in Helman 339).[3]

This chapter focuses on three narratives from that fluid, preimperial moment in U.S. history. *Jicoténcal* (1826) was published anonymously in Spanish by William (sometimes the imprints read "Guillermo") Stavely in a press run under auspices of the Protestant Episcopal Church.[4] Stavely also published a weekly newspaper, *The Philadelphia Reporter*, and a wide variety of literary, political, legal, and philosophical works in Spanish, Latin, and English, along with travelogues and even ship manifests.[5] *Jicoténcal* is a political treatise disguised, rather unsuccessfully it must be confessed, with an overlay of historical romance. In its own time it was praised for the "just and enlightened notions on political government and other important subjects" and for the compelling moral quality which makes it important reading for people like the freedom fighters in Spanish America and "those who lived through our own Revolution" who make common cause with such ideals (*Bryant* 336, 344). The same review, however, gently panned the book on narrative grounds: "the form of fictitious narrative is by no means a suitable one for the ample and free discussion of important doctrines" (337).[6]

Calavar; or The Knight of the Conquest: A Romance of Mexico (1834) and *The Infidel; or The Fall of Mexico. A Romance* (1835), both by Robert Montgomery Bird, are clearly linked novels focusing sequentially on two different moments of the Cortés expedition, temporally following directly upon the period described in *Jicoténcal*. These popular novels, written by one of Philadelphia's foremost literary figures,[7] were published by Carey, Lea, and Blanchard. The press was founded by Mathew Carey, in his day the most influential publisher in Philadephia, and was at that time operating under his son Henry Carey, where it continued to dominate the national book trade. In addition to Bird's works, Carey, Lea, and Blanchard published such well-known writers as James Fenimore Cooper and Washington Irving, among others. The Careys were especially interested in political and economic causes (Richardson 248), and Bird's novels fall squarely into a popular and much discussed mode of combining social commentary and exotic narrative siting. Reviews were extremely laudatory: "The work may fairly rank among the highest efforts of genius, and we do not scruple to pronounce it superior to anything of the kind which has yet emanated from an American press"; "It is, without question, the best American novel that has yet appeared"; "Suffice it to say, that *Calavar,* throughout, is a romance of very great interest. It will interest the imaginative . . . ; it will please the poetic . . . ; it will charm every lover of fiction" (*Infidel* II, 229). Prescott paid tribute to Bird's work in his *Conquest of Mexico.* Even the usually hypercritical Edgar Allan Poe was enthusiastic: he called *Calavar* "certainly the very best American novel, excepting perhaps one or two of Mr. Cooper's, which [he had] ever read" (cited in Williams, *Spanish Background,* I, 220), and his review of *Infidel* began, "The second effort of the author of *Calavar,* gives us no reason for revoking the favorable opinion which we expressed of his powers as a writer of fictitious narrative, in noticing the first. On the contrary, that opinion is confirmed and strengthened by a perusal of the *Infidel*" (582).

Following upon Walter Scott's wildly successful model for historical novels, there is an obvious interest in siting narratives in some kind of exotic locale as de rigeur for the genre. As Khatibi says perceptively in a different context, on the representation of the foreigner in French literature, "L'éxotisme n'est pas, ici, un folklorisme de surface, mais un secret de toute littérature, de ses paradigmes" [Here exoticism is not a superficial folklorism, but a secret of all literature, of its paradigms] (*Figures* 9). His acute commentary is equally applicable to these earlier period texts, where the paradigm of the Scottish historical novel has already imposed a certain recognizable shape on the genre. Beyond this rather superficial motivation (any exotic locale is equally useful; America is preferable to Europe), however, is there something that goes beyond the surface folklorism? What can we conjecture about the coincidence of these novels focusing on Cortés, and why precisely in this moment of thinking through the emerging national structures in the new American republics north and south?

I would like to suggest that both these texts see the (Spanish) colonial period as a long blank that can safely be ignored from the perspective of Republican sentiment, and that there are solid, traditional, nation-building reasons for so doing. Mexican thinker Octavio Paz would agree: "Most historians offer us a conventional image of New Spain: an intermediate stage between Indian Mexico and modern Mexico. . . . The official history presents it in an even more negative light: New Spain was an interregnum, a stage of usurpation and oppression, a period of historical illegitimacy. . . . Independence was a *restoration*" ("Foreword" xi–xii). In this politically charged context of a hypothesized restoration, it is not the long colonial period but more punctually the originary European encounter that urgently needs to be rethought and rethought at least imaginarily from the perspective of the conquered. Ironically, continues Paz, in the colonial period "New Spain wished to be the Other Spain: an empire, the Rome of America. A contradictory proposition: New Spain wished to be the realization of Old Spain, and this implied the negation of the latter" ("Foreword" xii). In Palumbo-Liu's terms, we might conclude that New Spain by definition cannot *be*, that the very nature of its existence becomes the cause of its fatal contradiction, and hence a further reason for consigning it to historical oblivion.

The Republic resolves this impossible otherness by projecting the lost and defeated other back upon the past as an invented version of itself. In this formulation, the other of old (European) Spain is not new (Mexican) Spain in the form of a spuriously imagined new imperial Rome, but its own internal others, resurrected in the process of recalling its violent and repressed indigenous past. Thus, the tragedy of the indigenous loss marking the initiation of the colonial period is balanced with and measured against the implicit celebration of the contemporary gain of independence. To apply Dominick LaCapra's suggestive formulation, the conquest is inscribed in Mexican culture as an originary trauma, transgenerationally transmitted, whereby contemporaries "may be possessed by the past and relive the hauntingly post-traumatic symptoms of events and experiences one may not have directly lived through" (8). This fraught heritage functions as an instantiating traumatic event, which in the context of a later event that somehow recalls it, triggers a traumatic response, a belated repetition compulsion (LaCapra 22). Because both the originary event and its resurrection are traumatic in nature, the entire enterprise is shot through with ambiguity, mysterious silences, and odd displacements.

The appeal to a heroic indigenous past is almost formulaic in all contemporary calls to revolutionary action. Just one example anchors the point, this taken from a widely diffused speech by Mexican independence leader José Morelos, who in an inspirational rhetorical gesture evokes the spirits of the heroes who serve as forefathers of that movement: these heroes include "shades of Indian ancestors who were victims of *gachupín* barbarity: Moctezuma, Cacahma, Cuauhtémoc, Xicoténcatl, and Caltzontzin" (cited in Lafaye 121). In this revolutionary appeal to a restored past, the noble Tlaxcalans and Aztecs are given a second chance, and that new opportunity is—interestingly enough—projected onto the imaginarily mestizo, actually creole, revolutionary leaders as the true heirs of Xicoténcatl and Moctezuma. The Aztecs are associated with this historical narrative as modeled through Rome in their imagined similarity to the emperors of classical antiquity, and their antagonists, the Tlaxcalans, represent the virtues of the Roman Republic. The remaining dramatic role is clear; the Spaniards are the barbarians at the gates in all three moments: the Roman past, the European colonial encounter, and the American independence movements.

For the novelist in early nineteenth-century Philadelphia, what is conceived of as two conflicting knowledge systems—America and Europe—have to be put into play on a clear ideological field, responding, among other factors, to the imperatives of postwar reconstruction and reevaluation of the former antagonist. Thus, if colonial history involves overlaying European values onto an American map, this overlay inevitably reshapes and restructures that map, detaching it from its pre-Columbian pristineness and disrupting its historical continuity. The American voice then operates as a subversion of that European text, intentionally silencing Europe by delegitimating its most salient representation on this side of the ocean: colonial discourse. The irony, of course, is that the recuperative effort rejects Europe in terms familiar to any Europeanist, looking to Europe's originary siting (the Roman empire) as a deep structure for legitimizing an anticolonial origin for an imaginarily different epistemological system located on the American continent.

In *Jicoténcal* the Tlaxcalan political and military organization bears straightforward homologies with the Roman Republican senate, an echo picked up immediately in contemporary reviews; says Bryant, for example, "it seems like an anecdote of Grecian or Roman greatness of mind" (339). Roman allusions overlying indigeneous heroes are similarly pervasive in Bird's texts, an echo that must have spoken as strongly to the U.S. public as to the creole elite readers of *Jicoténcal*, in an atmosphere where both Bolívar and Washington were artistically tricked out in togas for large public monuments. In Bird's English texts, a further critical framing perspective is given in the introduction to *Calavar*, where an indigenous Mexican historian hands over his precious manuscripts detailing the true story of the fall of Tenochtitlán to a visiting American, precisely because of the tourist's republican credentials, favoring American continental solidarity over potential *gachupín* perversions. At each point, the indigenous subject becomes linked with the strong moral genealogy of highly valued republican sentiment. There is, moreover, in these novels an ellision of difference and distance between the Roman and the modern versions, implicitly creating an investment in a universalized timeline and establishing a basis for rights and privileges that should naturally accrue to citizens sharing this cultural heritage, whether Roman, U.S., or Latin American.

Paz also describes how throughout history the "exaltation of the dead Indian past coexisted with hate and fear for the living Indian" (xvii); this observation is certainly true and well taken, although I need to add the caveat that there is no hint of a portrayal of any living Indian in any of these three novels, except for the single example of the mad historian, the indigeneous *cura* whose manuscript provides the pretext for *Calavar.*[8] The indigenous male, in any case, is fatally destined to tragedy and nonreproduction. In terms of the need to establish a continuous republican heritage, the contradictions of a heroic (but indigenous) past that must be resuscitated in modern revolutionary struggles are novelistically resolved through heritage descending solely through the female line, thus avoiding the problem of a living indigenous warrior in the present. Implicitly, the future hope of republican struggle is projected onto Marina's mixed-race son in *Jicoténcal,* as well as, presumably, Juan Lerma and Zelahualla's putative children in *Infidel.* The heroic indigenous potential forefathers are all tragically eliminated from the family tree in every one of these three novels.

Since the philosophical work involved in the construction of the American republics crucially implies a definition of national origins, the retelling of the story of a heroic resistance, even one relived as the acting out of trauma or couched in classical metaphor (where, for instance, Jicoténcal is a Republican leader in the imagined mode of the Roman Republic), offers a highly resonant venue for siting the nation. I can hypothesize that one issue of deep importance for the author of the Spanish text is the continuing colonial status of Cuba, even as other fellow Spanish colonies successfully achieve independence and recognition as new republics. This same historical circumstance provides an important clue as to why this tendentious novel was published anonymously. Whether the particular Cuban author is assumed to be Varela or Heredia, the case is the same, since both men were passionately involved in ongoing efforts to achieve independence for Cuba. The use of a fictional narrative as the vehicle for this commentary is innovative; but its motivation is in its deep structure closely attuned with the favored political metaphors of the time. In these novels, as in political addresses like those of Morelos, the claim to a particular national vision involves tracing back and reoccupying crucial symbolic historic spaces, and the historical claim grounds territorial ones.

Historical memory, as well as romantic genealogy, is, therefore, very much at stake in all these works. While it is by no means my point to evaluate these novels on historical grounds, both of the authors make explicit appeals to the authority of well-known historical texts in the body of their work.[9] Thus it is worth recalling briefly what was known about the colonial encounter with respect to Latin America in the United States at that time. One such source of information is Robert C. Sands, a contemporary scholar who wrote an expansive biography of

Cortés during this period (the book was first published in a Spanish translation made from the manuscript, and only appeared belatedly in English two years after Sands's death in 1832). Sands reports reading carefully among what are still the standard canonical texts today—Cortés's letters, de Solís, Guevara, Bernal Díaz de Castillo, Herrera—and he combines this primary text work with explorations among the works of contemporary historians of Mexico: William Robertson and Francisco Javier Clavijero are especially important. Clavijero's works, for instance, became available in translation in 1806 and 1817. Influential works by Gordon and Prescott, generally cited as the most important historical treatises of this period, were both slightly later than these novels; their books were published in 1832 and 1843 respectively. Sands is also aware that there are many gaps in his scholarship. He complains that "I am very much troubled by the want of books. . . . Some of the manuscripts [in the Library of Congress] are forgeries, beyond all question" (Williams, *Spanish Background* I, 392). This concern is echoed by Jared Sparks on other grounds with reference to the paucity of sources of information about current events in Latin America, a factor that exacerbates the difficulties of doing thick analyses: "our newspapers, the only vehicle of communication, have sent out as many errors as truth. . . . Our news is principally obtained from private letters of ignorant or disappointed adventurers" (unpublished letter, dated Boston, September 24, 1825, cited in Helman 345).

Even in Bird's novels, the lamentable state of available resources is decried. When the U.S. traveler proudly tells the Mexican historian that he has read de Solís, Clavijero, Bernal Díaz de Castillo, and Dr. Robertson, the irate priest interrupts him: "Basta! Demasiado! Enough—too much! What a niño, a little child, a pobre Yankee, have I fallen upon! That I should waste my words on a man who studies Mexican history out of the books of such jolterheads!" The *cura* explicitly claims the superiority of his indigenous countertexts, deriving his authority from the heritage of "Moteuczoma Xocojotizin . . . , Tizoc, of Xocotzin, and of Ixtlilxochitl" (*Calavar* I, 11).[10] Bird's fictional historian, thus, echoes a common lament among contemporary professionals in the field: an awareness of working from incomplete and defective sources that inevitably taint the historical text. At the same time, while the earlier period sources were understood to be inadequate and biased toward the European side of the story, some understanding of the magnitude of the Mexican tragedy was well known. Indeed, the absence of accurate assessments serves as an invitation to the responsible creative writer, whose work helps fill the gaps. The contemporary novelists, then, may offer a greater accuracy and realism than their historical counterparts. They do not, however, pretend to scholarly objectivity.

Bird, especially, laments the horrendous price of colonialism in breaking down a flourishing civilization, one that was strikingly advanced and modern avant la lettre.[11]

THE NOVELS

Jicoténcal was originally published in two slim volumes, and the only available modern edition is less than 150 pages long in total; in contrast, Bird's volumes are about 250 pages each, for 1,000 pages total in the two linked novels, about seven times the length of the Spanish-language text. The earlier Spanish-language novel is set in Tlaxcala at the moment of forging the alliance between the Spaniards and the indigenous republic, and it ends with Cortés's words, "Mañana salimos para Méjico" [Tomorrow we leave for Mexico City] (144/156). Bird's first novel begins almost exactly at the point where *Jicoténcal* concludes, as if taking up the story where the earlier author left off. There are three main sets of characters in *Jicoténcal*, set off in pairs so as to highlight the moral dilemma animating the text. The side of evil is represented by Cortés himself, a canny but treacherous man and unfaithful lover; the Tlaxcalan senator, Magiscatzin, who is led by greed and shortsightedness to betray his people's best interests; and Marina/Malinche, Cortés's translator and sometime mistress, who uses seduction to achieve her nefarious goals. The only villain who comes to a good end in this tale is Marina. When under the influence of new motherhood, she decries her dishonest lust for power and is converted to the purer charms of child raising. Ranged against these powerful villains are the doomed forces of good: Diego de Ordaz, an ineffectual and honorable Spaniard who is too decent to see the corruption right in front of his face; Jicoténcal, a great warrior handicapped by having to fight alongside the Spaniards under an agreement he knows is morally and politically corrupt; and Teutila, Jicoténcal's anodyne wife, the foil to the evil Marina.[12] Retrograde politics and selfish carnality go hand in hand in this novel; the action, such as it is between philosophical observations, involves Marina's attempts to seduce both Diego de Ordaz and Jicoténcal, and, in a parallel manner, describes Cortés's dishonest lust for Teutila. Both Jicoténcal and Teutila die tragically; the warrior by betrayal, his wife by self-inflicted poison as she attempts to assassinate Cortés.

Bird, says Gordon Hutner, "provocatively reminds us of the connection between regions and borders in US writing" (95). Certainly, Bird participated actively and consistently in the trend to write America and turn away from European subjects and sites, and he is attracted to the drama of encounter between two different cultural systems in his Spanish American fictions as well as those set on the U.S. frontier. His cultural ambivalence and the moral ambiguity in his South American works give rise to what Dahl calls a "dilemma of sympathy," which for the mid-twentieth-century critic manifests itself in what he sees as an annoying tendency "to not know on which side he really should be" (79). It is telling that Dahl much prefers Bird's later works, where the messy ambiguity about noble indigenous people in Mexico is resolved and Bird's works, for his taste, more successfully focus on the moral clarity of exterminating the dirty, ignorant savages in the U.S. borderlands.

Bird had a very clear literary plan, charted out in 1828 and held to firmly for the rest of his life: after youthful experiments in poetry, he turned to playwriting, then abandoned theater for novels. He had planned to turn at some point from novel writing to history, but died before he was able to move into this next projected stage in his career (Dahl 69). In the period immediately before his turn to fiction, he demonstrated a notable predilection for Roman (e.g., his wildly popular and consciously proto-abolitionist 1831 play *The Gladiator*, about Spartacus) and South American themes (other popular dramas by Bird include *Oralloossa, Son of the Incas* [1832] and *The Broker of Bogotá* [1834]). Although in 1834 Bird complained to a friend that Latin American topics were "too far-offish and Hebraic for our Johnny Raws of the States, who know and care as little about Mexico as they do about the moon" (Foust 89–90), he must not have been entirely convinced by his own words, since *Calavar* and *The Infidel* follow immediately upon this series of Spanish American–sited plays. He had originally planned to write eight novels on Mexico and Peru, including three more about Mexico, concluding with one set during the war of independence; however, his works after the two extant Mexican novels turn to the U.S. frontier. The indigenous thread and shock of encounter between whites and Indians remains constant in these later works, in a much darker version, notably in his most well-known novel, *Nick of the Woods; or The Jibbenainosay,* published after *The Infidel* in 1837. Based on a Kentucky legend, that later novel reaches beyond melodrama to a psychological exploration of a pious Quaker named Nathan Slaughter who is driven by the destruction of his family into orgies of violence against local Indians, alternating the murder of "red niggurs" with episodes of deep contrition.

The historical moment referenced in *Calavar* concerns the defeat of Narváez and the first combined Tlaxcalán-Spanish assault on Tenochtitlán; the novel proper concludes with an image of Cortés pondering his final assault on the Mexican capital, followed by an epilogue in which a returning conquistador visits a friend in Spain. Their conversation ends with a cliffhanger: "When thou art rested a little, I shall desire thee to speak, -for very impatient am I to know, -

what circumstances of marvel and reknown, of romance and chivalry, have distinguished the last days of Tenochtitlan" (II 251). This request opens directly onto the time frame of *Infidel*, as if *Infidel* were Fabueno's narrative response to the inquiry, a Spanish proletarian follow-up to the explicitly indigenous narrative in *Calavar*, where the text is supposedly written by Cristobal Johualicahuatzin/Cristobal Santiago Marhojo y Ixtliloxochitl.

Calavar concerns itself with the unwaveringly honorable don Amador de Leste, a member of the military brotherhood of San Juan, who has traveled to Mexico to serve don Gabriel de Calavar, a knight under Cortés's command. Accompanying him are a mysterious Moor, called Abdalla, alias Esclavo de la Cruz, whose real name is Alharef-ben-Ismail, and his son Jacinto (later revealed as his daughter Leila in disguise—she is also incited by her father to take on the role of an Aztec priestess, which she does convincingly for a good part of the novel). The most important romantic entanglement in this historical novel is that between the Spanish man and the Moorish woman. Amador provides the moral compass for this text, which details the course of his association with Cortés's forces, his honorable decision to abandon the battles, go back to Spain, and no longer participate in a war he sees as unjust. This decision is amplified in the working out of the course of his deep love for a woman of another race and culture, who has been innocently caught up on the losing side in two major wars—both the reconquista in Spain and the conquista in Mexico. Cortés in this novel is smart but duplicitous and vindictive; Calavar has a "sore infirmity on my brain" (I, 146) which makes him quixotic but highly unreliable since during most of the novel he is self-confessedly mad; Moctezuma treats the Spaniards honorably and foolishly expects honor in return from his enemies. For my taste, the most interesting character is Abdalla, a nobleman who acts like an abject servant, who is accused of being a traitor and a spy, but where the lines between perfidy and honor are never entirely clear. The Moor is a tortured soul who has been dishonorably treated in the Spanish wars against Granada, and so, quite reasonably in the moral structure of this novel, looks for righteous vengeance: the problem consists in his allying himself with the indigenous opposition to Cortés and dragging his daughter into his plans.

In *Infidel*, the blazing ambition and black heart of Cortés come even more to the fore, as he engages in a series of dishonest exchanges with the Indians and hypocritical interactions with the novel's protagonist, the much misunderstood and calumnied Juan Lerma.[13] Bird borrowed the name of his hero from a passing reference in Bernal Díaz de Castillo, which he cites as an epigraph to the novel: "un esforçado soldado, que se dezia Lerma—se fue entre los Indios como aburrido de temor del mismo Cortés, a quien avia ayudado a salvar la vida, por ciertas cosas de enojo que Cortés contra é tuvo, que aqui no declaro por su honor: nunca mas supimos del vivo, ni muerto, mala sospecha tuvimos" [a brave soldier named Lerma—he went among the Indians as though bored of fearing Cortés himself, whose life he had helped save, by reason of certain complaints Cortés had against him, that I won't mention here to preserve his honor. We never heard of him again, neither dead nor alive, we have a bad feeling about it]. Lerma's story is an extremely twisty and convoluted one, worthy of the most extravagant *novela de caballerías* or modern soap opera, involving lost children, treachery and lies, near incest, and final untangling with the revelation that Lerma is really Cortés's nephew and the rightful Count Castillejo de Merida, and that la Monjonaza, a nun in Cortés's lustful keeping, is not Juan's sacriligeous love interest but his twin sister. The novel ends with Lerma's return to Spain to live happily ever after accompanied by his lovely—and light-skinned—Aztec bride, Zelahualla. The epilogue reminds us, though, that Lerma's good friend Guatimozin, Moctezuma's successor as the Emperor of Mexico, is not so lucky.

In all of these novels, the most lauded and virtuous characters are more acted upon than acting; by modern standards, they are a strangely passive set of heroes, whose mettle is tested and character forged by their resistance to the villainous activities of their antagonists. The first sentence of *Jicoténcal* sets the stage for an inexorable tragedy whose course is already familiar to his readers: "estaba escrita en el libro fatal del destino la caída del grande imperio de Motezuma" [the fall of the great empire of Moctezuma was written in the fateful book of destiny] (3/7). The nobility of the indigenous protagonist, thus, is measured by his honorable and stoic endurance in the face of a defeat that the readers know is inevitable. Likewise, Bird explicitly establishes that in his work, passivity is an important heroic quality. In a letter to his friend James Lawson, Bird comments on the protagonist of *Infidel* in terms that are equally applicable to the protagonist of *Calavar* as well as to the cognate noble indigenous leaders in both his novels and in *Jicoténcal*:

> The character of Juan I meant to be 'passive'. . . . You are certainly wrong about the 'action, action, action' being as necessary in a novel as in a play. The deepest interest can be drawn from the sufferings of individuals incapable of resisting their fate, and even when they attempt no resistance. Such is found *The Bride of Lammermoor*, where the heroine is wax and the hero lead, clay, water, or anything. And that fiction, if you will take my word for it, is the most interesting and deeply affecting ever penned by the hand of man. The actors do nothing; but how one's tears drop over them. . . . (cited in Dahl 124).

By extension, the powerful effect that Bird ascribes to passivity is even more in evidence with his highly noble indigenous characters, who suffer outrageous Spanish whims with consistent dignity: Moctezuma, Guatimozin, Xicotencal, Techeechee the Ottomi ambassador, and so forth.

In their idealization of such intrinsically noble characters, these novels, especially Bird's, derive in a direct line of narrative descent from *novelas de caballerías*/romances of chivalry. Amador's name pays tribute to the most well-known novel of the tradition, *Amadís de Gaula* (1508), Cavalar is entirely quixotic, the indigenous warriors are compared to medieval knights (*Infidel* I, 194), and Lerma's story is as convoluted as its literary forbears. Like the heroes in Bird's novels, these fifteenth- and sixteenth-century romances—which were immensely popular, by the way, with Spanish conquistadores—follow the peripatetic tale of the strictly honorable hero, who typically falls into a series of unsought adventures occurring in a highly fabulous geography. These texts of courage define character and mainly prove courage rather than cleverness or aggressivity. In fact, in the romances, a highly canny warrior with an aggressive style is usually associated with the villains. At the same time, like other contemporary historical novels, these nineteenth-century romantic tragedies are meant to be cathartic and uplifting, aimed at a generation of readers whose experiences of the chaos of war and the exhilaration of nation construction are firsthand—ironically moving the reader to action precisely at the point where the character is most acted upon.

A HISTORY OF MORAL EPIDEMICS

Serious historical and moral/ideological claims clash with the understood frivolity of romance as the written medium chosen to convey an important message to an imagined body of lazy readers who eschew more intellectual treatises. *Jicoténcal* seems to have a particularly vexed relation to this problem. It is meticulous in citing its sources; for instance: "sobre este fundamento . . . va a hablar Antonio de Solís en su *Historia de la conquista de México* (libro V, capítulo XIX)" (128), referring the reader to that text as if the foregoing narrative were a citation in a scholarly tome. At the same time, internal evidence tells us that any exploration of historical, geographical, or cultural accuracy is so far beside the point in this novel as to be almost entirely ignored. Thus, the descriptions of the indigenous people, their customs, the geography that surrounds them, their culture, and their forms of social organization are entirely invented from whole cloth in this novel, with little or no actual knowledge of Mexico in evidence (*Jicoténcal* xx–xxi). The obvious conclusion is that the novel is meant less as a historical narrative than an emblematic moral tale, set somewhat awkwardly in an exotic setting so as to capture the eye and interest of a reading public already sensitized to the symbolic appeal of a vague indigenous past as the preferred model for thinking about the revolutionary present. Even more awkward in this novel are its efforts to match this emblematic history to a narrative flow that relies on romantic tensions of a conventional fictional sort; as Bryant writes, "the author has not been quite successful in the attempt to ally the feverish thirst of revenge with the peace and serenity of virtue" (343). In other words, the dramatic climax of the novel falls completely flat. But perhaps, as the early reviewer suggests, the interest of the author is not so much in the historical romance as in the discussion of current politics and forms of government, in trying to reach a wider market than could be accessed by a treatise on civil rights (337).

Calavar too is implicitly concerned with contemporary revolutionary struggles, as the frame chapter intimates, but it is more self-consciously aware than *Jicoténcal* of the situatedness of history and of the historian who brings his experience to bear upon a confused series of events that can be interpreted from more than one moral, national, ideological, and ethnic perspective. The framing prologue to the novel draws attention to the narrative's role as a specifically positioned historical discourse, and focuses on a series of issues surrounding the question of how historical memory invests itself with the trappings of romance. The novel begins with the ruminations of a U.S. traveler, looking out over the valley of Mexico from Chapultepec hill: "We live over thoughts which are generated by memory, and our conceptions are the reproductions of experience. But poetry has added no plenary charm, history has cast no over-sufficient light on the haunts of Montezuma. . . . One chapter only of its history has been written or preserved; the rest is a blank, . . . a secret, strange, captivating, and pregnant of possibilities. This is the proper field for romantic musings" (I, 1). This initial appeal to the propriety of romance immediately brings up the challenge of reconciling the fictional and historical in the genre of the historical novel, and speaks as well to the uneasy relation between experience and memory, as well as to the reproductions of experience which in the absence of poetry/romance can become sterile or misleading (the traveler's gendered metaphor of pregnant secrets is telling in this regard). The traveler's musings also open onto a theme that will pervade the introduction to the novel and inflect a staging of how the following narrative is to be read: how to represent a more accurate primordial history? In Bird's terms, the response is that the poet must collaborate to fill the blanks, resulting in the elaboration of a landscape more legitimate, if inevitably more romantic, than that deriving from the biased and incomplete accounts of earlier writers.

Thus, at its outset *Calavar* poses the problem of the relation between history and romantic musings, between the role of the philosopher and that of the poet, as well as the validity of imagination to fill in historical blanks. This meditation is interrupted (and supplemented) by the appearance of an indigenous Mexican *cura*, who sees in the traveler the proper repository for his secretly written and lovingly preserved counterhistorical account of the conquest of Mexico, a tale that also has close ties, at least in the traveler's later perspective—upon decoding the system that prevented him from reading it—to romance. The *cura* gives the traveler his histories, the true chronicles of the land, because he distinguishes in the foreign visitor a common cause between Mexican and U.S. republican sentiment, as well as a common philosophical bent. Almost the first thing the *cura* tells the traveler is, "I must speak with you, very learned stranger, for I perceive you are a philosopher" (I, 6). He retains this initial good impression despite his concern that the traveler is "a man with two souls; you are wise and you are foolish, and you speak bad Spanish" (I, 7). The credentialing, thus, as a philosopher, identifies the historian (*cura*) and romance writer (traveler) as people capable of and charged with organizing and conceptualizing the moral dimension of historical experience. To the degree that the traveler is wise, he is a philosopher; his foolishness is ascribed to his foreignness and his poetic bent.

On accepting the charge to disseminate this history in the United States where republican spirit is more advanced than in unreceptive Mexico, the traveler also takes on the task of editor, translating between two historical moments, two cultures, two ethnicities, and two views of how to infuse experience with meaning. Here, interestingly enough, the *cura*'s reason for choosing the traveler (his philosophical sensibility) proves to be at least a somewhat mistaken assumption on his part, as the traveler, who is more committed to romance, edits the history by concentrating on cutting the philosophy drastically in his version of the text: "the narrative was more verbose, but Cristobal lived in an age of amplification. . . . [The traveler/editor] shaved, therefore, and he cut; he amputated, he compressed; and he felt the joy of an editor, when exercising the hydraulic press of mind. This will be excused in him. He expunged as much of the philosophy as he could. . . . If it should be objected, that he has called the *Historia verdadera* a romance, let it be remembered, that the world likes romance better than truth, . . . and that the history of Mexico, under all aspects but that of fiction, is itself—a romance" (I, 22). Here too, the narrator sets "true history" against "romance," and explains this shift in title (if not content) on affective grounds ("the world likes romance better than truth"), while playing with the assumptions about both genres. In the pages that follow, of course, Bird offers both. In privileging romance over history, nevertheless, he moves the focus away from an emphasis on intellectual and moral insights and toward a more popular entertainment. The traveler in this manner bases his novel on "true history," while seasoning it with romance in both senses: as a fictional narrative, and a particular kind of narrative focusing on heterosexual love—something the *cura* would find a deformation of its primordial conceptualizing project.

In the *cura*'s harsh perspective, "the vale of Anahuac is not deformed for nothing; Christian man has ruined it" (I, 8). The traveler's own editorial infidelities are anticipatorily erased, and Europeanist deformations are displaced implicitly to a representative of these "Christian men" in the form of the pedantic Mexican scholar don Andrés. This seemingly respectable and in fact highly respected aristocratic creole overtly espouses racist sentiments, proudly bragging that he "knows nothing" about the indigenous past of Mexico, but nevertheless insisting that the *cura* is mad for imagining Cortés in a negative light and Moctezuma in a favorable one. In his version of the background to the *cura*'s crazy scribblings, don Andrés tells the traveler that the old indigenous priest had been mad ever since he was knocked around when taken prisoner while fighting in the war of independence at the side of Miguel Hidalgo (I, 17–18). In the interplay between the traveler and the *cura*, and later the traveler and the creole scholar, Bird reminds his reader that any "historia verdadera" is shaped by the historian's philosophical commitments and decisions about the meaning to be applied to the shape of the past. Because gaps exist, moreover, even the most careful historical studies have unavoidable inaccuracies based on a limited knowledge base. Furthermore, the individual idiosyncrasies of interpretation of what are known to be limited scholarly deposits of fact can easily be sidetracked by high coloring, come to be understood as undependable, and derive from sources suspected to be unreliable or biased.

Infidel too begins with reference to a traveler who, in this case while wandering the area around Lake Texcoco, cannot help but contrast past and present, to the detriment of the long and destructive colonial project: "the royal city of Tezcuco is now, though the capital of a republican state, a mean and insignificant village." The narrator contrasts this present decline with a glorious past: "they sowed the roadside with corn for the sustenance of travelers and the protection of husbandmen, built hospitals and observatories, endowed colleges and formed associations of literature and science. . . . As in the learned societies of modern Europe and America, encouragement was given to the study of history, poetry, music, painting, astronomy, and natural magic" (I, 14). Once again, as in *Calavar*, imagination supplements beyond the limits of the experiential, filling in the historical blank with narrative romance that allows access to the real, if not to the strictly verifiable, empirical evidence.

One of the most striking qualities of all these maneuverings in both Bird and *Jicoténcal* concerns the policing of textual boundaries as a political act framed in the language of virtue and moral imperatives. Bryant's review once again is apposite. Speaking from the perspective of the United States's successful revolution, he concludes about the Latin American independence revolutions, "we are morally certain, that in such a contest of an oppressed nation with its despotic masters, its character cannot fail to elevate and purify itself" (344). Such wars, then, bring out the inherent nobility in the warriors for the republican cause. Bryant's terms may at first glance seem very dated to us at the turn of the twenty-first century, yet the seductions of an appeal to morality have not faded in the highest policymaking levels and serve as the basis for contemporary calls to involve the country in international conflict. Similarly, moral judgments are often the underlying subtext to allegations about the hypocrisy of elected officials.[14]

The language of morality is distributed across the apparent political spectrum, attaching itself to virtuous individuals who respect their sworn commitments, but also hold themselves to a higher moral standard of conscientious objection when leaders behave immorally. The historical defeat of the indigenous forces in this war is particularly traumatizing because it directly contradicts the optimistic projection that the forces of right and progress will win out over the evil and the retrograde in the end. Once again, the stage is set in terms that link revolutionary-era republican values with an alleged heritage reaching back to Republican Rome, albeit curiously displaced in a nineteenth-century version of political correctness onto the great pre-Columbian culture of central Mexico. Thus, for example, Abdalla, in arguing the case for his shift of allegiance, compares Mexican to Roman generals, implicitly justifying his betrayal of the Spanish cause, which he as a defeated Moor was obligated to support, for the morally correct choice of aiding the Mexicans: "This is not a war of heaven against hell, but of tyranny against freedom.—I did see some sights, this day, upon the pyramid, which caused me to remember those noble Roman generals, who, in ancient times, were wont to devote themselves to death, for the good of the state" (*Calavar* II, 142). Explicitly, the terms of the battle are decoupled from the Christian concepts of good and evil and realigned with the pagan-cum-republican moral choice of tyranny or freedom.

This secular republican take on moral or ethical issues is persistent throughout the texts. Here is the traveler in the opening pages of *Calavar*, questioning the ways of Providence: "two mighty empires . . . were broken, and at an expense of millions of lives, barbarously destroyed; and for what purpose? To what good end?" It is precisely this line of inquiry that leads to the interruption of the *cura*, who, despite the implications of his own religious affiliation, is attracted to the traveler because he overhears this passionate speech and understands the traveler to be a philosopher (I, 5–6). Here again the play of history and romance comes to the fore, each tempering the other and providing a context for moral speculation. In this context, a reading of history without the leavening of ethical doubt can be dangerous. *Infidel* uses even stronger language than *Calavar* to make this point: "to one whose perverted imagination can dwell with pleasure on 'the pomp and circumstance of glorious war,' no better study can be recommended than the history of the siege of Mexico" (II, 91). Bird's narrator emphasizes that for this very reason he will skip over the disturbing scenes of violence. The tale of the war is of necessity perverted, by reason of the intensity of violence and gore, since the battle in effect lasted over three months. At the same time, it is another and very deep perversion to take pleasure in such suffering. Since this narrator has a higher motive, he therefore will not cater to such individuals, even if the result were to be to cure the reader of his perverse interest by virtue of an exposure to such excessive suffering.

Chapter XXI of *Calavar* is framed as a philosophical aside on the conquest. The narrator comments, "A history of moral epidemics . . . would add much to our knowledge of the mysteries of human character and human power, as well as the probable contingencies of human destiny" (I, 172). He details the obstacles against the indigenous forces at the time they were invaded—unreliable local allies, superstition, retrograde religion—but emphasizes that Mexico, despite its disadvantages, had attained a civilization level equal to that of Europe. The difference, he says, is the moral quality of the opposing forces, where the question of "moral epidemic" is definitely not linked to the simplistic reductionism of good versus evil. Chile, by way of contrast, suffered from no such moral epidemic, and in that region the indigenous forces were able to decisively defeat Spain, despite having no great civilization in which to anchor their resistance.

Thus, if Moctezuma's empire suffers from a debilitating moral epidemic that undermines Mexican forces, the Spaniards suffer from a different moral dilemma. In the case of the conquering forces, the problem is the inconsistency between their stated and sworn values, and the actions in which they are engaged, which are typically defined in terms of just/unjust. Bird makes it clear early on in these novels that it debases honor to inflict pain on an unworthy enemy or to engage in an unjust war (e.g., honorable Spaniards don't commit violence against women or children). Yet, one of the perversions of war is that the combatants frequently violate their sworn codes. Thus, for example, one Spaniard, de Morla, admits, "Señor, for the sake of lucre, we have done many unjust things" (I, 188). Amador, in trying to exculpate his leader, looks for mitigating factors: "I cannot believe that Cortes would adopt a course, that seems to savour so much of injustice, without a very discreet and politic object" (I, 211). The deepest conundrums of all are posed by the situation of making war against an honorable enemy whose cause is just. Amador ponders just this problem: "is it possible, then, . . . that these blood-thirsty barbarians are only seeking our lives, to liberate their king? Surely, we do a great sin, to slay them for their love" (II, 81). Moreover, the Spaniards make a generally bad showing in the war itself, since their allies the Tlaxcalans get the brunt of every battle and suffer the most casualties, while the Spaniards stay back "in comparative safety" (*Calavar* II, 41), a wholly dishonorable action in the terms set up by the novel. Finally, amazed and shocked by Cortés's bad treatment of the Aztec king, Amador loses respect for his leader and resolves to abandon a war that he can no longer fight with honor. In the second novel, a character named Sandoval inadvertently attests to the moral probity of the much-calumnied protagonist when he comments that "Lerma has the love of the dog Xicotencal, who loves nobody else" (*Infidel* I, 9). In each case, the moral choice for the Spaniard is to demonstrate a kind of conscientious objection, abstaining from participating in an unjust war against an honorable opponent.

If in Bird the traveler frames the novels in terms of philosophy while explicitly cutting back drastically on the philosophical content, the reverse is true in *Jicoténcal*, where the philosopher-commentator is the key figure. Indeed, it is no exaggeration to say that the moral question is the most important issue in *Jicoténcal*. Overall, as noted above, this is a text in which ideas are more important than action, and in which action basically serves as a pretext for philosophical meditation. These meditations have the explicit goal of defining a moral course—"el filósofo que examina con imparcialidad estos grandes sucesos encuentra su causa en el influjo que ejercen sobre los pueblos las virtudes y los vicios" [The philosopher who examines these events with impartiality finds the cause in the influence that virtues and vices have on all peoples] (49/55)—and separating truth from partial and biased reports so as to make moral judgment more efficacious: "El ojo perspicaz del filósofo sabe distinguir, entre el fango y basura que ensucian el papel de las historias, algunas chispas de verdad que no han podido apagar ni el fanatismo ni la servil adulación" [The philosopher's shrewd eye knows how to distinguish, among the mud and trash that sully the documents of history, some sparks of truth that neither fanaticism nor servile adulation have been able to extinguish] (120/131). For *Jicoténcal*, the terms of the conflict could not be more straightforward. On one side are the "republicanos valientes y aguerridos" [valiant and inured republicans] (3/7); a description later expanded to define the indigenous men more precisely: "el carácter de los habitantes era belicoso, sufrido, franco, poco afecto al fausto y enemigo de la afeminación" [The inhabitants' character was bellicose, long-suffering, frank, little given to pomp, and the enemy of effeminacy] (4/8). Their antagonists are "mercenarios vasallos de un tirano orgulloso" [mercenary vassals of a proud tyrant] (3/7). The only Spaniard who escapes this categorization as a despot is Amador/Juan Lerma's counterpart in the Spanish-language novel, a marginal character named Diego de Ordaz.

Interestingly enough, it is Diego de Ordaz who comes closest to serving as a counterpart to the indigenous hero as the point-of-view character in the novel. He argues passionately with Jicoténcal about the contrast in their forms of government. From his perspective, both monarchy and republic are honorable options, but he sees the Spanish strength in their oftentimes blind "fidelidad a su rey" [faithfulness to his king]. He discerns many problems with a more popular-based form of government (51/57), where the terms of the discussion between the two men perhaps recapitulate contemporary debates that in the United States were framed in terms of Jeffersonian versus Hamiltonian ideas of democracy. In an analogical manner, one of Bird's characters, de Morla, a Spanish soldier sympathetic to the indigenous cause, seems to see similar weaknesses in the republican system: "though these proud people, the commoners, call themselves free republicans, they are to all intents and purposes the servants of many masters; a sort of freedom somewhat more questionable than that of a nation governed by one king. . . . For my part I think them rogues to love us, their truest enemies, better than their domestic rivals, the people of Tenochtitlan" (*Calavar* I, 181).

The main flaw in the indigenous system described by the Cuban-American novel is that it, like the parallel structure depicted in Bird's world, suffers from a lack of strong leadership, what in other terms both writers see as the sort of moral epidemic that a more acute philosopher would be able to dissect fairly. Tellingly, the narrator of *Jicoténcal* focuses his attention on the Tlaxcalan senate, where a lack of vision and honorable statesmanship create serious problems, permitting a corrupt senator to influence his fellows into making the wrong decision by allying their people with the Spaniards. Nor is there a functional alternative for the indigenous peoples in this novel. The indigenous monarchy also suffers from an intractable and ultimately fatal problem. Moctezuma is cowardly and despotic; in a phrase repeated many times until it becomes almost the equivalent of an epic Greek epithet, he is consistently referred to as "el imbecile emperador" [the imbecile emperor] (e.g., 78, 101, 102).

Ultimately, the philosophical problem addressed most closely in this novel is not so much that of the specific form for the best modern government (all have advantages and disadvantages) but lack of morality that can undermine any social structure. Tellingly, the conquistadores are dishonest and un-Christian, and make only half-hearted efforts to dissimulate their intentions: "tomaron como pretexto de sus aventuras la propagación de una creencia que casi no conocían y que insultaban con su conducta" [took as pretext for their adventures the propagation of a faith that they hardly knew and that they had insulted with their conduct] (26/31). The deep hypocrisy of the Spaniards' position is described in debate in the Tlaxcalan senate, especially in the discourse of the other Jicoténcal, not the warrior but the senator, Jicoténcal el viejo [the Elder]. Here too a classical referent adds weight to the language and depth to the allusion. González Acosta observes that the speeches of Jicoténcal el viejo in this novel have been drawn on the model of Cicero's defense of the Republic, and like that classic Roman hero the indigenous American senator goes down tragically to defeat and death because as a highly moral man he cannot disregard his duties as determined by the senate (85). One of Jicoténcal el viejo's speeches reveals Spanish motivations in the charged language of satire: "su lenguaje es éste: 'Yo vengo a esclavizaros a vosotros vuestro pensamiento, vuestros hijos y vuestra descendencia, vengo a destruir vuestro culto . . . vengo a violar a vuestras mujeres e hijas; vengo a robar cuanto poseéis. . . . Mi soberana benignidad os reserva el alto honor de que seáis mis aliados para que perezcáis peleando contra mis enemigos' " [This is its language: 'I came to enslave all of you, your thinking, your children, and your descendants; I come to destroy your form of worship. . . . I come to violate your women and your daughters; I come to steal from you all that you possess. . . . My sovereign benevolence reserves for you the high honor of being my allies so that you might perish fighting against my enemies'] (10/14).

For the other side of argument, also emanating from the Tlaxcalan senate, the author of this novel quotes directly from de Solís, putting the Spanish chronicler's ventriloquized words into the mouth of the corrupt senator, Magiscatzin: "Mi sentir es que los admitamos con benignidad . . . si son hombres, porque está de su parte la razón, y si son algo más, porque les basta para razón la voluntad de los dioses" [My feeling is that we admit them with kindness . . . if they are men, because reason is with them, and if they are something more, because reason is satisfied if it is the will of the gods] (7/11–12). Strikingly, the corrupt politician uses the voice of reason and divine will, whereas the incorruptible one argues from rhetorical projection. If, following Bryant, we are to understand the function of historical narrative in the 1820s as that of speaking to recalcitrant reason through the medium of romance, then Jicoténcal el viejo's Ciceronian projective address more accurately captures the spirit of the narrative enterprise, despite its classical rhetorical trappings, and despite the narrator's clear predilection for emphasis on the abstract issues. At the same time, the narrator's compulsion to philosophical interruption and interpretation is short-circuited by Magiscatzin's intervention, which very much partakes of this mode, intensifying the historical irony of a corrupt Indian speaking in the words of the Spaniard reproducing the voice of Indian reason. In the conjunction of the two, the narrator's warning about the potential problems of the republican model is most deeply felt; the voice of reason becomes lost in perversions of rhetoric and the actual experience of traumatic violence.

INDIGENOUS VOICES

These debates bring to the foreground of analysis the question of how these narratives locate and define the voice of the defeated and dispossessed indigenous peoples. One of the most powerful moments in either of Bird's novels is the long and earnest speech of Masquaza-teuctli, the Lord of Death and Guatimozin's ambassador, to a disgruntled and inattentive Cortés, who continually interrupts the embassy with other business. Each of Masquaza-teuctli's succinctly made points begins with the repetition of some variation on "hear the words of Guatimozin" as the context for the presentation of each of a series of six symbolic gifts. Thus, for example, Guatimozin gives Cortés a history codex, refuting Cortés's claim to the land by saying that there is no evidence of justification for such a prior claim in Mexican history. Also, since Spaniards are gratuitously handing out Bibles and preaching the story of Christ, he counters by giving the Spaniards books detailing Aztec religious practices and their legal system, explicitly so that these newcomers can begin to assimilate themselves to the American civilization they have encountered and presumably will enter: "Take this book, and learn how to worship the gods: religion is a good thing and will make you happy. Take this book also, and understand the laws of men: justice is a good thing, and will make you happy" (*Infidel* I, 198–99). Cortés also receives a bag of enemy skulls, a bundle of corn, a pile of gold and jewels, and last, a collection of warlike implements to symbolically warn him of the indigeneous response if Cortés fails to be satisfied with the other five more benign presents. The ambassador concludes, in words that echo the speech of Jicoténcal el viejo in the earlier Spanish-language novel: "What is the Lord of Castile, that Guatimozin should call him master? What is Malintzin that Guatimozin should make him his friend? . . . His religion is murder, his law robbery: he is strong, yet very unjust" (204). Masquaza-teuctli's frustrating and frustrated effort, crucially positioned near the end of the first volume of *Infidel*, has a double purpose. It reminds the reader of Cortés's barbarism, while reconfirming the highly civilized reasonableness of the indigenous counterpart. At the same time, since Cortés ignores the ambassador's words and is insultingly disrespectful to an honorable foe, it is left to the contemporary reader, who presumably has a very different understanding of the issues at play, to become Masquaza-teuctli's real, appreciative audience. The pathos of the situation, thus, inspires the reader to a reasoned, moral response. This overturning of the historical relations of power corresponds closely to the rewriting of the historical record in favor of indigeneous heroes as a feature of the creole independence movements.

Significantly, the final words in this novel are a reference to Guatimozin: "He merited a higher distinction, a loftier respect, and a profounder compassion, than men will willingly accord to a barbarian and infidel" (II, 228). This resonant last sentence suggests that the entire novel needs to be reimagined from the perspective of the rhetorical slippage in the use of the term that gives the work its title and that serves as the novel's last word. In dominant Latin American creole and U.S. white cultures, it is the non-European ethnic who is tagged with the depreciatory epithet "infidel" as a way of keeping the other in his place. Yet, of course, the term is not only highly identified with a Euro-U.S. dominant culture mind-set, but in Bird's work, is more typically used by those representatives of the Spanish culture whose own judgment is suspect. Cortés and his corrupt sycophants call their indigenous allies as well as their foes infidels, a term that is also used for the Moor in *Calavar* and generally connotes not only otherness but dishonorable faithlessness as well. Of course, in all three of these novels, it is the Spaniards who more fully embody the the denotation of the term: they are cynically non-Christian, care nothing for honor, and consistently fall into the role of the barbarian horde overrunning a Romanesque civilization. In raising the question of what "men will willingly accord," Bird implicitly reminds us that history is written by literate winners, and that in this case it needs to be rewritten from the perspective of justice, from the margins of the colonial episteme. "Infidel" in this manner becomes a highly ironized term, ostensibly referring to the Aztec leader, but more obviously applicable to the despicable Cortés, and Bird's work, to borrow a phrase from Palumbo-Liu, "points up the disjuncture between what the imagination proffers and the limits of narration as historical act" (43). It insists upon the historical and moral necessity of querying received knowledge.

Take, for example, the *cura*'s subversive history, of which "Una crónica de la Conquista de Megico, y Historia verdadera de los Conquistadores, particularmente de esos Caballeros á quienes descuidaron celebrar los Escritores Antiguos"[15] has been supposedly excerpted, transcribed, translated, and edited by the Yankee traveler, a somewhat unreliable mediator given his northern prejudices and bad Spanish. The traveler/editor tells us that the *cura*'s many books contain "the annals of Aztecs and Toltecs, of Chechemecs and Chiapanecs, and a thousand other *Ecs*, from the death of Nezahualcojotl, the imperial poet, up to the confusion of tongues" (*Calavar* I, 20–21), but strikingly, he has chosen from among this wealth of material the one text with a heavy European focus. Thus, the Yankee ignores all the indigenous histories to offer for circulation only the present material, an alternative Spanish history focusing on the honorable unsung conquistadores, leaving the massive body of the other histories to an unbroken silence. Since the *cura*'s own investment lies more significantly in the indigenous chronicles than in the chapter on the Spanish conquest, the reader might well imagine his horror at having his work so greatly truncated and traduced.

Not only is the content of the *cura*'s complete works deeply influenced by his indigenous heritage, so too is the structure and presentation. The *cura* explains the peculiarities of his chosen format: "you perceive, that this volume, done up after the true manner of ancient Mexican books, unrols [sic] from either end. The first pages, and the last, of each volume, contain duplicates of the first and last chapters, done in Mexican characters: the rest is in Spanish, and, I flatter myself, in very choice Spanish. *Hoc ego recte*—I knew what I was about" (14). At least four languages make their appearance in this brief explanation. The cura is speaking in English, referring to a text in Spanish and Nahuatl, and authorizing himself by way of a Latin quotation. The physical ordering of the material is non-Western; the traveler later discovers that it is more highly ciphered than the *cura* originally intimated as well. The editor cannot follow the text upon solely unrolling it; sentences break off, and the text seems to jump randomly from one historical point to another. However, he eventually discovers the reason in the *cura*'s seeming insanity; order is created out of a chaotic-looking text by folding and reading it in a particular way.

From another perspective, the *cura*'s post-Columbian codices partake of some of the complexities of their historical referents. Jorge Cañizares-Esguerra reminds us that most indigenous codices were actually painted during the colonial period and are themselves already engaged in a bicultural understanding, making the indigenous people of Mexico "active participants in the arts and sciences of the Renaissance" (271). They were, for instance, considerably more open to the new cultural materials than has often been allowed them, and were "avid consumers of Renaissance grotesquerie" as well as students of Ovid and Titian (274). Such understudied or unrecognizably multilayered histories are very much to the point in Bird's novel, which presciently hints at some of the more knotty issues engaging scholars today.

How much information the reader may need in order to understand the chosen narrative presents another problem, one that requires careful negotiation among the scholar's intent, the editor's preferences, and the reader's expectations. Here again, there is an ironic distance between the traveler-editor and the narrator of the novel, where the latter enjoys a fuller understanding and thus a greater ability to select wisely from the massive quantities of material available. The narrator, on the other hand, is more discerning and more aware of the philosophical stakes:

> In the prosecution of his purpose, our historian, the worthy Don Cristobal Ixtlilxochitl . . . is sometimes seduced into the description of events and scenes of a more general character, not very necessarily connected with his main object. . . . The difficulties that beset a historian are ever very great; nor is the least of them found in the necessity of determining how much, *or how little*, he is called upon to record; for though it seems but reasonable he should take it for granted that his readers are entirely unacquainted with the matters he is narrating, and therefore should say all that can be said, this is a point in which all readers will not entirely agree with him. Those who have a smattering of his subject, will be offended, if he presume to instruct them. For our own part, not recognizing the right of the ignorant to be gratified at the expense of the learned, we have studied as much as is possible, so to . . . present his readers chiefly with what they cannot know. (*Calavar* I, 204–05)

Bird's many pedagogic asides and his long footnotes constantly destabilize the text, creating conflicts of authority and opening the space for readerly doubt about the nature of the narrative/romance in the reader's hands. Here, for example, at the end of the prologue to *Calavar*, a footnote instructs us: "For fear that the reader, from the specimens of Mexican words he will meet in this history, should imagine that the Mexican tongue is not meant to be *spoken*, we think fit to apprise him that all such words are to be pronounced as they would be uttered by a Spaniard. . . . Esto importa poco á nuestro cuento: basta que la narracion de él, no se salga en un punto de la verdad—*Don Quijote*" (*Cavalar* I, 22).[16] To be able to pronounce Nahuatl words like a Spaniard, of course, the reader must minimally have some knowledge of Spanish, an expectation borne out in the concluding phrase. Strikingly, the footnote is capped by a disclaimer of sorts in the form of a quote from the premier romance of all time, the Spanish classic *Don Quixote*, where *Don Quixote*'s appeal to its own veracity gives this footnote a similarly ludic access to historical authority that is both insisted upon and revealed as spurious.

Bird's novels were written rapidly, yet clearly he is deeply concerned with questions of language, of the differential weightings of terms, and of the slippages and misunderstandings that occur when translating between cultures that imperfectly understand each other's speech. Nahuatl presents a problem he grapples with continually throughout both novels, and an awareness of a Spanish undertext in the official history of the conquest permeates his work. The text is peppered with Spanish and Nahuatl words, sometimes without translation, especially when the context is clear: "the birds are at rest . . . all save the little madrugadores . . . and the centzontli" (*Infidel* II, 72). Of Juan Lerma's new clothes, the narrator says, "the *bragas* and *xaqueta*, at least were from the wardrobes of the general" (*Infidel* I, 124). Before attacking the forces of Narváez, Cortés makes a stirring speech to his troops, where one of the key words in his final peroration remains untranslated: "it is certain your innocence could not be made apparent to his majesty, until after the gallinazos had picked the last morsel from your bones" (*Calavar* I, 150). Conversation in general is a particularly favored spot for multilingual play, as it allows the author—a well-known former playwright—to experiment with characterization through the oral texture of voices. In this case, he captures the confusion of a soldier being woken up in the middle of the night from a sound sleep: " '*Fuego! Quien pasea alli?*' grumbled the voice of Lazaro . . . , '*Fu! El muchacho!*—I am ever dreaming of that cursed Turk . . . *Laus tibi, Christe*! —I have a throat left for snoring' " (*Calavar* I, 204). Here Bird emphasizes the rhythmic and sonoric qualities of Lazaro's instinctive cry of "Fire" and his subsequent mumblings, terminating with the Latin prayer and falling back to sleep. "Moro! Moro! Tlatoani Moro!" cheer the defenders of Tenochtitlán when Abdalla survives a Spanish attack on their defenses (*Calavar* II, 160), combining Spanish and Nahuatl terms. As with the title "tlatoani," Spanish and Nahuatl are frequently preferred for professions and titles throughout these volumes: "boticario," "alguazil," "teuctli," "tlaméme"; as well as for foods: "tortillas," "chocolatl"; and for native animals and plants.

The reader at times knows more than the characters, as when Amador is invited to a feast where the main dish is turkey (*guajolote*).

When Amador asks Salvatierra to identify the delicious fowl they are eating, his host replies that it is "a sort of great pheasant, the name of which I have not yet schooled my organs to pronounce. . . . It is a kind of peacock. . . . [O]ur soldiers have sometimes, for want of a better name, called it *el Turco*" (*Calavar* I, 77). Because the reader is introduced to the Nahuatl name, as well as the modern Spanish version of it, we are in a position of superiority to the hapless conquistador, and as fellow Americans are better able to understand the bilingual joke of the pheasant/peacock/Turco/turkey.

Salvatierra's inability to learn Nahuatl is emblematic of a leitmotif in these two works—the corruption of native Mexican language when mispronounced by inept Spaniards, and its selective recuperation by a modern counterhistory. For instance, when describing the obsidian-studded club that serves as a common indigenous weapon, he adds the comment that "the *maquahuitl* was speedily corrupted by the Spaniards into *macana*" (*Infidel* I, 56). More important, the reader is presumed both to want to know the accurate name and to prefer the corrupted version, more amenable to Spanish (and presumably English-trained) tongues. Once the authority of the narrator is established by the introduction of the authentic term, the corrupted version is used consistently throughout the text. The Nahuatl words resonate with this heightened authenticity, but are too hard to pronounce, as for example: "the imperial standard, which, in the tongue of Mexico, bore the horribly uncouth title of Tlahuizmatlaxopilli, was conspicuously visible" (*Calavar* II, 221). As with indigenous artifacts, flora, and fauna, so too the indigenous characters' names tend to be corrupted into more Spanish-friendly forms: "Quauhtimozin . . . which is given here in its original and genuine harshness, that the reader may be made acquainted with it, though it is not intended to substitute for its far more agreeable and familiar corruption, Guatimozin" (*Infidel* I, 148). Or, in another example, note this exchange around the campfire, referring to a woman who will loom large in this novel, identified as the youngest of Moctezuma's daughters, where the shifting sound of her name and its loss of signification when corrupted is precisely the point of the conversation.

> . . . said Villafana, . . . "the youngest of all, and, in truth, the prettiest, as I have heard, for I never beheld her, who was called Cillahula,—"
>
> "Zelahualla," said Bernal Diaz. "It is a word that signifies—"
>
> "It signifies nothing, so long as thou give it not the proper accent," said Guzman with infinite composure. "Her true name is Citlaltihuatl. . . . The name may be interpreted the Maiden of

> the Star or Celestial Lady; for so much is expressed by the two words of which it is compounded."
>
> "I maintain," said Bernal Diaz, stoutly, "that the word Zelahualla is more agreeable of pronunciation . . ."
>
> "I grant you that," said Guzman. "Nor is the corruption so great as that of many other names you have recorded in your journal. . . . We will call the princess, then, Zelahualla . . ." (I, 50–51)

The process of Hispanicization has already begun, so that when Juan meets the princess in the garden, it is already Zelahualla with whom he falls in love and whom he converts to Christianity. At the same time, Bird halts the deformation of names at the euphonious Castilianization of Citlaltihuatl to Zelahualla, eschewing the full erasure of identity of renaming in baptism suggested by the historical evolution of Malintzin to Malinche to Marina.

While the male antagonists are the focus of attention in all these novels, the treatment of these characters is relatively unproblematic, since the greatest ambiguity in their characterization involves the author's conscious decision to focus on more or less passive, meditative heroes in a context that seems to call for a ripping adventure yarn. These articulate, noble men—both Spaniards and indigenous people—define the counterhistorical thrust of the morality tale by inverting the perspective derived from official history. I would argue, however, that while relegated to a minor role, the textual disturbance caused by the introjection of the romance aspect of the historical romance leads to an even greater instability in the narrative universe. The naturalization of Citlaltihuatl the Aztec princess into Zelahualla the Christian wife offers one such troubling of the conventional romance happy ending, where the princess does not reveal her real identity as a condition for marriage, but rather assumes a foreign, albeit more euphonious one. This contrasts sharply with the like-to-like tradition of the founding family romances typical of the Anglo-European model. In that tradition, the honorable young man of the *novela de caballerías* typically discovers that he is really a prince and hence a suitable bridegroom; in the fairy-tale version, Cinderella's natural nobility earns her the love of the king's son. In both cases, the man and woman are demonstrably of the same ethnicity and either possess an inherent nobility that shines through superficial trappings despite an underprivileged upbringing or can fall back on the heritage of blood and critically positioned birthmarks to testify to their genetic fitness for rule. Cross-ethnic matches are ignored or specifically excluded. Significantly, in one of the best-beloved novels by the man most associated with energizing the historical novel, Walter

Scott's *Ivanhoe*, the budding romance between the lovely Jewess and the noble hero is doomed from the very beginning because of the prohibitions on mixtures of people from different ethnicities.

In contrast, both Bird's novels and *Jicoténcal* to some degree have to come to terms with the very different founding narrative of Mexican identity, which posits an originary couple of an indigenous woman and a Spanish man, where the woman may be a princess or a slave, and the man's nobility is always somewhat in question. Of course, the indigenous man remains notoriously absent from that founding myth. In these novels, following upon the Mexican mythic/historical tradition, the indigenous warrior must be both a heroic presence organizing the text, so that his figure becomes available to be resuscitated in later days as a model for modern revolutionary endeavors, and he must be very rapidly and completely erased from history in favor of the mestizo offspring of his sister and daughter. He is locked in a detemporalized zone between past defeat and present victory, so that early nineteenth-century revolutionaries must be reminded of his potent history, even as they are implicitly tasked to remember that his is a story that has been forgotten or ignored, and so must be remembered, remade. He is passionate and eloquent, but his words, like those of Masquaza-teuctli, are not heard for four hundred years. The indigenous woman, on the other hand, in the version of the conquest narrative recuperated in these novels, has a continuous presence, but no autonomous speaking role. She remains in the background as one of the interchangeable princess-brides of Spanish soldiers, or at best, in Marina's case, serves as a translator for another's words. In any case, she must give up her native identity for Christian motherhood, in this manner retaining a symbolic presence as the mother of the nation. Hers is a liminal status, bearing children and contributing a blood quotient to her offspring but not herself serving as a cultural mediator.

The historical role of Marina/Malinche is perhaps the most crucial in this regard, though the narratives under discussion here displace the emphasis away from the conqueror and his very able interpreter to deal with the ur-couple of Marina and Cortés as background characters rather than the focus of romantic interest. For Bird, Marina is relegated to a very minor, though wholly positive, role, making her alliance with Cortés an entirely uncomfortable one in narrative terms, since the conqueror is seen at best in a very ambiguous light. Bird prefers his central couple to be completely virtuous; thus, while Marina is frequently mentioned in both novels, Bird focuses his romantic plots on other, less morally fraught miscegenated couples. In *Calavar* he explains her minor role as follows: "at this period, many Spaniards had acquired a smattering of her tongue, and could play the part of interpreters; and, for this reason, Doña Marina will make no great figure in this history. Other annalists have sufficiently immortalized her beauty, her wisdom, and her fidelity; and it has been her good fortune, continued even to this day, to be distinguished with such honors as have fallen to none of her masters" (II, 21–22). In this way, Bird makes a clear distinction between the actions of Marina, who acts honorably in her efforts to facilitate conversations between the Spaniards and the indigenous peoples by translating accurately and faithfully, and Cortés, who dissimulates his real intentions and so fools his interpreter into unintentional misinformation.

In *Jicoténcal*, on the other hand, Marina is omnipresent, and she serves as an important foil to Cortés in the evolution of the plot. In the first instance, she is evoked as an object reason to distrust the Spanish leader. As Diego de Ordaz comments in a conversation with Fray Bartolomé de Olmedo, Cortés "hace ostentación de sus amores adúlteros con esa india, quizás víctima de su seducción" [he almost boasts of his adulterous affair with that Indian woman, who is maybe a victim of his seduction] (12/16), a worrisome action that the honorable young Spaniard reads as an indication of deep character flaws. Seduction is, in fact, the keynote in all matters pertaining to the indigenous woman; once seduced, she learns from her master how to seduce and readily employs her talents at his behest and on his behalf. When we meet Marina herself a few pages later in the narrative, it is already as Cortés's willing ally in crime. She serves as an "astuta y falsa amiga" [astute and false friend] to Teutila, who in her naive and Native innocence expects virtue and honesty of her fellows. Marina, a willing apprentice to her dishonorable master, is aware of this inherent indigenous nobility of mind and easily seduces Jicoténcal's young bride: "no sospechando en ella las artes y el dolo de los europeos, supo emplear con más efecto la corrupción y la intriga, en que hizo grandes progresos" [the natives did not suspect in her the guile and deceit of the Europeans. She was able to employ corruption and intrigue more effectively, activities in which she made great progress] (32/37). For good measure, she also seduces Jicoténcal: "el bravo tlascalteca cayó poco a poco en las redes de su astuta y hábil compatriota" [the brave Tlaxcalan slowly fell into the web being spun by his able and astute compatriot] (53/59), which leads to absolute agonies of remorse on his part when he comes to his senses (58/65). She also seduces the one Spaniard who has been resisting her wiles, and who holds virtuous chastity in high regard: "Ordaz era joven; doña Marina era hermosa y amable, y . . . Un tardo desengaño vino a sacar al honrado Ordaz de su letargo después de cubrirlo con vergüenza" [Ordaz was young, doña Marina was beautiful and kind, and—too late did the honest Ordaz come out of his lethargy and he was covered with shame] (42; original ellipsis/48). For the reader who may not be entirely certain of what narrative sins were covered by the authorial ellipsis, Ordaz shortly after this scene expresses his deep anguish that he might have fathered a child with her (59/66).

Marina eventually realizes, however, that her indoctrination into Christianity through moral and physical seduction was superficial and lacking—or that perhaps the religion itself sponsors criminality—and comes to a new commitment to the ways of righteousness in fear of death as she undergoes the labors of childbirth: "quizá la Naturaleza podrá en mí más que la corrupción" [Perhaps Nature will be stronger in me than corruption] she suggests in a childbed confession to Fray Bartolomé, which she later shares with Ordaz as well (90/98). The responsibilities attendant upon her new baby, along with the example of Teutila, prompt her to rethink her too-easy conversion; these virtuous models "la llamaron dentro de sí misma y principió a tomar gusto por las dulces habitudes de la virtud" [struck a chord within her, and she began to take pleasure in the sweet habit of being virtuous] (108/119). In a long conversation with her chaplain, Marina explains her reasons for rejecting the hypocritical and dishonest excesses of the Cortés expedition, calling for a faith that aligns itself with practice, rejecting Christian doctrine, at least until such time as the practitioners can demonstrate its teachings through virtuous example:

> Cuando yo seguía mi culto sencillo y puro, pues que salía de mi corazón; cuando yo era idólatra, segun tú me llamabas, yo fui una mujer virtuosa . . . pero desde que fui cristiana, mis progresos en la carrera del crimen fueron más grandes que las hermosas virtudes de Teutila.
>
> Abjuro para siempre de una religión que me habéis enseñado con mentira, con la intriga, con la codicia, con la destemplanza y, sobre todo, con la indiferencia a los crímenes más atroces. La doctrina se predica con ejemplo, y, cuando éste se ha ganado el respeto, el entendimiento se sujeta a la convicción. (109–110)
>
> When I observed my simple and pure worship, well, it came right from my heart. When I was an idolater, as you referred to me, I was always a virtuous woman . . . but from the moment that I became a Christian, my progress along the road to crime was greater than the beautiful virtues of Teutila.
>
> I renounce forever the religion that you have taught me with lies, with intrigue, with greed, with misery, and especially with indifference in the face of the most atrocious crimes. Doctrine is preached through example, and when it has earned

> respect, understanding is held through conviction. (121, translation slightly modified)

Fray Bartolomé is outraged and wholly unable to respond to Marina's call for accountability in religious practices. Strikingly enough, however, her concerns strongly echo those of Diego de Ordaz, and both are mediated through dialogues with the priest at different points in the novel. This confluence of protorepublican anticlerical thought, which they share as well with the explicit conclusions of the philosopher-narrator, suggest an alternative understanding of the Mexican originary family at this historical bifurcation of paths figured in the sixteenth-century conquest and its nineteenth-century redemption. If the mestizo children of postindependence narrative decry the historical criminality of their putative forefather, Cortés, and his evil cohort, the betrayer Marina, *Jicoténcal* offers an alternative historical siting. In this story, the old historical narrative is given a new twist. Cortés is victorious, the virtuous indigeneous couple of Jicoténcal and Teutila are betrayed to their death, foreclosing the possibility of an indigenous line of descent, but the future holds out the limited redemption of an unspoken alternative pairing that supplements the losses of recorded history: a redeemed and repentant Marina, the noble and honest Diego de Ordaz, and the child, the future of the race, which could be as easily Ordaz's son as Cortés's.

Bird resolves his narratives more traditionally with a formal marriage, in both cases a miscegenated one. In *Calavar*, Bird is careful to set the scene for an openness to such cross-ethnic pairings by having his characters discuss the relative merits of indigenous American versus Spanish Moorish women as brides. De Morla, who is in love with an Aztec lady, believes that the daughters of Mexican nobles "if converted to the true faith, would make more honourable wives for Spanish hidalgos than the Moorish ladies of our own land," to which Don Amador, who has a past of his own with Moorish Leila, responds, "these Mexican princesses may make very good wives when true Christians, I can well believe; but I have my doubts whether they have any such superiority over the Moorish ladies" (I, 189-90). Even more forcefully, in *Infidel*, Cortés argues for the fitness of the marriage between Juan Lerma and Zelahualla: "as for this princess . . . know that she is a daughter of Moctezuma, the descendent of a thousand kings; and the Count of Castillejo will carry with him to his castle, a bride more noble than ever entered it before" (II, 213). It is, perhaps, too much to expect that Bird's Lerma would follow the example of his historical forerunner and disappear into the indigenous community, rather than having his indigenous wife disappear in a Spanish castle; the permeability of racial lines is already an unusual enough step in this romance.

Importantly, in both *Calavar* and *Infidel*, in very different ways, the bride's ethnicity serves as a plot device rather than a scandal. Indeed, while Bird subscribes to the paler-skin/greater-virtue model, he does not automatically associate beauty and whiteness with European descent. He notes that many of the indigenous beauties have lighter skin than Spanish men, hence confusing the typical pigmentation schema by applying a sliding comparative scale. Thus, for example, the narrator describes the princess Zelahualla: "Her skin was, for her race, wonderfully fair; and yet there were, even among the men of Mexico, skins much lighter than those of some of the Spaniards, of which Guatimozin was a famous example" (*Infidel* II, 48).

In *Calavar*, the love story revolves around the wildly improbable juxtaposition of a disguised Leila and her erstwhile Christian beloved, who does not recognize her until near the end of the second volume, despite the many hints she gives Amador, which include recounting to him their own story of star-crossed love. The young woman, dressed in male clothing as the servant boy "Jacinto," is greatly loved by all the Spanish troops, and his/her marked effeminacy is excused because of the boy's courteous and helpful behavior and excellent singing voice. Jacinto/Leila's father is the dishonorably treated Moorish nobleman, Alharef-ben-Ismail, alias Esclavo de la Cruz, alias Abdalla the Moor. Abdalla is a contradictory and morally ambiguous character who commits treason against his Spanish colleagues but has a morally comprehensible reason for doing so, who is fierce and strong in his political convictions but behaves in a groveling and abject manner so as to ensure his child's safety and well-being. Abdalla is betrayed by the Spaniards, forced to convert to Christianity, and enslaved. When freed by Amador, he joins the Cortés expedition, only to abandon the allied forces as soon as they reach Tenochtitlán so as to lend his expertise to the opposing indigenous forces. Having no safe haven for his daughter, he brings her along on his adventures, dressed as a boy, and has Amador swear to protect him/her. Out of filial duty, Jacinto/Leila accompanies her father to the Mexican side of the war and rallies their forces by enacting the role of an Aztec priestess. It is precisely in the moment at which the disguised Leila takes on this new role that Amador, who believed her dead, imagines his beloved resurrected in another form:

> In the centre of the train on a sort of litter, very rich and gorgeous, borne on men's shoulders, and sheltered by a rich canopy of green and crimson feathers, stood a figure, which might have been some maiden princess, arrayed for the festival, or, as she seemed to one or two of the more superstitious Castilians, some fiendish goddess, conjured up by the diabolical arts of the priests,

> to add the inspiration of her presence to the wild fury of her adorers. . . . Just as she was about to be concealed from them forever, the divinity, priestess, or princess, whichever she was, turned her body slowly around, and revealed to them a face of a paler hue than any they had yet seen in the new world, and, as they afterwards affirmed, of the most incomparable and ravishing beauty. (II, 48–49)

Leila never satisfactorily explains her role in the war effort as an Aztec priestess; the reader is meant to understand that she participates in these events out of laudable devotion to her father while remaining absolutely faithful to her Christian beliefs. At the same time, the slippage among the three identities—Moorish woman, Christian boy, Aztec priestess—points to a particularly striking narrative crux symptomatic of all three of these texts: how to articulate the liaison between Western and non-Occidental cultures and histories. The supposed Spanish openness to cultural mixing through marriage to properly Christianized Moorish women provides a model for a New World racial and cultural amalgamation; by the same token Jacinto becomes available as a potential wife because she is revealed as an Aztec priestess, and her Moorish father must die for her to take on her real identity as Leila. There is in this shifting alliance and ethnic negotiation a hint of the multiple understandings of the nature of hybrid cultural identity that in these novels has a particularly American and republican flavor. While the issues necessarily remain undecidable in the pressures of the historical moment of conquest, the novels point beyond that moment, to a time in which the potential children of this union will resolve the quandary by finding a way to articulate the hopes for the future.

With *Infidel,* the narrative becomes considerably darker. *Calavar* takes place before the definitive conquest of the Aztec capital; *Infidel* (subtitled, *Or, The Fall of Mexico*) describes the final days of Tenochtitlán. The conceit of a fall pervades the entire narrative; the plot is far more intricate than that of the previous novel and has a greater gothic quality. While in *Calavar* the weight of moral ambiguity falls on the Moor, in *Infidel* that function rests upon a mysterious fallen woman, called la Monjonaza or Infeliz, but whose obviously symbolic given name is Magdalena. Magdalena is presumed to have been raped as a young girl, thus compromising definitively her good name, and she has subsequently taken religious orders. She claims that she is innocent, but her reputation is completely lost because of a deathbed lie by an enemy swearing to her lack of virginity; she is considered "the base, the fallen, the degraded" (I, 141). As the novel begins, she is Cortés's "fancy" (I, 177), though the suggestion of the crime of blasphemy, punishable by death, would attend any sexual congress with a nun (137). Cortés is insanely jealous of Juan Lerma, whom Magdalena loves; the unhappy woman dies of a broken heart when she discovers that Juan is her twin brother and her feelings for him are entirely incestuous.

This dark story of personal betrayal and dark loves contrasts with the central love story of the novel, the innocent and chaste relationship between Juan and Zelahualla. Perhaps one of the most striking elements of this novel is that the ambiguously fallen woman is the only Spanish noblewoman to appear in either of these works, and her virtuous counterpart is not a white woman but an indigenous princess. The contrast between them could not be more stark. Where Magdalena's life consists of one disaster after another and continual association with evil men, Juan meets Zelahualla in a perfectly pastoral garden setting: "in a green nook, exceedingly sequestered, and peculiarly beautified by banks of the richest flowers, were five Indian maidens, three of whom danced under the trees on the smooth grass, to the sound of a little pipe or flute. . . . The other, half kneeling, reclined hard by, fastening a chaplet of flowers around the neck of a fawn. . . ." In contrast with the dark-complected and darkly robed Magdalena, the princess and her companions display a classical elegance in their dress; they are: "young, pretty, and robed with such simplicity as might have become the Hamadryads of Thessaly" in richly embroidered white *huipiles* (II, 46). The Spaniard falls in love with Zelahualla at first sight, a fortunate fall and one that offsets the unhappily fallen state of the Spanish woman and, in the larger world, the fall of the Mexican city. Juan immediately begins to teach her about Christianity, the truth of which she instinctively understands and accepts: "With good hearts, Juan Lerma and the princess of Mexico, moved among the corruptions of superstition, uncorrupted; and preserved to themselves, unabated and unsullied, the pure and gentle feelings, which nature had showered upon them at their birth" (II, 74).

Where Juan and Zelahualla are able to retain a foothold in the pastoral oasis despite the travails of war, *Jicoténcal* consistently puts pressure on the sanctity of the *locus amoenus* by actualizing the scene of violation at its heart. Two contrasting stories of invasion point up the moral turpitude of the Spaniards, who respect neither beauty nor virtue. At one point in the novel, Teutila is on a trip to Zocothlán, and she runs into two fellow Tlaxcalans, who have in their charge a Spaniard "enteramente desnudo y tan fuertemente atado que le era imposible todo movimiento" [entirely naked and so tightly bound that it was impossible for him to move] (121–22/133). In response to her inquiry, the Tlaxcalans tell her that the man invaded the peace and harmony of the *bosque* to fall upon a local matron innocently going about her business: "su brutal lujuria consuma el crimen atroz que no me atrevo a nombrar en su presencia" [with brutal lust he consummated the atrocious crime that I do not dare to mention in your presence]. The man and his two sons, upon hearing the woman's screams, try to come to the rescue, only to "descubrir al malvado, que estaba sobre su infeliz víctima ya desmayada" [we found him lying on top of his wretched victim, who had already fainted]. Their efforts to save the woman are in vain: "al perder su honor perdió también la vida" [upon losing her honor she also lost her life] (122–23/134). In contrast, Teutila's story of her first encounter with her future husband, when they were on opposing sides in a war, could not have been more different. A similar encounter takes place, in that Teutila is going about her peaceful business in a pastoral setting when she runs into her people's enemy: "caí yo a tierra sin sentido. Al volver en mí, me encuentro en los brazos de Jicoténcal" [I fell to the ground unconscious. When I came to, I found myself in the arms of Xicoténcatl]; instead of raping her while she was unconscious, however, he rubs her hands, and splashes water on her face to help her regain her senses. Subsequently, she fully expects to be treated as a slave and instead is accorded great respect, to the degree that Jicoténcal offers her honorable marriage (19–20/24–25).

The theme of rape or near rape pervades the novel and reminds the reader of the "tan natural consecuencia de los vicios de un gobierno arbitrario y desmoralizado" [such a natural consequence of the vices of an arbitrary and demoralized government] (124/136). The narrator describes Diego de Ordaz's seduction by Marina in terms that very nearly approximate violation. Cortés, likewise, nearly rapes Teutila and is only stopped by the intensity of her resistance: "Teutila perseveró en su mismo silencio y con éste, triunfaba siempre de su insolente tirano. Al fin al violencia y la fuerza hubieran quizá consumado el crimen si los gritos espantosos que daba la inocente víctima . . . no hubieran causado una alarma en el campamento" [Teutila persevered in her silence, and through it all she always triumphed against her insolent tyrant. Violence and force would have finally consummated the crime had the frightening screams of the innocent victim . . . not caused great alarm in the encampment] (71–72/79–80). In *Jicoténcal*'s world, this lack of respect for the individual reflects the lack of order and moral purpose among Cortés's troops; moreover, in the larger social context it also describes a specific strategy for disrupting the virtuous local government and bringing it down. Thus, not only do they sanction physical rape, a crime that embodies their degenerate morality, Cortés and Magiscatzin symbolically also have their way with the republican senate. Their proposal for an alliance "triunfó de la débil resistencia de algunos pocos senadores que se opusieron inútilmente a la prostitución y envilecimiento de la autoridad soberana de Tlascala" [triumphed over the weak resistance of a few senators who showed useless opposition to the prostitution and debasement of the sovereign authority of Tlaxcala] (107/118). Thus, the city-state is like a woman mistreated by her putative lover and forced into an unsanctified liaison, just as dishonorable warfare turns a blind eye to the abuses of individual soldiers who invade peaceful lands and rape and murder virtuous women. Both women and the land need care and protection, since their beauty is delicate and can easily be destroyed, their fragile virtue irretrievably lost. The narrator makes this point explicitly: "La soberanía de los Estados es como el honor de la mujer" [the sovereignty of states is like a woman's honor] and similarly needs to be preserved intact because once lost it can never be regained (107/118). Cortés, thus, is doubly reprehensible since he not only engages in unjust war that disrupts a good and honest government to replace it with an arbitrary and tyrannical one, he also sullies the virtue of both women and the State with his corrupting acts.

If we return to the question that started this analysis, the inquiry into "what, exactly, America is to be" (Palumbo-Liu), these early texts insistently point to an epistemological system that operates at the margins of, and frequently in opposition to, the structures of knowledge inherited from the European colonial experience. These texts all go back to an unquestionably American founding moment, rethinking the received history by speaking from the margin of the episteme, radicalizing it by privileging the perspective of the indigeneous American forms over those imposed upon this continent by conquerors from the other side of the Atlantic. It is, perhaps, too easy a critique to signal the ways in which a European-derived perspective still governs the moral thrust of these works: their privileging of whiteness, for example, or the approximation of native Mexican cultures to imagined Roman Republican forms.[17] González Acosta's citation from an unpublished manuscript by Nancy Vogeley is apposite: "esos escritores transplantados contribuían a la formación de discursos nacionales y de nuevos públicos lectores en sus áreas respectivas. . . . [Y]o quiero argüir que su esfuerzo temprano para desarrollar la conciencia con ayuda de la narración de la historia, aunque sea una reliquia, es un ejemplo valioso del discurso descolonizador, evidencia de un tipo de historia potencialmente útil, que parece haberse perdido en el nacionalismo del siglo XIX" [those transplanted writers contributed to the formation of national discourses and new reading publics in their respective areas. . . . I want to argue that their early effort to develop a consciousness with the aid of historical narration, even a vestigial one, is a valuable example of a decolonizing discourse, evidence of a potentially useful type of history, that seems to have gotten lost in nineteenth-century nationalism] (256). Both Bird and the author of *Jicoténcal* explicitly present counterhistories that interrupt the presumed hegemonic memory by offering an alternative reading of the trauma of conquest as a founding myth with continental reach and repercussions.

At the same time that these early historical novels posit a rethinking of the European-derived systems of thought and governance, they also remind us contemporary readers of an important historical dialogue that we twenty-first-century Americans often forget, a conversation that is continental in scope, multilingual in presentation, multiracial in sensitivity, and postcolonial in ideology. The texts by these two writers, written within a decade of each other in the same city and published in different languages, engage implicitly the analysis of an abstract American citizen, referencing the concept of "American" as a general term implying an identity common to both the U.S. and Latin American republics, and reminding the reader that an American history would naturally concern itself with the collaborative continental struggle for independence from Europe. In this struggle, the early history of the United States is as likely to be written in Spanish or Nahuatl as English, and Xicotencatl, Bolívar, and George Washington have equal claims to the role of the prototypical American hero.

chapter three

Crossing: Vega, González Viaña, Fuentes, Oropeza

IN 1829, A SPANISH-AMERICAN civil servant named Jorge W. (George Washington) Montgomery adapted Washington Irving's story "Rip Van Winkle" into Spanish under the title of "El serrano de las Alpujarras" and published it in Madrid in a volume called *Tareas de un solitario*, where neither Montgomery's nor Irving's names appear anywhere in the text.[1] The next year, Henry Wadsworth Longfellow chose several stories from that book, reedited them in a volume titled *Novelas españolas*, and made that volume required reading for students of Spanish at Harvard, thus in effect turning Irving into a Spanish author. "Rip Van Winkle" was, and remains, one of Irving's best-known stories; it has also been considered notoriously difficult to translate because of the very particular local flavor deriving from its New York Dutch elements.[2] In his Andalusian version of the tale, the Spanish-American translator shifts the locale of the story entirely, changing both continent and historical setting. His protagonist is named Andrés Gazul, and instead of encountering Dutchmen in the Catskills, he wanders into a flamboyantly described Moorish setting in Andalusia. The Dutch kegs become Moorish opiates, and the cultural subtext no longer has to do with the transition between colonial and independent status in the United States, but the influence of Moorish culture on a peaceful man who after being drawn into the Moorish festivities is crowned king of Granada before falling into a drugged stupor.[3] Like Rip, he awakens and returns to his village to find that years have passed. At the end of the story, Andrés Gazul recovers from his strange adventure to become a respected patriarch. This seemingly innocuous story was viewed with some suspicion in its own time, and the original volume, *Tareas de un solitario*, is extremely rare, perhaps partly because it raised the hackles of Spanish censors, "who saw libel and treason against the King in the Spanish version of 'Rip Van Winkle' " (Williams, "First Version" 190–91).

This anecdote about "Rip's" adventures in the Iberian peninsula would be relegated to a historical curiosity today, were it not for the fact that it speaks so clearly to the issues of translation across cultures and the political consequences of such often-fraught bicultural exchanges. It adds another fillip to the story to remind ourselves that Irving's original is itself bicultural, and that the American author acknowledges his debt to a previous, European-based, cultural export. The narrator of Irving's original story hints that this folktale had already crossed the ocean in the other direction to come to his hands, and, in a tongue-in-cheek comment, the "editor" of "Diedrich Knickerbocker's" histories humorously credits his own sources: "The foregoing Tale, one would suspect, had been suggested to Mr. Knickerbocker by a little German superstition about the Emperor Frederick der Rothbart, and the Kypphauser Mountain: the subjoined note, however, which he had appended to the tale, shows that it is an absolute fact, narrated with his usual fidelity."[4] Thus, Irving informs his readers that he has borrowed a German tale and adapted it to a U.S. context. In making this transition, the American writer highlights the competing ethnicities involved in the sequence of Dutch and British colonialism in the New World and their subsumption under the flag of the United States as an independent nation, albeit somewhat imperfectly, as attested by the hasty repainting of George III as George Washington on the inn sign. In crossing the ocean again to Spain, the tale that is returned to Europe retains the context of an encounter between competing ethnicities in a space and time outside normal history and geography, and moreover acquires a different ideological charge as a dangerous political parable attacking the Spanish monarchy.

This tale of adaptation and readaptation, of crossing and recrossing the oceans and borders and historical times, has a textual as well as a thematic analogue, and the Moorish adaptation of the story is peculiarly apropos both in the context of Irving's corpus and with respect to the argument I hope to elaborate in this chapter. Irving from a very early age was deeply intrigued by fifteenth- and sixteenth-century Spanish military expeditions, including both the conquest of Mexico and the capture of Granada, and was interested in colonial chronicles as well as contemporary Spanish *novelas de costumbres.*[5] Even before leaving the United States for his extensive travels in Europe, Irving wrote numerous Moorish-inspired fragments of prose and folkloric sketches.[6] He eventually lived for seven years in Spain, and—among others—was a close friend of the prominent novelist Fernán Caballero (Cecilia Böhl von Faber), who was delighted by the work in his *Sketch Book* and found it inspiring in her own *artículos de costumbres.*

The version of the Rip Van Winkle story told by "Diedrich Knickerbocker" focuses on the ethnographic results of a serious scholar who had conducted scrupulous historical research into the history and customs of New York State. "Rip" is one of a series of supposedly carefully authenticated histories from that region. The protagonist of the tale is a good-natured man, well liked by all in his small upstate village. The bane of his life is that he is terribly henpecked by his wife, "a termagant" and "terrible virago"; though the reader could well find sympathy for poor Dame Van Winkle, since she is burdened by a large family and a feckless husband: "the great error in [his] composition was an insuperable aversion to all kinds of profitable labor." To escape her nagging, Rip goes off squirrel hunting, comes across the strange Dutchmen, parties with them all night, and wakes up twenty years later to find his wife dead and the world changed. Most notably, the village inn where he passed so many happy hours has become the Union Hotel: "he recognized the sign, however, the ruby face of King George, under which he had smoked so many a peaceful pipe; but even this was singularly metamorphosed. The red coat was changed for one of blue and buff, a sword was held in the hand instead of a skeptre, the head was decorated with a cocked hat, and underneath it was painted in large characters, GENERAL Washington." Other more able critics have analyzed the visual imagery of this story, as well as the political moral tale encoded in the twenty-year sleep; what I want to briefly highlight here is Irving's criss-crossing of ethnicities, customs, and literary styles such that the rubbing together of two formerly antagonistic groups resolves itself in an uneasy and ideologically charged peace. Whether in its German, U.S., or Spanish versions, this is a story that always has a political import, though the target of critique differs drastically depending on the presumed audience.

In 1982, Puerto Rican author Ana Lydia Vega revisited this old story and published a Caribbean adaptation of it with her "Cráneo de una noche de verano" [Cranium on a Summer's Night]. Rewriting from a perspective outside the continental United States, from a position of otherness to the dominant-culture ethic that people like Irving have in contemporary times come to represent, Vega adopts the voice of a Puerto Rican drug addict who wakes up from a bad trip only to wander into the celebrations attendant upon the declaration of Puerto Rico as the fifty-first state. The story, thus, at best encodes the Puerto Rican ambivalence about the relation of their nation to the imposing cultural and political pressures coming from the North. More exactly, it points to the ideological and cultural challenges of being a U.S. citizen, but not quite accepted as a "real American," of living within a community that perceives itself as misshaped/deformed by its relation to the United States. Vega is clearly in dialogue with the received canons of both countries; at the same time, in putting them together in a promiscuous juxtaposition of texts and voices, she calls them both into question. As Juan Gelpí notes: "con la obra de Ana Lydia Vega se cruza un límite, una frontera: en ella estamos decididamente fuera del canon" [with Ana Lydia Vega's work one crosses a limit, a border: with her we are decidedly outside the canon] (183). This is true in various senses, not the least of which pertains to the fact that Puerto Rico, while technically part of the United States, remains largely outside U.S. literary consciousness, and while culturally part of Spanish America, suffers from a lack of national status. At the same time, her sharp, modern rewriting of "Rip" captures some of the political urgency of the original tale, which in its time pointed to the uneasy accommodations between an earlier conqueror and now-conquered people (the Dutch settlers), in a state that is making the transition between secondary British colonialism and a new, still fluid, unexpected and perhaps undesired, independent status, one where the dominant culture retains an unmistakably British-inflected Otherness.

Within the context of the U.S. dominant culture imaginary, Puerto Rico has a very restricted role, making it extremely challenging for writers like Vega, who in her collection *Encancaranublado* [Cloud Cover Caribbean] speaks to and against the U.S. corporate/colonial model from within a Caribbean basin discursive structure. Hers are, in Gelpí's words, "escrituras a la intemperie" [rough weather writing] (183). Ana Lydia Vega's collection of short stories identifies with the Caribbean in general, though she writes specifically within a Puerto Rican perspective. This outsider situation with respect to the imperial United States is not unique to the Puerto Rican author. The nature of the Puerto Rican colonization, however, allows Vega to play with a rich subtext that includes riffs on what are now canonical U.S. literary texts identified with the United States' WASP cultural core, such as the works of Washington Irving. Moreover, she implicitly reminds us that when we go back to Irving's work with the historical context in mind, the shock of encounter among conflicting languages, discourses, and cultural communities is very much the point, and very much a part of Irving's preimperial United States that was only just beginning to define itself as an independent nation in counterposition to the old colonial power. In staking her claim to "Rip Van Winkle" and rearticulating it for a very different cultural and political setting, Vega implicitly calls for a reimagination of the possibilities for understanding a relation to primordial literary spaces, inserting Puerto Rico firmly into the palimpsestic landscape.

The rich subtextual debate thus engendered bears the marks of layers of competing visions and multiple reappropriations. In his analysis of C. L. R. James, Grant Farred succinctly captures the vexed nature of these simultaneous and conflicting patrimonies:

> The Caribbean is always an "imagined" rather than an essential community. Since "half" of the Caribbean "belongs to someone else," and "half" of its inhabitants "belong somewhere else," the region itself is a diasporic settlement. And because "half" of its population and "half" of its "history" are "imported," and a great deal of wealth (its natural resources, its culture, its people) is exported, the Caribbean can only be fully grasped by going beyond it. (Farred 35)

Similarly, in the introduction to *Puerto Rican Jam,* the editors of the volume write: "most intellectuals frame Puerto Rican struggles within a nineteenth-century model of colonialism in which the colonized lived in daily confrontation with the invader on their own soil and thus are unable to properly contextualize Puerto Rican cultural practices" (Grosfoguel, Negron-Muntaner, and Georgas 10). The question, thus, is "not whether Puerto Ricans even 'have' a culture or if that culture is corrupt or 'penetrated,' but rather in what ways do Puerto Ricans imagine themselves in culture as part of communities" (15). The solution, they conclude, is to make use of mimicry and masquerade, especially the "mimicry of subversion where the deliberate performance of a role does not entail identification" (27).

For Ana Lydia Vega, and as we shall see, for González Viaña, Carlos Fuentes, and Margarita Oropeza as well, the narrative of culture and border crossing is marked and enriched by the play of us/them, by the stylistic and thematic exchanges between national cultures and iconographic gestures. These texts expose highly conflicted relations to an ineluctable U.S. hegemonic power that at one level will inevitably interpellate them according to an unavoidable representational logic. At the same time, the chain of identification and representation is so overdetermined that in effect these crossing narratives create highly ironized contexts for thinking outside the box. Vega's *Encancaranublado,* as well as González Viaña's *Los sueños de América* [American Dreams], Fuentes's *La frontera de cristal* [*Crystal Frontier*], and Oropeza's *Después de la montaña* [After the Mountain] offer narratives derived from the subject position of individuals typically unobserved and unobservable, border-crossing subjects who defamiliarize the literary landscape by subjecting others to their gaze.

Santiago Castro-Gómez comments, for example, that the normative understanding of modernity in Latin America is necessarily different in kind from the Euro-American, and that this temporal belatedness reflects a qualitative distinction in theoretical structures of thought about modernity: "a diferencia de lo acaecido en Europa, la consolidación de la modernidad cultural en América Latina no precede al cine, la radio y la televisón, sino que *se debe* precisamente a ellos. . . . La modernidad en América Latina desafia, entonces los marcos teóricos generados por el 'proyecto de la modernidad' " [Unlike what happened in Europe, the consolidation of cultural modernity in Latin America did not precede film, radio, and television, but *owes itself* precisely to them. . . . Modernity in Latin America, therefore, challenges the theoretical frames generated by the 'project of modernity']. It is precisely this antinormativist perspective that Castro-Gómez analyzes in his work delving into the still relatively unexplored territory of modern Latin America's philosophical difference from, and potential contributions to, the metropolis (3–4). There is in this argument a strong claim for a supplementary reading of this Euro-identified theory, one that comes from the South, from the peripheries of modernity. Even further: this southern take on theory, suggests Castro-Gómez, will not only serve as a supplement to the metropolis, but can provide the foundation for a countertheoretical stance that will challenge some of modernity's most basic and assumed premises. In a parallel manner, Vega, González Viaña, Fuentes, and Oropeza supplement U.S.-based narratives of immigration to the United States with their own, Latin American–based takes on this familiar phenomenon, creating the possibility at least for a transnational communication circuit.

Martín Hopenhayn asks us to think about the possibilities of a globalization that "podría movilizar energías liberadoras. Me refiero al enriquecimiento transcultural, al encuentro con el radicalmente-otro. . . . Más que respeto multicultural, autorrecreación transcultural: regresar a nosotros después de pasar por el buen salvaje, ponernos experiencialmente en perspectiva, pasar nuestro cuerpo por el cuerpo del Sur, del Norte, del Oriente . . . " [could mobilize liberatory energies. I refer to the transcultural enrichment in the encounter with the radically other. . . . More than multicultural respect, transcultural self-reinvention: to return to ourselves after having passed through the noble savage, placing ourselves experientially in perspective, passing our body through the body of the South, the North, the East] (32–33). Both Hopenhayn and Castro-Gómez, in this brief capsule, serve as exemplars of representative projects for Latin American engagement and dialogue with the challenges of thinking globally from outside the Euro-American axis. They are the others within the purview of the globalized theoretical network, the oppositional thinkers who frequently serve to remind metropolitan totalizing thinkers of the local particularities and regional realities that offset as they undergird theoretical analyses. The questions they pose are essential ones; furthermore, the nuanced engagement with thinkers such as these men reminds us of a crucial blind spot in much first-world theorizing, and provides a resource for deeper and more powerful thinking.[7]

VEGA'S DISLOCATIONAL POLITICS

Ana Lydia Vega engages in a sort of sleight of hand by which the location of cultural capital is redefined in a defamiliarizing gesture of dislocation, shifting the ideological ground while retaining certain familiar markers. As suggested above, "Cráneo de una noche de verano" offers an excellent case in point, providing us with a Spanish adaptation of "Rip Van Winkle" that is at least as faithful to the original as the Montgomery translation, and reminding the reader as well that the original "Rip" was not just a quaint folktale, but also a pointed political allegory about the ethnic and ideological frictions in the new, and still unstable, United States. The Montgomery adaptation, while not as well known as the original, adds another layer to the already palimpsestic political and social allegory, suggesting how texts change meanings as they cross borders into another language. This observation is not unique to Montgomery, of course; Irving has already anticipated it in his tongue-in-cheek evocation/dismissal of the story's potential German roots. The putative "origin" of the story continually recedes behind its local masks, but in each case creates political trouble. In her version of this story, Vega pays homage to the New England traditions undergirding contemporary U.S. dominant literary culture and undermines them at the same time, going back to a version of "Rip" that echoes the now-faded political satire of Irving's original. Güilson, like Rip, is a marginal character in his society, though of course each holds the central location in his respective story. As Aníbal González says of Vega, in terms equally applicable to Irving: "En todos estos relatos, los personajes son estereotipos, caricaturas o entes personificados cuyas mutaciones e interacciones ilustran una moraleja que unas veces se nos anticipa en los epígrafes y otras se nos presenta de manera más tradicional al final del cuento" [In all these tales, the characters are stereotypes, caricatures, or personified beings whose mutations and interactions illustrate a moral that sometimes is anticipated in epigraphs and other times is presented in a more traditional form at the end of the story] (294).

Rip is a lazy Dutch-descended drunkard, a familiar type in colonial lore; Güilson a modern drug addict, a stereotypical sight in modern Puerto Rico. Mysterious Dutchmen identified with the colonial explorer Hendrick Hudson give Rip strong drink, and he falls asleep in a colonial monarchy only to wake up as an old man in the United States. In the case of Vega's character, a dealer named Yuniol "lo había embollao con guasas y lo había atosigao de ácido y de pepas hasta las tetas,"[8] providing the hapless antihero with modern, metropolitan-derived drugs such that he loses consciousness for what seems to have been several days (or perhaps many years?). He suffers from at least the illusion and perhaps the reality that he has become an old man "más plegao que un culo y tras un plegao sin dientes" (82). Yuniol's drugs send him on a "tripeo jeviduti que creía que ahí mismo lo iba a soltar la guagua e la vida" (83).[9] Like his earlier counterpart, Güilson passes out with his nation still under a (secondary) colonial government and regains his senses and returns to the street during the festivities associated with Puerto Rico's new status as a U.S. state, with the entire city seemingly out in the streets celebrating and the Police Band "tocando algo así como el himno americano en tiempo e merengue" (85).[10]

A large rickety building called the Union Hotel has replaced Rip's friendly Dutch inn in Irving's story, and Rip laments that "there was a busy, bustling, disputatious tone about it, instead of the accustomed phlegm and drowsy tranquillity." In Vega's modern version of the story, Güilson retires to his favorite gathering place, only to find "el fóquin cafetín estaba cerrao. Y el restaurán de lao también. Y el sitio chino también. Y hasta el friquitín cubano, men, que no cerró ni pal entierro e Muñoz."[11] Where Rip wonders what happened to the local Dutch heritage of phlegm, Güilson theorizes that maybe all his fellow citizens "se había embarcao to el mundo pa los niuyores buscando el bille" (83).[12] In each case, the "inn" or the "cafetín" serves as the space of encounter with a radical change in society; likewise, in each case the protagonist attempts to rationalize the changes and create a narrative to account for the inconsistencies.

In the end of their respective stories, the protagonists must come to terms with a changed reality. Rip Van Winkle settles back into his role as a good-for-nothing layabout, happily freed from the demands of his long-suffering wife. For Güilson, the revelations are too overwhelming for him to process successfully. With the exception of "una vieja [que] jirimiqueaba sin consuelo" (84),[13] the entire Puerto Rican social and political spectrum has come together to celebrate their own qualified version of independence. Drug-sick and wavering on the balcony, Güilson reaches a point of no return: "Cuando se vino a dar cuenta de que iba pabajo sin remedio, Yuniol lo estaba agarrando por el cuello y faltaban dos segundos pa que la bomba de tiempo que tenía setiá entre ceja y ceja le volara en mil fóquin cantos la cabeza" (86).[14] Finally, in both stories the apparent frivolity of the topic shadows a more somber meaning. In Vega's story, the exuberance of the language—what Barradas calls "la identificación y exaltación del lenguaje popular—contaminado y agresivo, y por ello, vivaz y redentor" [the identification and exaltation of popular language: contaminated and aggressive, and for that reason, vigorous and redemptive] (553)—anesthetizes the reader to the shock of Güilson's death. In Irving's earlier story, the tale proper is multiply hedged, by a traveler who enjoys strange scenes both at home and abroad, by an editor who downplays Knickerbocker's work as trivial, and by two rather ominous-sounding epigraphs: one from Lyle, prefacing "The author's account of himself": "so the traveller that stragleth from his own country is in a short time transformed into so monstrous a shape, that he is faine to alter his mansion with his manners, and to live where he can, and not where he would," and the second, to the story proper, from Cartwright: "Truth is a thing that I will keep Unto thylke day in which I creep into my sepulchre."

Güilson represents a type of what María Milagros López calls "lite subjects": "rather than cultivate material life, they aspire to form and style. . . . They are 'people of the surface.' . . . Their knowledge is more of a counterfeit type, marginal to institutional knowledge" (126–27). Because both the narrative voice and the point-of-view character correspond to the margins of society, Vega's satiric commentary on institutions and structures of knowledge is particularly strongly focused from the outsider perspective; because hers are "lite subjects," their understanding is both suspiciously tainted and highly unreliable. Yet, of course, we have no other countervailing voice. In a sense, just as we are warned ironically about the suspiciously gullible nature of narrator Diedrich Knickerbocker in the original "Rip" as the source for a history "too well authenticated to admit of a doubt"; in Vega's story, too, the readers are asked to accept the authority of an unreliable narrator, who contextually speaks from and identifies with the Puerto Rican drug subculture. The nation, in these stories, is a chronotope that rests upon the unstable base of a fiction told by a marginal and questionable narrator: an outsider's imagined construction of a vaguely invented state.

Lite subjects pervade the most well-known and anthologized story of Vega's volume as well. The title story, "Encancaranublado" (an English translation has been published under the title "Cloud-Cover Caribbean"), according to Aníbal González, "se parece a . . . aquellos chistes étnicos tan conocidos, en los que un americano, un ruso y un puertorriqueño, por ejemplo, se encuentran y comparan las virtudes relativas de sus países. . . . Los personajes de este cuento son estereotipos nacionales sin mayor elaboración, situados en el contexto de una alegoría política" [is similar to those well-known ethnic jokes in which an American, a Russian, and a Puerto Rican, for example, meet and compare the relative virtues of their countries. . . . The characters in this story are national stereotypes without any elaboration, situated in the context of a political allegory] (293). Here as in "Cráneo," the narrative—this time a literal story of crossing—is centered on marginal and stereotyped bodies that anchor the allegory/joke. In this story, however, the narrative perspective is that of a more privileged speaker from a social class considerably higher than that of the narrative subjects, a position explicitly shared with the reader. Barradas defines this style succinctly: "en Vega, el interés está en producir el choque entre lo popular y lo culto, el discurso de los personajes de sus narraciones no se asimila al de la voz narrativa de las mismas" [in Vega, the interest lies in producing a shock between the popular and the elite, the discourse of the characters in her narrations is not assimilable to their narrative voices] (552). Vega calls it "un sancocho . . . es como una lucha de clases a nivel de lenguaje" [a stew . . . it's a class war on the linguistic level] (Berríos 10B). The deployment of jostling high culture and popular culture language registers creates a good deal of the narrative effervescence, and at the same time tempers the antic humor with political purpose.

"Encancaranublado" begins on the open sea between the Caribbean islands and Florida, with a Haitian boat person confronting the reality of "ese mollerudo brazo de mar que lo separa del pursuit of happiness" [this muscled arm of sea that separates Atenor from the pursuit of happiness] (13/106). In rapid succession, the unlucky Haitian unwillingly takes on two shipwrecked passengers: a Dominican and a Cuban, whose entry into the boat makes it rock to the rhythms of merengue and rumba respectively. The two Spanish speakers immediately establish their control over the Haitian's boat and all its contents, settling down to argue over the comparative difficulties of living under a system with no whores (Cuba) or one with so many prostitutes that they serve as a major export product (Dominican Republic). Indeed, the Cuban's explicit model for achieving the American Dream involves emulating a cousin who began as a humble pimp and rose to ownership of a tony *casa de citas* [escort service]. The Haitian, Antenor, meanwhile "siguió jugando al tonto. De algo tenía que servir el record de anafabetismo mundial que nadie le disputaba a su país" [played dumb. Our undisputed world record illiteracy rate might pay off here, he thought] (17/108).

The jockeying for pride of place among the three men is invalidated brutally at the end of the story, where the joke of three men in a boat is given a double punch line; for bilingual readers and for (presumably) monolingual Puerto Ricans sensitized to the United States' racial politics. As the men are rescued from their perilous situation of an unlucky boat and depleted supplies, they are pulled aboard a Coast

Guard vessel. Immediately, the blond, blue-eyed U.S. captain orders, "Get those niggers down there and let the spiks take care of 'em," which the narrator immediately follows with: "palabras que los incultos héroes no entendieron tan bien como nuestros bilingües lectores" [words which our untutored heroes did not understand as well as our more literate readers will] (20/110). The second punch line is a combination of acid commentary and an ironic gesture of support from the darkness of the clearly symbolic ship's hold. It takes the form of a sobering warning given by one of the "spiks," a black Puerto Rican, who tells his fellow Caribbeans that "esos gringos no le dan na gratis ni a su mai" [a gringo don't give nothing away. Not to his own mother] just before passing them dry clothing (20/111).

On a first reading, it seems oddly strikingly that Ana Lydia Vega, often identified as the foremost feminist writer in Puerto Rico, includes no counterpart to the much maligned Mrs. Van Winkle in her "Cráneo," and no women characters among her boat people in "Encancaranublado." There is only the figure of the single crying older woman in the first story; in the latter, the male bonding through vaguely dismissive references to prostitutes past, present, and desired in the future, and a gesture toward the sacred feminine figure of the mother in the Puerto Rican's warning to his fellow Antillians. Yet such gaps can be oddly revealing. On the one hand, this absence reproduces a kind of satirically tinged voyeurism into the supposedly privileged male-only spaces that Vega and Lugo Filippi also eloquently parody in their contemporaneous short story "Cuatro selecciones por una peseta" [Four Songs for a Quarter], where four down-and-out male friends meet in a bar to complain about the women in their lives. Vega elsewhere calls this modality, with striking concision, the "pobres-puertorriqueños-oprimidos-por-el-imperialismo-yanqui pero a la vez sinvergüenzas opresores de sus pobres-puertorriqueñas-oprimidas-por-el-imperialismo-yanqui mujeres" [poor-Puerto Rican-men-oppressed-by-Yankee-imperialism but at the same time shameless oppressors of their poor Puerto Rican-oppressed-by-Yankee-imperialism-women] ("Bípeda" 45). On the other hand, the time-traveling drug addict and the shipwrecked refugees ironically reproduce a modality familiar to the readers from traditional stories of adventure and migration. These stories focus on and valorize a transient male subject to the exclusion (and historical forgetting) of female fellow migrants/fellow citizens. As James Clifford famously argues, white men travel, colored men migrate, and women of all ethnicities stay home (passim). Vega echoes and parodies the male migratory tale, by which a certain homosocial genealogy insistently shapes narrative.

Furthermore, in the juxtaposition of the captain's voice from on deck with the voice of the Puerto Rican from the depths of the hold,

Vega makes an explicit commentary on the U.S. dominant culture's efforts to control the location of those racially and culturally disenfranchised individuals who, despite the energy they expend on creating genealogies or denying them, have never been granted a proper place within the imaginary order of U.S. society. Yet, of course, the denial of cultural uniqueness in itself operates as the confirmation of an assigned space and order (if only down there with the spiks), erasing national identities in favor of a single racialized otherness relegated to the fringes of U.S. subjectivity. Thus, the refugee boat creates one sort of identitarian struggle related to Caribbean insularity; the Coast Guard vessel invalidates those distinctions to impose another identity that contains and absorbs local differences. Ironically, by throwing the Haitian, the Dominican, and the Cuban together in the hold with the Puerto Rican, the captain relegates them to a similar marginality, but also implicitly sets the conditions for the actual—as opposed to the ideal—process of assimilation to the United States. The action of crossing from boat to boat, from Haitian to U.S. territory, produces ethnicity in the U.S. sense.

It is particularly appropriate that Ana Lydia Vega sets this story on the ocean, floating between the islands left behind and the United States not yet achieved. Many recent commentators have pointed out that the structure of Puerto Ricanness itself can be defined by a concept of a translocal social space, by the traveling between two national poles. Thus, for example, Sandoval Sánchez suggests, "The so-called 'floating identity' of Puerto Ricans is articulated not only between two geographical spaces but also in the creation of a space in midair where identity intersects, overlaps, and multiplies" ("Puerto Rican Identity" 197). On the one hand, a traditional concept of immigration requires well-established and visibly policed borders separating clearly delimited states, so that the identity established in crossing can be defined and confirmed. On the other, the floating nature of Puerto Ricanness sharpens perceptions about ahistorical safeguards affecting the U.S. dominant culture's sense of self. Unlike the Haitian, Dominican, or Cuban, each of whom is identified in kind of narrative shorthand with their local music and a sketch of a stereotype, "Encancaranublado" makes no similar cultural claims about the Puerto Rican; he alone is entirely defined by the floating existence itself, by the Coast Guard ship.

In their introduction to the special section on Puerto Rico in *Social Text,* Juan Flores and María Milagros López address this "floating identity" from a different perspective. They assert that Puerto Rico "is surely a paramount instance of the present-day 'heterotopia' " (94), evoking a term most famously associated with Michel Foucault. Says the French theorist, "I am interested in certain [sites] that have the curious property of being in relation with all the other sites, but in such a way as to suspect, neutralize, or invert the set of relations that they happen to designate, mirror, or reflect. These spaces, as it were, which are linked with all the others, which however contradict all the other sites, are of two main types." For Foucault these two sites are utopias, which have no real place, and heterotopias, among which Foucault includes ships, which are both specific sites and nonplaces, and which are "capable of juxtaposing in a single real place several spaces, several sites that are in themselves incompatible" ("Of Other Spaces" 24–25). Vega's allegorical story both evokes and evades utopia with its stereotypical three men on a boat, and then more strictly inserts itself into heterotopic space with the arrival of the Coast Guard. Typical understandings of history are bracketed in the heterotopic space, and likewise heterotopias interrupt normal temporality, forcing a revision in relations of time and space. The refugee boat and the Coast Guard ship, then, both serve parallel theoretical functions as othered spaces outside of and inimical to normal historical sites, though their ideological charge in this story is directly opposed. This floating space operates in a register similar to the alternative and equally familiar metaphor of "la guagua área" [airbus]; both ship and airplane represent the mobile border space. In this way, Vega establishes a dialectic tension between at least two temporal and social frames: dominant historical time and sociopolitics of space versus a concept of floating subjectivity.

In this collection of stories, Vega instantiates the heterotopia thematically, but also more subtly, linguistically, in her use of shifting registers and styles ranging from high culture to street slang, in her promiscuous mixing of languages, in the aggressive deployment of loan blends and Spanglish sprinkled throughout her text. She also makes extensive use of local cultural references best understood from within the Puerto Rican context, as when Antenor swallows his anger at the Dominican's depredations "desde su pequeño Fuerte Allen" [from inside his little Fort Allen] (18), encoding here a too-succinct reference to a U.S. military installation in Puerto Rico used as a holding ground for illegal Haitian immigrants. Similarly, in another instance the narrator of "Cráneo" describes a scene by way of a pop culture reference that non–Puerto Ricans might find highly obscure: "y to el mundo más callao que . . . pal capítulo final de Cristina Bazan" (85).[15] In both these stories, Vega privileges the sound of Puerto Rican voices, projecting an able mimicry of the traditional oral storytelling style, and utilizing numerous direct addresses to the presumed listening public. Thus, in "Encancaranublado" her narrator says at one point, "no me pregunten cómo carajo se zapatearon a los tiburones" [don't ask me how in hell they kept the sharks at bay] (19/110), and "Cráneo" opens with a direct appeal to the listeners: "Ustedes perdonen que les venga a bajar del up del viernes social pero se lo voy a vender como me lo pasaron a mí: calle, pa llevar" (81).[16] The pan-Caribbean reach of the stories is reflected in their trilinguality; a Spanish dominant discourse sprinkled with key phrases in French and English. Vega's work will perhaps strike her readers neither as systematic nor profound, yet the lite subjects and the heterotopic spaces speak urgently to the multiple crossings of subjective and ideological identities.

GONZÁLEZ VIAÑA: AMERICAN DREAMS

Eduardo González Viaña's recent collection of short stories, *Los sueños de América* [ambiguously "American Dreams" or "America's Dreams"] provides another point of entry into a more nuanced theory related to the conundrums associated with coming to the United States. The stories in the volume continually catch the reader off-guard; their narrative location tends to be slightly askew from readerly expectations, forcing us to recognize the U.S.-centrism of both dominant culture and traditional Latino/a contestatory discourses emanating from the United States, reminding us as well of the blind spots deriving from certain Latin–American privileged locations as well. The title story of the volume is typical in this regard. Set in Berkeley in the late 1980s, the story details a series of encounters between a Latin American writer and an eighty-year-old gringo named Patrick, who may be a Communist who fought in the Lincoln Brigade during the Spanish Civil war or alternatively may be a CIA agent. At one point early in the story, the narrator comments, "la verdad es que América me parecía un artificio literario en las supuestas historias españolas de Patrick, o una muestra de su adicción por la literatura de Hemingway" [the truth is that America seems to me a literary artifice in Patrick's supposed Spanish stories, or a sample of his addiction for Hemingway's literature] (180). Complicating the referent still further, "América" in this quote is purportedly a young Spanish woman who fights with the Republican forces and has taken on the pseudonym out of her love for Patrick and to honor his homeland. The series of cultural referents (Berkeley, Spain, Peru) and the complicated lines of storytelling are tangled indeed—América passes through three different narratives of ambiguous political affiliation, none of which can be fully authorized by any grounding authority.

The entire volume is full of similarly tortuous artifices. His characters are typically described as invisible people, plagued by shadows and haunted by disappearances both atrocious and mundane, people whose most common mode of social intercourse involves near encounters, or disencounters, or mutually misunderstood exchanges. These characters suffer from prescient dreams, and if their waking lives are almost too full, they have yet to find a way to articulate them in narrative form. One of the most common complaints involves the inability to tell a story: because the cultures are incommensurate and there is no context for common dialogue, because the storyteller is invisible to the social network around him and thus goes unheard, because the writer has no English and would be laughed at.

A character in one of González Viaña's stories recalls, "no se olvide que la mayoría de los norteamericanos dispone de una geografía diferente a la que se usa en otras partes. . . . En muchos colegios y universidades, los estudiantes creen que su país se llama 'América' y limita por el sur con una nación llamada México de la cual provienen los hispanos. Buenos Aires, Montevideo, Lima, Bogotá y Quito, según eso, están en México" [don't forget that the majority of North Americans make use of a different geography than what is used in other places. In many colleges and universities, students believe that their country is called 'America' and is bounded on the south by a nation called Mexico which is where Hispanics come from. Buenos Aires, Montevideo, Lima, Bogotá, and Quito, according to this geography, are in Mexico] (240–41). U.S. citizens are not the only people in the hemisphere ignorant of the particularities of American geography. In another of his stories, González Viaña describes a conversation between new immigrants from Peru and Guatemala in which the Guatemalan solicits the assistance of his fellow Latin American to locate a proper forest in the United States where *naguales* might have fled. He is astounded when the Peruvian university professor expresses his ignorance of *naguales* in general, a fact familiar to any Guatemalan child (57–58). This story, with gentle humor, points to the cultural incommensurability between countries that are often collapsed in the U.S. imaginary, and reminds us that an educated Peruvian from Lima and a campesino from Guatemala, despite superficial similarities of language, have very little in common except the circumstance of coincidentally meeting in the state of Oregon, U.S.A. (which the author of this collection of short stories ironically describes as a state "en el lejano Oeste, sobre cuya existencia real la gente tiene algunas dudas" [in the far West, about whose real existence people have their doubts] (162). Here too, the very fact of contact itself creates new realities; in the case of these two characters, Oregon—the imaginary locus—is the catalytic factor that interpolates them into U.S. *latinidad*; at the same time, the form of this newly Latino identity derives from the encounter between Peru and Guatemala in a third space of personal investment, in the mutually contesting and revisionary sense of cultural selves evolving from this contact.

One of the most successful stories in the volume is "Esta es tu vida" [This is your life], ostensibly rerunning an episode from the Spanish-language network's variation on a famous U.S. show dating to the early days of television. Like the original show, the story's pretext involves reuniting in a Miami studio key individuals from the honored guest's past for an evening of surprises and celebration. In this case, the honored guest is distinguished businessman and *orgullo latino* Dante León. In this richly imagined story, González Viaña successfully mimics not only the hype involved in the staged recognition event, but also opens up the question of what it means to talk about a person's "life" on various levels: that which is constructed for a television audience for a particular political and social purpose, that which has been really lived, the roads not taken, and the choices and regrets involved. Thus, for instance, from the outside Dante León is an extremely successful individual, a role model, a fitting example of the small and highly visible group that represents Latin pride in terms of U.S. measures of achievement. At the same time, this superficial appearance of success came with a high price: León has given up his country, the woman he loved, his dignity, a life he understood, "y, en cierta forma, a todo lo que hacía mi identidad personal. Y también a todo lo que me parecía perfecto en este mundo" [and, in certain respects, everything that made my identity personal. And also everything that seemed to me perfect in this world] (278).

León's deep regrets, the loss of self that accompanied the step-by-step process of choices that brought him to this point and this place, remain silenced in the celebratory television event. More: León's nostalgia for what he has lost grates uncomfortably against the double story of the American Dream as stereotypically imagined from U.S. dominant culture, and as adapted by Miami Latino culture in an unrecognized assimilationist gesture. The program has no real interest in León or his life in terms of a cautionary tale about the cost of living between Latin America and the United States and having to sacrifice the former to satisfy the latter. Instead, the story ends with the grand finale of the program and the unveiling of the parting gift, hidden behind a door in a studio mock-up of the Statue of Liberty: a Mercedes Benz car "full equipo de calidad Liberty" [fully loaded, Liberty quality]. In the final scene, the studio technicians "prendan otra vez los faros de la Liberty y apunten a los ojos de Dante para que no se quede dormido, para que no se desmaterialice y para que tenga tiempo de contar a los que van con él toda su vida y milagros en los Estados Unidos" [switch on the Liberty's lights once again and point them at Dante's eyes so that he doesn't fall asleep, so that he doesn't dematerialize and so that he has time to tell everyone with him about his life and the miracles in the United States] (282). This episode seems a perfect example of the phenomenon described by Khatibi in "The Colonial Labyrinth": "Memory survives in melancholy. . . . The implosive memory dreams up therefore an imaginary exchange. It implodes in two ways: on the one hand, it closes itself in the nostalgia of a dead time and its entropy; on the other hand, it *endures* the present as if it were a dream, or rather, a nightmare" (10). León's past, the memories of loss, cannot sustain themselves in the "reality" evoked by the American Dream—on the contrary, his memory of an alternative and unreachable past can only survive in melancholy daydream. The collision of Dream and dream implodes in Liberty's blinding headlights; the present is endured as if it were a dream; the inaccessible past is locked in the nostalgia for a dead dream. The movement of nostalgia and melancholy in the context of a media extravaganza celebrating a commodified Dream reminds the reader of what happens when an individual loses his bearings in time and space, no longer able to articulate precisely what his life is, or is about, in this site of cultural collisions. In González Viaña's stories, the Statue of Liberty or the local Safeway store offer cultural markers that provisionally and very ambiguously serve as overdetermined symbolic sites for these cultural collisions, as well as the actual locations for the crisscrossing (non)exchanges among the invisible people within U.S. borders.

FUENTES'S INTERNALIZED BORDER

In contrast with the fluidity of the border space in Vega and González Viaña, in the two Mexican writers studied here the border is always fixed. Says Sandoval Sánchez: "If for Mexicans the border/*la frontera*, a tangible and horrible reality, is both a dream to cross over and a nightmare if caught or deported, for Puerto Ricans it is a figurative one where tragedy is translated into humor and always mediated through sarcasm, cynicism, mockery, parody, and irony" ("Puerto Rican Identity" 198–99). In both cases, the metaphor of crossing is situated in a political space anchored in discourses of the body and how certain ethnically marked bodies locate themselves or are interpelated into the politics of U.S. dominant culture. However, while the significance of the "crossing" image retains its potency, when we move from the Puerto Rican Ana Lydia Vega and Peruvian-American Eduardo González Viaña to the Mexican writers Carlos Fuentes and Margarita Oropeza, the fluid, heterotopic understanding of space in the Caribbean writer is replaced by a more juridical relation to the borderline, and the immigrant's insertion into specific urban sites. Palumbo-Liu, referring specifically to Asian Americans, poses queries that are especially pertinent to this discussion of the Mexican writers as well: "How have they variously taken possession of a place in the nation and been dispossessed of it? . . . How have race and ethnicity, those markers of difference, entered into the negotiations over 'common ground'? And finally, how have imagined claims to space and place clashed with juristic ones or coincided with them, and how is the imagination of space linked to political and racial ideologies of nation?" (217). Perhaps the easiest response to Palumbo-Liu's provocative questions is that the imaginary location of the Mexican-American border region (as opposed to the sociopolitical one) tends toward dystopia, and all the complex negotiations of self and space pass through this projection.

While Carlos Fuentes has always been an attentive and prolific commentator on U.S.-Mexico relations, until the mid-nineties his published works reflected little direct engagement with border issues. It is not surprising, given the dramatic events impacting both Mexico's northern border (especially the tensions and recent legislation concerning migrant flow to the United States) and its southern one (the 1994 Zapatista uprising in the southern border state of Chiapas timed to coincide with the implementation of the North American Free Trade Agreement [NAFTA]), that Fuentes would in recent years focus his creative eye on national identity at the site of its greatest pressure. It is past time, he hints, for central Mexico to turn its attention to the previously ignored fringes of national culture so as to interrogate both the nation's recent past and its future prospects.

In a series of articles written in 1994, some of the more important of which have been reprinted in *Nuevo tiempo mexicano,* Fuentes repeatedly expresses his concern about U.S. economic, cultural, and political inroads into Mexico while reiterating his support for NAFTA and the need for Mexico to integrate itself into a global economy. Fuentes negotiates this difficult balancing act by assuring his readers that Mexico is well positioned to deploy native creativity in the service of change, while maintaining pride in national sovereignty. Written at approximately the same time, the conclusion to his sweeping overview of Latin American culture since Columbus, *El espejo enterrado* [*The Buried Mirror*], phrases his call to action in more measured, elder-statesman-like tones: "En medio de la crisis, la América Latina se transforma y se mueve . . . mediante elecciones y movimientos de masas, porque sus hombres y mujeres están cambiando y moviéndose. . . . Tal es la política de la movilización social permanente, como la llama el escritor mexicano Carlos Monsiváis" [In mid-crisis, Latin America transforms itself and moves, through elections and mass movements, because its men and women are changing and moving. . . . Such are the politics of permanent social movement, as Mexican writer Carlos Monsiváis calls it] (*Espejo* 387). It is this question of constant movement and change as it impacts on a strong national identity that most exercises Fuentes's inquiries in his controversial 1995 novel-in-stories featuring El Paso-Juárez, *Frontera de cristal.*

In both his fictional and nonfictional works, Fuentes has focused intensely on the question of how to define an authentic national culture within the parameters of a politically circumscribed entity: what he calls "la nación legal" [the legal nation]. In his fictions, these debates typically crystallize around a strong male figure. Thus, his Artemio Cruz served famously to describe the midcentury corruption of the revolutionary spirit into a quasi-global industrial enterprise. Similarly, Fuentes himself notes that *Cristóbal Nonato* [*Christopher Unborn*] presciently foresaw the central government's implication in the corruption and narcotraffic scandals of 1994 ("la literatura fantástica latinoamericana tiene un problema y es que se vuelve literatura realista en unos cuantos años" [Fanstasy in Latin America has the problem that it becomes realist literature in a few years] *Nuevo tiempo* 76–77). By a natural extension of his double role as fiction writer and political commentator, Fuentes's immediate response to the uprising in Chiapas was to argue its importance in both national political and literary terms. His early articles on the topic discuss the Zapatista revolution in the context of other revolutionary actions in 1712, 1868, and 1910 as well as in parallel to fictions by Juan Rulfo and Gabriel García Márquez. Likewise, in his early articles on Chiapas, he refers patronizingly to charismatic spokesman Marcos as a revolutionary-cum-culture critic "[quien] ha leído más a Carlos Monsiváis que a Carlos Marx" [who has read more Carlos Monsiváis than Karl Marx] (*Nuevo tiempo* 116, 126). If it is not too much of an exaggeration to say that Fuentes's response to the southern border conflict has tended toward normalization of the Chiapan indigenous people into a ready-made centralist reality/fiction of the sort for which he is already justly famous, then on the other hand his engagement with the powerful northern border is most cogently expressed in his diatribe/novel *Frontera de cristal*, in which he addresses powerful economic trends through fictional representations of typical actors in this political drama.

Unlike the southern border, which is rich in indigenous tradition (the other within) and natural resources but poor in influence, in the northern border area Mexican creativity intersects directly with the transformative force of U.S. economic might (the other outside). A few years ago, Carlos Monsiváis, whom Fuentes quotes so approvingly in other contexts, published an article in a volume on NAFTA in which he underlines the political, social, and cultural cost of the traditional division between Mexico City and the rest of the country: "Se sanctificó el juego de los opuestos: civilización y barbarie, capital y provincia, cultura y desolación. Desde principios de siglo . . . cunde una idea: la provincia es 'irredimible,' quedarse es condenarse" [the play of oppositions was sanctified: civilization and barbarism, capital and province, culture and desolation. From the beginning of the (twentieth) century . . . an idea has propagated: the province is 'unredeemable,' to stay is to be condemned] (197). From Mexico City's point of view, the northern border has been imagined as perhaps the most "unredeemable" of all the provincial representations, the least authentically Mexican part of the nation, the region most culturally, linguistically, and morally corrupted due to the unfortunate influence of the United States. This region is also, largely post-NAFTA, forcing itself on the Mexican national imaginary as the fastest growing and most prosperous region of the country. Necessarily, then, the engrained oppositional fiction of barbaric desolation rubs uncomfortably up against the economic reality of a booming industrialization that serves as a human magnet to inhabitants of less prosperous parts of the country.

Both *Nuevo tiempo mexicano* and *Frontera de cristal* are notably silent on the northern border's potential contributions to Mexican national culture (in contrast with the almost purely cultural role he envisions for the Chiapan revolutionaries and their ready availability for fictional reimagination), and he consistently refers to the long northern borderline between Mexico and the United States, à la Anzaldúa, as "la herida" [the wound] or "la cicatriz" [the scar] (e.g., *Nuevo tiempo* 200) where transnationally imagined Mexican entrepreneurship meets U.S. xenophobia. Fuentes implicitly inserts his work into this volatile arena, and does so with an assumption of considerable authority on the nuances of U.S. culture, given his early childhood experience and his frequent adult visits to the United States.[17] Roberto Ignacio Díaz also notes that "Fuentes has often stated that, as a bilingual person—he was raised partially in Washington, D.C.—he could very well have chosen to write in English; the fact that 'everything' has already been said in that language made him choose Spanish instead" (189). In so doing, Fuentes reiterates once again, as he has so often in past narratives, the amazingly persistent centrist psycho-narrative of Mexican national identity derived from the midcentury work of thinkers like Octavio Paz and Samuel Ramos. Estelle Tarica summarizes this phenomenon well when she comments that Mexican identity is mostly succinctly and accurately defined as a crisis of masculinity. This crisis is provoked to a large extent by the doubled awareness of a powerful, English-speaking nation to the north, and a rich but somewhat shamefully accepted indigenous heritage at home. Tarica continues: "The origins of the Mexican nation lie elsewhere, not in a transculturated reality but in 'pure' Mesoamerican Indian culture, in the Aztec 'nation' which the Spaniards conquered and violated. . . . [A] teleological narrative of progress linked to modernization . . . does nothing to alter the fact of the original violation. This originary violation always remains a violation that cannot be restituted" (ms 8–9). In Fuentes's telling division of intellectual territory, Mexico's southern border evokes this lost origin, as a nostalgic remainder/reminder of that pure and masculine Indian; the northern border, in contrast, is not only modern and Americanized, it is shot through with persistent metaphors of feminization and violation.

Fuentes, then, perhaps unwittingly (or unwillingly) addresses in this novel the traditional dichotomies of Mexican fiction, where an interrogation of the tight imbrication of provincial identity and deviant female sexuality has often been particularly pronounced. In a manuscript on female prostitution in Tijuana, Gudelia Rangel Gómez writes a concise summary of the working of this stereotype:

> Como puede observarse en el proceso histórico de Tijuana, tanto su crecimiento poblacional como su desarrollo económico han ido de la mano de actividades estigmatizadas o consideradas prohibidas en otros lugares, esto ha provocado que la concepción generalizada de la ciudad haya sido un proceso de feminización de Tijuana; identificada primero con una "dama generosa" que permitió mejores niveles de vida a su población, posteriormente una "joven coqueta" que atraía hombres para "perderlos" y finalmente la visión que se tuvo de una "prostituta decadente y grotesca" que utilizaban aquellos que pasaban por Tijuana. (30)

> As can be observed in the historical process of Tijuana, both its population growth and its economic development have gone hand in hand with activities that are stigmatized or considered prohibited in other places. This has created a generalized concept of the city as a process of feminization of Tijuana; identified first as a "generous lady" that allowed for a better standard of living for its population, then as a "flirty girl" who attracts men to their perdition, and finally the vision of a "decadent and grotesque prostitute" used by all those who passed through Tijuana.

Rangel Gómez's reading of Tijuana's infamous international image as a meat market for the United States—U.S. men cross the border to purchase sex from Mexican women, while Mexican men cross the border to sell their labor in U.S. fields—is a potent one, suggesting that from both central Mexico and the United States there arises a tendency to feminize the border in a particularly marginalizing and stigmatized manner. The northern border, in this respect, confirms the primacy of centrist notions about the provinces by antinomy. By setting border inhabitants outside the traditional construction of the motherland (*madre patria*) as a domestic space writ large, they help define the normalized space, holding up a distorting mirror to central Mexico's sense of itself as a nation of decent women and hardworking men. *Frontera de cristal* likewise inscribes the border existence as a particularly privileged location—simultaneously strange and familiar—to explore the regionally-and gender-bound nature of discursive constructions of Mexicanness itself.

While Fuentes is clearly familiar with Monsiváis's (and others') arguments about the cultural (non)status of the northern border in the Mexican imaginary, he is also extremely well read in the works of U.S.-based culture critics and theoreticians, where border studies are currently enjoying a boom. From both sides of the U.S.-Mexico border, the region has been in recent years submitted to intense scrutiny both as an apocalyptic space of a rejected past/present, and—curiously—as the best hope for a utopian project for the future. And while these two sets of discussions often occur in a parallel manner, much of the discourse echoes those issues that both societies uneasily abject or repress or, curiously, celebrate, often through an exoticizing lens.

In their introduction to a recent volume, *Border Theory*, David Johnson and Scott Michaelson summarize recent contributions to the astonishingly popular theoretical formulation of border studies in the United States. They note the hundreds of conferences, articles, and books organized around this topic, making it what they call "one of the grand themes of recent political liberal-to-left work across the humanities and social sciences." They continue, in a perceptive and pointed conclusion: "In the majority of this work, interestingly, the entry point of 'the border' or 'the borderlands' goes unquestioned, and, in addition, often is assumed to be a place of politically exciting hybridity, intellectual creativity, and moral possibility. The borderlands, in other words, are *the* privileged locus of hope for a better world" (2–3). I think Johnson and Michaelson are absolutely accurate in this summary, and only add to it that, interestingly enough, the general direction of this liberal-to-left work exactly inverts the traditional dominant culture (both U.S. and Mexican) stereotypes about Mexico's northern border as a place of deplorable cultural mixing, intellectual and creative vacuum, and immoral depravity: the equal and alternative apocalyptic vision. In these recent theoretical recuperations of the border, the characterization as a "locus for hope" can occur precisely only to the degree that the U.S.-Mexico border's concrete location is undermined and the border region becomes u-topic, a floating signifier for a displaced self.

Carlos Fuentes's *Frontera de cristal* offers a salient and unusual example of a blend between Mexican centrist thought and U.S.-high-culture border theorization. For Fuentes, the political border is less important than the symbolic one: the division between developed and underdeveloped nations, first and third world. As he says in one of his millenary-inspired articles, "Here in Tijuana, in Cuidad Juárez, en Matamoros, all of Latin America begins" ("Milenio," quoted in Van Delden 199). Unsurprisingly, given Fuentes's narrative trajectory of focusing issues through typical figures, it is what one character calls *la frontera interior* (279), which dominates in this work of fiction, and the question of an authentic national identity locates itself only—or most persistently—in relation to displaced individuals who travel, frequently voluntarily, deep into gringolandia.

The *frontera* of the novel follows the flight of first-class passengers between Mexico City and New York City, and includes on its border itinerary such equally alien and familiar sites as the deserts of Sonora, the vegetable fields of California, Chicago high rises, and a Cornell University student apartment in Ithaca, New York. Often, limits and borders seem to be arbitrarily set, as in this comment from the perspective of Mexico City debutante Michelina Laborde e Ycaza, on a border city's central plaza in the first chapter of the novel: "hasta aquí llegó el barroco, hasta el límite del desierto. Hasta aquí y no más" [the Baroque came this far, to the very edge of the desert—to this point and no farther] (16/9). The reader is left to wonder, on the one hand, if this (historically and geographically located) end of the baroque signals the end of high culture and the beginning of low gringo imports, or if, on the other hand, this profoundly uneducated, opportunistic young woman is merely making another display of her unwitting ignorance. In either case, a line is drawn in the sand between fussy Mexican baroque artifacts and U.S. architecture's clean, modern lines. The point, however, is not geographical or cultural accuracy; Michelina's observation describes a psychic rather than physical boundary line. Alternatively, in a strange blurring effect, Juan Zamora superimposes a bridge over the Río Bravo in Juárez on a bridge over Fall Creek in Ithaca. Even in the context of a solipsistically imagined internal border, surely this is one of the weirder collapsing effects in recent fiction. In such a context, it is no wonder that, en route to New York City on the same Delta flight as Michelina and rich industrialist Leonardo Barroso, Lisandro Chávez ponders his conclusion that "Ya no había país, ya no había México, el país era una ficción o, más bien, un sueño mantenido por un puñado de locos" [there was no homeland anymore, no such thing as Mexico; the country was a fiction or, rather, a dream maintained by a handful of madmen] (191/170–71).

The first chapter sets the tone for this novel-in-stories with the incongruous arrival of arrogant, uneducated, aristocratic Michelina in Campazas on a whimsical response to her godfather's invitation to hop aboard his private plane and fly out for a visit. The first words of the novel, "No hay absolutamente nada de interés" [there is absolutely nothing of interest], which Michelina quotes from her guidebook, are confirmed by her personal observation: "No vio nada. Su mirada le fue secuestrada por un espejismo: el río lejano y más allá las cúpulas de oro, las torres de vidrio. . . . Pero eso era del otro lado de la frontera de cristal. Acá abajo, la guía tenía razón: no había nada" [She could see nothing. Her gaze was captured by a mirage: the distant river and, beyond it, golden domes, glass towers. . . . But that was on the other side of the crystal frontier. Over here, below—the guidebook was right—there was nothing] (11–12/3–4). Later she complains even more forcefully: "no hay absolutamente nada en Campazas de interés para nadie, forastero o lugareño, chilango o norteño" [there is absolutely nothing of interest in Campazas for anyone, outsider or native, city person or northerner] (25/17). Michelina's complaint, so forcefully reiterated in the first chapter/story of the novel in both direct quotes and indirect authorial discourse, efficiently reinstates the centrist's contempt for the northern border region so succinctly described by Monsiváis in his summary of that antagonism, and captures as well the yearning of the Mexico City elite toward the delights imagined on the other side of the border. Here, as Michelina insists, there is nothing, only desert, the end of civilization, the limit point of hoary colonial monstrosities like the baroque, of interest to no one at all. There, on the other side, across the border, are the shining glass skyscrapers of modernity. Michelina's greatest disappointment is, of course, that she belongs politically to the uninteresting side, while yearning for transborder acceptance that she can never fully achieve, for all her aristocratic background and megadollars.

In a sense, Michelina poses the question that drives all of the characters in this novel. The northern Mexico borderlands are consistently drawn as absolutely empty and entirely without interest, except for the narrowly defined self-interest of greedy maquiladora plant operators. Yet Mexican citizens confronted with the border experience are required to choose—and to choose this blankness both for reasons of national pride and for a vaguely defined loyalty to an implicitly centrist-defined heritage of cultural richness and hypermacho virility. Furthermore, like Michelina, they more often than not make these choices in an intellectual vacuum. In *Espejo* Fuentes writes, "Es fácil de cruzar la frontera ahí donde el río se ha secado o los montes son solitarios. Pero es difícil llegar al otro lado" [it's easy to cross the border there where the river has dried or the mountains are isolated. But it is difficult to arrive on the other side] (371). The difficulty for the Mexican citizen desirous of participating in the goodies across the border resides not just in the literal "tierra de nadie" [no man's land] at the borderline and the checks created by surveillance of the area by U.S. immigration patrols, but also in the difficulty of arrival in a metaphorical sense. Another of the characters in this novel, Emiliano Barroso, ventriloquizing his children's complaint against him, explains long-windedly that life on the borderline forces certain unwelcome decisions: "nos obligaste a justificarnos, a negarte, afirmar todo lo que tú no eres para ser nosotros. Ser alguien. Ser del otro lado. . . . Si creces en la frontera tienes que escoger: de este lado o del otro" [You forced us to justify ourselves, to deny you, to affirm everything you aren't so we could be ourselves. Be someone. Be from the other side. . . . If you grow up on the border, you have to choose: this side or the other] (115–16/101). More often than not, such choices are made willy-nilly for them. People are categorized and locked in place, unwelcomed in the United States, unwilling to identify with an unwelcoming landscape back across the river.

In *Nuevo tiempo mexicano,* Fuentes summarizes the problem concisely: "Estados Unidos ha tenido éxito en todos los renglones en los que los mexicanos hemos fracasado. . . . Vivimos un fracaso nacional lado a lado con el máximo *success story* de la modernidad" [The United States has been successful in every aspect in which we Mexicans have failed. . . . We live a national failure side by side with the greatest success story of modernity] (86). This dramatically fraught vision gives the entire book a Jekyll/Hyde aggressivity (Fuentes himself uses this metaphor in a 1986 article published in *The Nation* and repeats it ten years later in *Nuevo tiempo mexicano* for its explanatory force in describing border existence, 86) as borders are cut and recut, crossed and recrossed: feminine–masculine, margin–center, poor–rich, Mexico–United States, outpost of the past–threshold of the future, vast cultural resources–impoverished technological obsession. And yet, of course, as Michelina fails to recognize, but the reader inevitably must note, the yearning for the crystalline dream on the other side is merely a mirage, created out of straining her eyes in Mexico's strong northern desert sun.

Thus, the first chapter/story sets the stage for an impossible journey to the other side, and the inescapable entrapment in the dusty nowhere of the border town. Moreover, it enforces the stereotypical centrist reading of the border as a cultural vacuum. In the second story, focusing on Juan Zamora, the hapless Mexican medical student living his border experience in upstate New York, the narrator adds another crucial element to the reader's apprehension of the structure of this tale. Juan, the narrator tells us, cannot face his own truth: "él va a estar de espaldas al lector todo el tiempo" [he wants to have his back to the reader the whole time] (39/29). The narrator directly informs the reader that this turning away derives from shame, that Juan speaks out of deep and unrelenting pain about the way his social consciousness and commitment to his people have been sidetracked by his sexual obsession with a rich young fellow student whom he nicknames, following the lead of Conrad's eponymous novel, "Lord Jim." The emotional depth of his tale in some sense counterpoints the frivolity of Michelina's; nevertheless, the net effect of Michelina's shamelessness and Juan's anguish is precisely the same. Both perspectives create specific expectations about the location and identity of the implied reader of this narrative. For both of these characters, and for the implied reader as well, the border area, however defined, is an empty space, at best a staging area for transients on their way from the center to the north, important because social movement and change coincide at the international boundary. And yet, because it is an indiscriminate and empty flux, it cannot anchor imagination. It is that messy, leaking *herida*; like the characters, doomed to femininity/feminization. Like Michelina, Juan in looking away from his Mexican reader is looking toward the United States, turning her/his back not on *fronteras* actual or crystalline, but on central Mexico.

In *Frontera de cristal*, the only characters who escape this Manichaean division do so at the terrible price of multiply wounding interior divisions. Thus, for example, José Francisco, who muses, "Lo que es de acá es de acá y también de allá. Pero ¿dónde es acá y dónde allá, no es el lado mexicano su propio acá y allá, no lo es el lado gringo, no tiene toda tierra su doble invisible?" [What belongs here and also there. But where is here and where is there? Isn't the Mexican side his own here and there? Isn't it the same on the gringo side? Doesn't every land have its invisible double?] (278–79/150), and he adds, "Yo no soy mexicano. Yo no soy gringo. Yo soy chicano. No soy gringo en USA y mexicano en México. Soy chicano en todas partes" [I'm not a Mexican. I'm not a gringo. I'm Chicano. I'm not a gringo in the USA and a Mexican in Mexico. I'm Chicano everywhere] (281/252). José Francisco thus embodies the repressed "doble invisible" of both cultures, the "allá" for whatever local "acá" he happens to inhabit. The political-cultural identity marker, "soy chicano en todas partes," is also and most significantly in this novel an index of deeply seated, binational discrimination. The Michelinas and other elites of central Mexico may yearn for markers of U.S. prosperity, but they hold no brief for their Mexican-American brethren whose provincial origins, lower-class background, and unacceptably ethnic features relegate them conceptually to the underclass in Mexico as well as the United States. White-bread U.S. citizens see José Francisco and his ilk as potentially deportable illegal aliens irrespective of their ability to trace a genealogy of four hundred years of continuous residence in the same (now U.S.) territory.

In its Jekyll/Hyde fashion, Fuentes's narrative draws strong and sometimes offensively stereotypical characterizations, and, like other pop culture derivations of Robert Louis Stevenson's famous literary figure, makes no attempt to resolve the absolute schizophrenic split between competing versions of reality. Mexico, he suggests earnestly through one of his characters, is through illegal immigration well on its way to retaking the territories now occupied by the U.S. Southwest—a rather tired cliché that is the basis of innumerable jokes in both countries. The problem, this dyspeptic character muses, is that Mexicans do not have the tools to deal with the implications of this demographic phenomenon. He asks himself: "treinta millones de personas, en los Estados Unidos, hablaban español. ¿Cuántos mexicanos, en cambio, hablaban correctamente el inglés? Dionisio sólo conocía a dos, Jorge Castañeda y Carlos Fuentes" [thirty million people in the United States spoke Spanish. But at the same time, how many Mexicans spoke decent English? Dionisio knew of only two, Jorge Castañeda and Carlos Fuentes] (69/57). The point of this strange observation is driven home in another text, in *Nuevo tiempo mexicano,* where Fuentes remarks casually about a conversation he had over dinner with Bill Clinton in the U.S. president's private vacation retreat on Martha's Vineyard (156). It's a fairly good bet that Fuentes's fare at this presidential dinner was not the overcooked chicken that Dionisio complains about in his endless series of university "banquets." Thus, the problems of bad food and bad English run in tangent and, strangely enough, intersect as well with lack of access to the highest levels of public policy in the United States. On the one hand, then, aristocratic, educated, English-speaking folks like Fuentes are welcomed to the rarefied summit of social and political exchange, whereas poor grunts like Dionisio have been relegated to the outer fringes of academic irrelevance in earnest speaking engagements in Missouri, Ohio, and Massachusetts (though to be sure, the reader is bound to reserve judgment on U.S. university life as the worst of all possible fates).

At the same time, Fuentes seems to suggest a direct relation between being forced to eat tired lettuce with heavy "French" dressing in a university dining facility and doing stoop labor in the lettuce fields of California. With an echo of Alfonso Reyes's famous exclamation, "¡Qué cultos son estos analfabetos!" [How educated these illiterates are!] (*Nuevo tiempo* 122), Dionisio sighs over the U.S. phenomenon of power without culture in contrast to the sophisticated grace and aristocratic manners of even the most powerless Mexican illiterate (78), an observation that sits uneasily on the page with the same character's dismissal of Mexican ability to deal with the consequences of the population explosion in the U.S. Southwest. Sophisticated Mexican culture apparently has no power against engrained U.S. bad taste, unless the sophisticate in question is Carlos Fuentes himself, where excellent English will presumably free him from the horrors of chicken-fried steak sans *salsa ranchera* to make it palatable.

Dionisio, Michelina, and Juan are all, as must be clear at this point, crudely drawn characters, more inoffensively clownlike than dramatically Dr. Jekyllian. Yet, in placing in their mouths well-known and much restated clichés and earnest truisms about U.S.-Mexico relations, in offering no counterpoint to their projection of Mr. Hydian evil onto a vaguely defined U.S. environment, Fuentes risks having all of *Frontera de cristal* fall into strident propagandism. In this respect, *Frontera* once again is rhetorically very close to some of the more dramatic essayistic commentaries in *Nuevo tiempo.* There, for example, Fuentes draws a direct comparison between former California governor Pete Wilson and Adolph Hitler, between pogroms and the Holocaust in early twentieth-century Europe and contemporary anti-Mexican legislation in the United States' most populous state, and seems to hint that the genocidal movement in the latter may be even more poisonous than Hitler's final solution because of an overtly racist quality: "La clase política de California, vergonzosamente, ha atizado la campaña antimexicana. . . . Hitler necesitó judíos. . . . Pero la xenofobia y el racismo desembocan en el *pogrom* y el campo de concentración. Antes de salir a cazar mexicanos . . . los racistas norteamericanos deberían ver la película de Spielberg *La lista de Schindler.* Pero los judíos de Polonia eran blancos. La fobia contra los mexicanos tiene un nombre y un color: racismo" [The California political class, shamefully, has roused the anti-Mexican campaign. . . . Hitler needed Jews. . . . But xenophobia and racism led to the pogrom and the concentration camp. Before going out to hunt Mexicans . . . North American racists should see Spielberg's movie, *Schindler's List.* But the Polish Jews were white. The phobia against Mexicans has a name and a color: racism] (*Tiempo* 110). The tone of this comment is quite different from Dionisio's annoying cliché about bad food, yet it resonates in a similar register. Trivial or profound, both statements take a stereotype, elevate it to a truth, and exaggerate it to hysteria.

Underlying both statements, informing both Fuentes's and his characters' hysteria, is a half-admitted, half-concealed structure of desire. Mexico may in this construction metaphorically represent Jekyll and the United States embody Hyde, but at the same time the United States is wealth and power and success, just across what should be an irrelevant political boundary, except for the fact that neither Mexico nor the United States wants to dissolve it. The United States and Mexico are a study in contrasts at all levels, and the existence of a sharply defined border helps keep binaries clean and (presumably) cultures separate and pure. At the same time, the United States and Mexico are a single unit, a continuity of land and culture, "Hermanos Anónimos" [Brothers Anonymous] (119/105). And again: the United States is Mexico's desired and corrupting other, the magnet of spoiled rich girls and earnest students, of desperate campesinos and visionary industrialists, of internationally celebrated writers and hapless midlevel academics. It is the very essence of that which they cannot *not* want to inhabit, and so it is ideologically normalized as that absolutely alien space that once was home, has always been home, and will be again. In *Espejo,* Fuentes writes poetically, "cuando el trabajador hispánico cruza la frontera mexicano-norteamericana, a veces se pregunta, ¿acaso no ha sido ésta siempre mi tierra? ¿Acaso no estoy regresando a ella?" [when the Hispanic worker crosses the Mexican-U.S. border, at times he asks himself, Isn't it true that this has always been my land? Isn't it true that I am returning to it?] (373), and in *Frontera* his character Emiliano Barroso echoes this sentiment in almost the same words when he argues that the migrant workers "regresan a su propia tierra; nosotros estuvimos antes aquí" [They're returning to their own land; we were here first] (120/105).

There is another valence to the Jekyll/Hyde metaphor as well. In the original story, Jekyll is a mild-mannered and well-meaning medical doctor; his violent alter ego Mr. Hyde is the result of a scientific experiment gone terribly wrong. Following upon the familiar Gloria Anzaldúa metaphor of the borderline as an open wound, Fuentes too recurs repeatedly in his work to the image of this "tensa frontera común entre México y Estados Unidos: no una frontera, escribí una vez, sino un cicatriz. La herida se está abriendo de nuevo" [tense common border between Mexico and the United States: not a border, I once wrote, but a scar. The wound is opening again] (*Tiempo* 109). The concluding essay of the volume *Nuevo tiempo mexicano* recapitulates this favored metaphor: "¿No una frontera, piensa uno a veces, sino una cicatriz? ¿Se cerrará para siempre, volverá a sangrar? ¿Cicatriz o herida?" [Not a border, one thinks at times, but a scar? Will it close forever, will it bleed again? Scar or wound?] (200). As a logical extension, the character in *Frontera de cristal* most closely associated with the wounded border is the gay former Cornell medical student, now a physician, whose function is to take cognizance emblematically of the "enfermedad de la frontera" [border sickness] (273/244) in the final pages of the novel. It is, naturally, a wounding that is physical (the violence against Mexicans takes a graphic form, including two central characters shot to death at the international border), but more important for this novel, the border is lived as a psychic illness that transcends any specific geographical location.

Juan Zamora's transborder consciousness creates a palimpsest out of Ciudad Juárez and Ithaca, New York. Just before the climactic final scene of bloody death, Zamora indulges in reminiscence so as to more firmly anchor this parallel: "Parado frente al puente de Juárez a El Paso, Juan Zamora recuerda con una mueca ingrata el tiempo que vivió en Cornell" [Standing opposite the bridge from Juárez to El Paso, Juan Zamora remembers with a grimace of distaste the time he lived at Cornell] (274/245). When we turn back to the second chapter of the novel and to his depressed and embarrassed description of his days in Ithaca as a student, we can already see in germ the origins of this unusual conflation. Upon describing the wintry small town, the narrator notes, "Juan se siente, casi, en México, en San Juan del Río o Tepeji, esos lugares donde a veces iba de excursión" [Juan feels—almost—as if he's in Mexico, in San Juan del Río or Tepeji, places he's visited from time to time on holiday]. Ithaca is already, by an odd metaphorical linkage, identified as a Mexican town. Even more crucially for this extended metaphor, like the U.S.-Mexico border, Juan feels Ithaca too is organized around an inescapably present wound: "La barranca de Ithaca es un gran tajo hondo y prohibitivo, pero por lo visto también un abismo seductor" [The gorge in Ithaca is a deep and forbidding ravine, apparently a seductive abyss as well]. The difference between border experiences, he seems to suggest, is that while the seduction of the international border is horizontal (to cross over to the other side), the compulsion of Ithaca is vertical, the attraction of heights and depths: "Esa barranca es el vértigo en el orden de ese lugar" [The gorge is the vertigo in the order of this place] (42–43/32–33). In Juan Zamora's repeated dream, he and his homosexual lover Jim Rowlands plummet deliciously to their deaths in the Ithaca gorge: "se miran, sonríen, se ponen ambos de pie sobre la cornisa del puente, se toman de la mano y saltan los dos al vacío" [They look at each other, they smile, they both stand at the edge of the bridge, they take each other by the hand, and they jump into the void] (64/54). This dream is the index of Juan's shame at his weakness of mind and body upon falling in love with, and being abandoned by, an aristocratic young white man. On another level, of course, his entire career—and not just his student love life—has from some perspectives taken this sharp downward turn, from the enchantments of the north to the "vacío" [void] of the borderlands where he ignores slights about his sexuality and tends the illnesses of drug addicts and AIDS sufferers. For Juan Zamora, then, the border is a human garbage pit of disease and violent death, the counterpart and counterpoint to Ithaca's clean water-cut gorges, a place where he redeems his humanity and his shame in service to others.

Juan's meditations in the final chapter of the novel are interrupted by the call of "médico, médico" [doctor, doctor], and while the fragmentary narrative is interrupted at this point, the reader soon learns that he is called from his solitary thoughts by the violent death of Leonardo Barroso, assassinated on the Juárez-El Paso international bridge (275, 292–93/247, 262–64). It is far too late to help the rich international investor; nothing can be done to piece together the broken body. In fact, as the narrator makes sure to remind us, the damage to the cranium is so severe that Dr. Juan Zamora does not even recognize in the shattered cadaver his benefactor, the man who sent him to Cornell in the first place. The irony of this lack of connection is underscored in the last narrative vignette of the novel, which describes small-time gigolo Rolando Rozas, self-importantly reporting the incident in his battery-less cellular phone as he passes by the accident scene on his way to El Paso to look for another gullible young woman to seduce.

Despite all these negative images and insistently enforced negative stereotypes, the novel nevertheless intermittently insists upon visualizing the border region both cynically and optimistically as a place of human possibility where differences embrace and cohabit. Fuentes codes this alternative vision in the image of glass, which both gives the novel its title and serves as a leitmotif running through the entire fiction. The symbolic resources of the image cluster glass-mirror-mirage are familiar to any reader of Fuentes's recent work, where they appear almost obsessively, serving as the dominant metaphor in works as different as *El espejo enterrado* and *Gringo viejo*. Already in the first paragraphs of the first chapter of *Frontera de cristal*, Michelina establishes the importance of this image. Looking out over the desert as she arrives in the nowhere town of Campazas, she yearns toward the other side of the border, only to find her gaze interrupted by a mirage and "torres de vidrio . . . frontera de cristal" [glass towers . . . crystal frontier] (12/4).

Fuentes emphasizes this metaphor even more insistently in the title story/chapter of this fiction, "La frontera de cristal." This story is set in New York City, where the narrator focuses on a hallucinatory excess of glass in that border town's great skyscrapers. Fuentes imagines an almost surreal glass building as the setting for this narrative—"muros de cristal, puertas de vidrio . . . pisos . . . de un cristal opaco" [glass walls, glass doors . . . floors . . . of opaque glass]. The ubiquity of absolute transparency all around her tempts office worker Audrey, in a manner parallel to the seductions of Ithaca's gorges on Juan Zamora, with the attractive vertigo of the depths: "y a veces le gustaba que su mirada se desplomase cuartenta pisos conviertiéndose, en el trayecto, en copo de nieve, en pluma, en mariposa" [and at times she liked to feel that her gaze fell forty stories, transforming on the way into a snowflake, a feather, a butterfly] (204/182–83). Like Juan's repeated nightmare of jumping from Triphammer Bridge into Fall Creek Gorge hand in hand with Jim, Audrey's dream too involves both falling and flight in various senses of the words: falling in love, falling to her death; flight up from the depths, flight from an intolerable situation.

Inevitably, this most poetic of the stories included in the novel focuses on a transborder encounter. Audrey, working in her office, looks up to see Lisandro Chávez cleaning windows from the outside. As Lisandro gradually wipes away the layer of grime, "la transparencia del cristal fue develando el rostro de ella" [the transparency of the glass restored her face] (206/184); she too receives a clearer and clearer visual image of the man on the other side, seeing in Lisando her dream lover and the opposite to her disappointing ex-husband. Interestingly enough, Audrey in this sense serves as the counterpart to Michelina from the first story, for while Michelina looks through a mirage toward the glass towers on the other side of the geographical border, Audrey, the inhabitant of the glass tower, looks across the border of the window frame into a Mexican's face and reads it as an "espejismo" [mirage] (208/186). For inhabitants of both sides of these various borders, then, the gaze involves a duplicitous gesture, mirroring the self, desiring the other, unaware that the object of desire is a mirage.

For Lisandro, too, the unknown office worker figures in an invented narrative about her life in which he projects onto her the image of his desire such that "deseó intensamente tenerla, tocarla aunque fuera a través del cristal" [He wanted badly to have her, touch her, even if only through glass] (209/188). This tale of a fugitive encounter on the fortieth floor is doomed, of course; the gringa and the Mexican man remain irremediably "separados por la frontera de cristal" [separated by the crystal frontier] (210/188). In the final section of the story, Audrey writes her name on the sparkling glass in lipstick; he responds only with his nationality before exchanging a chaste and passionate salute: "los labios se unieron a través del vidrio," and when she opens her eyes, he is gone [their lips united through the glass] (211/189). It would be easy to overread this ultimately silly poetic scenario as a surreal vision of transborder safe sex; more important to Fuentes's narrative vision, however, is the emphasis it places on reaffirming the centrality of the glass/border metaphor.

José Francisco, the hippie-biker Chicano, is the unlikely author of the novel's most redemptive gesture, and the one that brings together the implications of this repeated image pattern focusing on a concept of the border that is as impermeable and as transparent as glass, of a mirrored self and a miraged other. He deals in contraband literature, carrying Mexican manuscripts to El Paso and Chicano writings to Juárez, zipping back and forth across the bridge on his motorcycle, dealing in mutual understanding, "para que todos se quisieran un poquito más" [so that everyone would love one another a little more] (281/252).[18] When he is stopped by agents from both sides of the border looking for drugs, he encourages them in their search through his bags, insisting that he is carrying subversive writing. He watches the puzzled agents throw the papers into the air, helps them empty his bags, follows the scattered manuscript sheets as they float across the river on the breeze, sees people in Juárez grabbing for them, and "lanzó un grito de victoria que rompió para siempre el cristal de la frontera" [gave a victory shout that forever broke the crystal of the frontier] (282/253). A pragmatist might ask what the actual, functionally illiterate Spanish-, Yaqui-, or Mixtec-speaking people waiting at the edge of the river to cross over to the other side for day work raking gardens or cleaning houses might in fact make of the dense theoretical and philosophical meditations of Antonio Cornejo Polar, or what redemptive power Denise Chavez's or Sandra Cisneros's English-language stories (all cited as examples of these subversive papers) might have to any Mexican other than Carlos Fuentes and Jorge Castañeda, the sole exemptions the novel cites to a generalized inability to deal with the English language. Fuentes' point, however, seems to be the familiar one of the trickle-down effect of a faith in paper, his own *Frontera de cristal* being an exemplary text, for liberatory political action. The metaphor of the glass border serves as a mirror of the self and a mirage of otherness; once illusion is dispelled, the glass disappears, mutual understanding rules, and Lisandro and Audrey can (theoretically) enjoy a real kiss.

The novel does not end quite so idealistically, but rather returns to a more somber tone in the two closing narrative vignettes of the novel, both focused on violent death, the first involving a group of twenty-three immigrants brought across the river by Gonzalo Romero and murdered on the other side of the border by a gang of white supremacist skinheads (285–88/256–59); the second on the assassination of maquiladora owner Leonardo Barroso. At the same time, in the italicized poetic interludes between vignettes, and in the final italicized section of the novel, Fuentes evokes the image of the young Chicano flinging his papers in the air: "*al norte del río grande, / al sur del río bravo, / que vuelen las palabras*" [to the north of the río grande, / to the south of the río bravo, / toss the papers], leading to the final words in the narrative, echoing pre-Revolutionary Mexican president Porfirio Díaz's most famous pronouncement on U.S.-Mexican relations: "*pobre México, / pobre Estados Unidos, tan lejos de Dios, / tan cerca el uno del otro*" [poor Mexico / poor United States, / so far from God, / so near to each other] (296/266).

Frontera de cristal, with its explicit borderlands focus, suggests a need to interrogate this old Porfirian claim more rigorously rather than merely repeat a catchphrase from the turn of the last century. Accordingly, Fuentes's final gesture shifts the dictum from its original complaint about an unequal relation ("pobre México, tan lejos de Dios, tan cerca de los Estados Unidos") [poor Mexico, so far from God, so near the United States] to a shared burden in which the United States and Mexico mirror each other as equal sufferers of cultural proximity, one that José Francisco's airborne writings will have some role in alleviating. Implicitly, equivocally, the old centrist focus (Mexico City, New York City) gives way metaphorically to a new understanding of the concept of center, based in those territories that represent from each side the limits of individual cultures, but in a more global understanding, the contact zone and thus shared center between them. This center is both the utopia where cultural exchange will flower and barriers will be broken down, and the dystopia where the realities of intermingling result in violent death.

From both of the traditional cultural centers, of course, the borderlands represent an unattractive emptiness, the no-man's-land between the limit of the baroque and the beginning of the glass towers, the red zone of transgressive and abjected sexuality linked to a traitorous femaleness. In her discussion of the sexual interface of colonial encounters, Ann Laura Stoler offers a helpful point of departure for an analysis of this trope. Her work focuses on what she calls the "analytic slippage between the sexual symbols of power and the politics of sex," and asks the important questions, "Was sexuality merely a graphic substantiation of who was, so to speak, on the top? Was the medium the message, or did sexual relations always 'mean' something else, stand in for other relations, evoke the sense of *other*... desires?" (346). Despite, or perhaps because of, its shocking physicality, control and manipulation of the sexualized trope serves both central Mexico and U.S. dominant discourses as a salient instrument of textual authority in constructing and controlling discussions about the dangerous attractions of a degraded border reality. The continuing resonance of this image reveals unsuspected weaknesses and fault lines in much Mexican, Chicano, and mainstream U.S. theoretical meditation on any national self-image as a function of a play of ossified notions of masculinity and femininity.

Frontera's emphasis on contemporary social movement, on images of center and limit, picks up on and develops a common theme in Fuentes's recent writings. More important, the uneasy jostling of cultures and clichés in *Frontera* underlines and undermines Fuentes's traditional narrative reliance on centrist imagery and strong male figures. In an essay in *Nuevo tiempo mexicano,* he comments that "el viaje es el movimiento original de la literatura" [the trip is the original movement of literature], and that such quests lead inexorably back, "comunicarnos de nuevo con el mito del origen" [connecting us once again with the myth of origins], making of all journeys a psychic "viaje al centro del origen" [trip to the origin's center] (27). While he is reluctant to specify more narrowly, Fuentes does agree with his friend Martín Caporrós that "México tiene un *origen*" [Mexico has an *origin*] (55), which is apparently singular in both senses of the word. When this origin and this journey are described in centrist terms, implicitly harking back to Tenochtitlán, Fuentes is on familiar ground, dealing with the deeply rooted complexities of a sedimented cultural base. However, when the journey is a literal one, and involves a transborder migration through a zone defined as culturally empty, our author runs into difficulties.

Interestingly enough, Fuentes in *Tiempo* evokes the image of the mandala to describe a parallel metaphor for Mexican history, one that helps him resolve the impasse. He writes that "el arte de los antiguos mexicanos" (the art of the ancient Mexicans; i.e., the Aztecs, the central Mexican dominant culture at the time of the conquest) returns obsessively to mandala-like figures, "diseños basados en un esquema de cuatro rectángulos en torno a un círculo que es un vacío" [designs based on a scheme of four rectangles surrounding a circle that is a vacuum] (207). In some sense, *Frontera de cristal* describes exactly such a mandala-like structure, reinventing a centrist perspective but now translating it from Tenochtitlán to Juárez, and localizing this empty center on the northern border between Mexico and the United States. In Fuentes's poetic, metaphoric vision, this invented borderlands subscribes to the old, stereotypical Mexican centrist calumny about the northern border in its emptiness and lawlessness. At the same time, it imitates the contemporary U.S.-based border theory projection of the region as a site of intellectual creativity and social and political hybridity.

In the end, however, Fuentes's mandala and his journey to the origin decry a common basis. Both vacuum (Michelina's desert of the opening pages) and cultural center (José Francisco's redemptive floating papers at the end), Carlos Fuentes's border enters current discussions less as an accurate reflection of the U.S.-Mexico region and its complex politics and social interactions than as a mirror held up to that experienced border crosser himself.

OROPEZA'S IMMIGRANT NIGHTMARES

While U.S. and Mexican dominant cultural discourses are differentially weighted in Fuentes and Oropeza, in each case the border itself delimits the conflict, propels the narrative into existence, and clarifies ideological, cultural, and ethical stakes. Fuentes' evocation of a reflective border space and its effect on its inhabitants is echoed in another key with Oropeza's focus on the unsituatedness of the migrant worker who finds her perceptions distorted by the shock of encounter with U.S. culture. Similarly, his concern with the real and metaphorical perversion of an internalized border finds an analogy in *Después de la montaña*'s real and metaphorical search for "hom." Both novels emphasize the question of how to define situatedness when the characters' social and political condition is one of displacement, and ask us to think about what it means for a migrant to belong anywhere at all. In each case, the meditation on issues of identity and location is staged in an unfamiliar and largely projected space: the border region for the centrist Mexican, the United States for the Sonoran, in both cases calling to mind and at the same time disturbing stereotypical notions of the relationship between gender and nation. Of particular interest is Oropeza's explicitly female-gendered take on these issues, through a narrative detailing the fictional life history of Adelaida Quintero as she struggles to accommodate herself to the alien system north of the border in which she finds herself living and working. In contrast with Fuentes, Oropeza's encounter with the American Dream is differently tracked, open to compromise and modification largely through the reader's oversight onto the spectacle of the protagonist at work and at home, in an accumulation of the trivial details that make up an ordinary immigrant life.

Fuentes, we might say, allows for abstraction and theory in the strong sense of the term; his novel-in-stories, accordingly, is fragmented among a large cast of characters from across the social spectrum. Oropeza, on the other hand, focuses on the impact of large political and economic structures at the microlevel of an individual body internalizing the economies of a globalized labor market. This work, tellingly prologued by Miguel Méndez and published a generation later than that author's most well-known work, *Peregrinos de Aztlán* [Pilgrims from Aztlan] (1974), picks up on themes highlighted in that earlier Chicano novel, carrying them forward into the 1990s. Like the earlier Chicano writer, and in a very different register than the centrist Mexican, Oropeza highlights a particularized subjectivity with its demands for satisfaction of mundane physical needs, and the transformations in identity that gradually evolve from the particular social situation in which the protagonist finds herself. Even further: dislocation naturally leads to the recreation of culture in another register.

Méndez organizes his prologue to Oropeza's work around one of his favored metaphors, that of "peregrinaje" (7; pilgrimage), and suggests that while *Montaña* "no es novela encaminada de intención a la protesta o testimonio documental. . . . Es . . . reflejo de aconteceres; pormenores de lo que es la circunstancia del mexicano en trance de migrante que pasa por los EE.UU. sin la debida documentación" [is not a novel intentionally directed toward protest or documentary testimonial. It is a reflection of events; the particulars of the circumstances of the Mexican in the life stage of a migrant who passes through the United States without the necessary documentation] ("Prólogo" 6). It is, he hints, a novel written in the same register as his own work, combining social consciousness with artistic value. In the precise reverse of Méndez's, "pilgrims" like Chuco, however, who travels to Mexico and learns to come to terms with his Mexicanness through reaffirming his Chicano identity, Oropeza's Adelaida offers a transposition of a Mexican worldview onto the United States, and in so doing also describes the other side of the coin: the always uneasy coming home to a newly emerging Chicana sense of self.

Adelaida is explicitly referenced in the first sentence of almost every chapter of the novel, providing an insistently located anchoring point of view for this migrant text. The novel follows her through twenty years in the United States, first as an illegal worker, then as a settled homeowner and legal immigrant, ending with her sale of her house in the United States and return to Mexico when she is sixty years old. Throughout this long period, Adelaida's most persistent fear is one of rootlessness and spritual homelessness. The novel begins with a series of dislocations: "Adelaida llega y siente el temor de que, de nuevo, ese lugar no sea para quedarse" [Adelaida arrives and fears once more that this might not be a place where she can stay] (23). When she finally is able to purchase a small house in the United States, her garden becomes the site at which her yearning for stability comes to apparent rest: "El jardín, inmóvil y vivo, es para ella el paréntesis de quietud espiritual en que hace mucho tiempo aprendió a refugiarse" [The garden, live and immobile, is for the the parenthesis of spiritual quietude in which she has learned long ago to take refuge] (59). The garden/refuge can serve nevertheless only as an unstable parenthesis in her daily life and in travels and, as such, points to the uncertainty at the core of Adelaida's life, disguising what she later realizes is a vacuum in her heart that has never been filled. There is, she comes to understand, a vast difference between "volver a casa" (which in this novel almost always tends to be laden with culturally specific references to returning to Mexico) and "going home" (which refers to her personal house in the United States).

The difference between "casa" and "home" (or "hom" as Oropeza frequently writes the word, so as to capture both the grain of a Mexican voice and the alienness of the concept) is at the heart of this novel. Adelaida's most concentrated desire is for a place to belong; at the same time, her migrant life has indelibly stamped her with foreignness. The northern house that seemed a potential haven earlier in the novel becomes merely the most notable place where her melancholy concentrates: "La soledad es un cuchillo. . . . Corta la tarde y está acabando sin remedio con su convencimiento de que en el Norte se encuentra la felicidad" [Loneliness is a knife. . . . It cuts the afternoon and is irremediably finishing off her conviction that she can find happiness in the North] (113). Yet, when Adelaida finally makes the decision to sell her house and move back to Santa Rosa, she almost immediately realizes that after twenty years in the United States her ideas and expectations no longer match those of her fellow townsfolk. The novel ends with her understanding that she cannot, in any spiritual sense, "volver a casa"—a romantic dream in any case—since the drive that sent her into the United States, and the experiences she lived there, have made her into a different person; or perhaps they have defined her difference even before she set out on her migrant journeys: "Presiente que se dará por vencida aunque todavía, dentro de poco tiempo, sentirá el impulso de salir otra vez a buscar eso que siempre ha sostenido sus huesos y la ha hecho caminar sin descanso" [She foresees that she will give up, although still, very shortly, she will feel the impulse to leave once more to seek that which has always sustained her bones and has made her travel ceaselessly] (137).

"¿A dónde pertenece?" [Where does she belong?] (88) Adelaida muses as she fills out her residence papers in the U.S. consulate. When her friend Rosenda insists "California es mi patria" [California is my homeland] (67), Adelaida is scandalized, but the other woman's point of view has effectively been placed into discourse by this statement both for our and for Adelaida's consideration. The reader of the novel realizes that by slow degrees Adelaida too is coming to understand the attractions of imagining herself as a Californian Chicana, although she would never articulate this position so forcefully. At the same time, Adelaida registers, almost subconsciously, a series of actions and behaviors that mark her increasing distance from the values she associates with her homeland. For example, already in her early years in the United States she demonstrates her independence in going to dances accompanied by another woman, and paying her own entrance fee, rather than waiting for a man to ask her (37–38). On visits to Mexico, she compares the tranquility and freedom of her life in the United States unfavorably with what she now sees as the repression of women in her home country (72); by the same token, she decides that she cannot and will not tolerate any longer the kind of abject poverty typical of her homeland (77). This woman who in Mexico had never lived alone, in the United States learns "el valor que tiene disponer de un lugar exclusivamente suyo" [the value of having a place exclusively for oneself] (47) and celebrates the purchase of her new house with a trip to McDonald's for mega-hamburgers. Oropeza underlines this shift in cultural perspective in other ways as well. Shortly after purchasing the house, Adelaida meditates on the Mexican migrant workers in California fields, describing their lives and customs as if they were strange and foreign: thus turning her countrymen into the "them" against which she measures her own newly settled "us" (51). One of the main differences between the resident "us" and the newly arrived "them" is, of course, that of perspective; they burn brightly and fast, live for the day and for the delight of spending their handfuls of dollars. Adelaida notes that, in contrast, she "comienza a pensar de otra manera en su futuro" [begins to think of the future in a different way] (91). Unlike the stereotypical Mexican spendthrifts against whom she gauges her own plans, she dreams of managing her money carefully, purchasing large items on credit, learning to drive a car and to speak English, and also of dumping her current unsatisfactory boyfriend for a better one.

One of the most important markers of this change in perspective revolves around Adelaida's increasing command of English, which is carefully developed in the text through a nuanced evocation of the stages and contradictions in her evolution from terrified migrant to resident Californian. There is a gradual shift from merely registering the use of impossibly alien concepts in a strange and twisty language to an assimilation of many of these same concepts into her own speech, along with the cultural presuppositions that underlie them. Thus, for example, the newly arrived Adelaida meticulously describes the *friwey*, categorizing it as a strange and marvelous sight; she is uncertain how to understand her cousin Anselmo's comment, "ya casi estamos en *hom*, Ady" [we are almost home, Ady] (13); she almost breaks into tears at the strangeness of the *breik* and the "media hora de *lonch*" at work, at the oddity of a food called "*hat dog*" (23–24); she has to come to terms with the alien U.S. obsession with time: "*Taim is money* alcanzó a oir algunas veces" [time is money, she was able to hear sometimes] (19). In each of these cases, the fracturing of mispronounced English words over a basically standard Spanish syntax creates a sense of estrangement. There is a violence done to the linguistic expressions with this insertion of fractured English, creating halting and opaque phrases that correlate perfectly with Adelaida's own struggle to comprehend. These English expressions are words that stand out doubly in the text, both because they reference things and concepts for which Adelaida has no Mexican equivalent, and because the slight distortion of the English spelling reminds us that they as yet have no firm contextualization in her new existence either. While each of these words points to a key signifier with specific cultural overtones: freeway culture, the U.S. idea of home, the structure of a factory workday, U.S. overreliance on a fast-food diet, a fixation on productivity by the clock; Adelaida still has no way to assess them, so they jostle in overheard speech as untranslatable dissonance interrupting her still fluid standard Spanish.

When Adelaida begins to take English classes, the formalized ESL exchanges offer little real assistance with this problem, since the memorized dialogues remain disconnected from her experienced reality. Deeply anguished by the unexpected solitude and culture shock of life in the North, stressed from days of pressured, repetitive work, she goes to class to learn how to say things like, "¿Ar yu japy in yur work? Yes, ai em japy" (31). It is no wonder that the similar question on the part of her companions at work, "¿Ar yu ol rait?" fills her with fury (25). Adelaida's trips to work on the bus are daily experiences in what she interprets as an intentionally exclusionary practice:

> . . . sigue el inglés apericado, gritón, salpicado de españolazos que la desespera porque se pierde en una intermitencia de imágenes en su mente que al fin de cuentas no le dice nada. . . . Se siente muy mal nadando entre objetos bonitos, gente güera y calles pavimentadas; entre mexicanos que no hablan para que se les entienda, sino para acompañarse en esta isla que es su lengua a medias, en ese mundo de cosas ajenas que los rodea. (16–17)

> . . . the screaming, parroted English keeps on, sprinkled with Spanish words that make her desperate because she gets lost in intermittent images in her mind that in the long run don't tell her anything. . . . She feels very bad floating among pretty objects, blonde people, and paved streets, among Mexicans who don't speak so that they can be understood, but rather to accompany themselves in this island that is their halfway language, in this world of alien things that surrounds them.

Adelaida is alienated by the newness and the strangeness of the cultures around her, both by the U.S. English-dominant one, and by the Chicano culture she registers as a "halfway" experience of marooned islanders in the midst of a *güero* sea. Her own position is aligned with neither of these two but, as a newly immigrant Mexican, she locates herself within an invisible third community of those like her who "todavía habla un español limpio" [who still speak a clean Spanish] (19) and retain close family and cultural ties in Mexico. Nevertheless, it is worth noting that the key word "todavía" (still) already hints at the changes to follow, at the instability of language in the border region, and the futility of applying prescriptive definitions of linguistic purity to borderlands practice.

One of the indices of her transformation is that later chapters of the novel register her speaking in just this combination of English and Spanish she once found incomprehensible and off-putting in her earlier days in the United States. This change is imperceptible to her, but clearly evident to the reader, who notes her bubbling enthusiasm about the prospects for her new life as well as her code switching in describing to herself her adventures in house hunting: "Tiene, sobre todo, una *yarda* enorme. . . . Lo mejor de todo es que tiene un *garach* largüísimo, para guardar su carro. Se arregla pronto con el agente del *ril esteit*. . . . En la siguiente esquina hay un super de chinos; a pocas cuadras está un *key mart*" [It has, above all, an enormous yard. . . . The best of all is that it has a really long garage. She quickly makes arrangements with the real estate agent. . . . On the next corner is a Chinese supermarket; a few blocks away is a Kmart] (99). This evolution from uncomfortable illegal immigrant to happy California homeowner would seem to mark the end point of this personal journey, just as her Spanglish indicates her newfound comfort level with the formerly alien concepts associated with her dominant English-language setting. Here, in germ, is the paradigmatic immigrant experience, leaving Mexico behind for an affirmative and empowering *Chicanidad*.

Matters are not resolved quite so easily, however. Early in her novel, Oropeza's point-of-view character tells herself, "Esto es el Norte, Adelaida, se dice, y no es el sueño que tenías desde los dieciseis años, ahora es cierto" [this is the North, Adelaida, she tells herself; it's not the dream you had since you were sixteen years old, now it is real] (13). Presciently, however, this newly visible border reality (we could almost call it the actualization of Adelaida's American Dream) metamorphoses into a cryptic phrase: "pesadillas de noche, amanecer de silencio" [bad dreams at night, dawning to silence] (21). In Oropeza's novel, the saga of immigration is completed in the cyle of return and disillusionment that allows Adelaida to finally define her difference against her expectations of a common culture. In his article "Cosmopolitan Patriots," philosopher Kwame Anthony Appiah defines what he calls a "tribal fantasy" that models national culture on an imaginarily homogenous ethnic, linguistic, social, and religious system. This tribal fantasy, he suggests, organizes discourses about presumed common cultures: "Where the common culture of a group is also, in this way, at the heart of an individual's culture, I shall say that individual is 'centered on the common culture'; and I want to make it part of the definition of being centered on a common culture that those who are centered on it think of themselves as a collectivity, and think of the collectivity as consisting of people for whom a common culture is central" (99–100).

By extension, I would posit that both the dominant cultures (in the United States, in Mexico) and resistant cultures (Chicano culture, northern border culture) necessarily and strategically streamline and homogenize their understandings of each other and of themselves in the crucible of these national and transnational conflicts; the very essence of a common culture, after all, is the ability to generalize about categories and qualities required for membership. And it is precisely to the extent that the concept of a common culture comes into question that the reactive forces of dominant culture production move to shore up its sagging acceptance. Thus, for example, the central Mexican worry about northern border economic and cultural contamination and southern border indigenous rebelliousness that can be most accurately traced in the outpouring of moderate to hysterical affirmations of an essential Mexicanness post-NAFTA; thus, too, the U.S. obsession with such slippery and ill-defined concepts as "family values" and its recent grassroots anti-immigrant movements; thus once more, in another register, the extraordinary outpouring of studies from European and North American academic centers attempting to articulate a theoretical framework for an indifferently anchored subject of study called "border theory."

The point of this novel, however, is to direct us in precisely the opposite direction, to ask us to look for the difficult heterogeneity rather than the easy commonality. In Oropeza's narrative, the uncertain and differential evolution of what might be considered an emerging Chicana consciousness rubs up against clichéd presumptions about U.S. dominant culture practices and also against a romanticization of provincial Mexican life. "Pesadillas de noche," muses Adelaida, "amanecer de silencio"; to some degree the two Mexican novels break down neatly along this boundary line. Fuentes's nightmare-wracked reinvention of the cacophonous voices of the many migrant souls who populate his multifaceted crystal frontier finds its counterpart in Oropeza's focus on a single migrant woman whose meditations on her mostly domestically oriented dreams jostle against her literal and metaphorical silencing in both U.S. and Mexican communities. At the same time, each novel evokes a geopolitical and cultural space of multiple crossings, one that is far more heterogenous than conventionally transnational. When we add the perspective of Puerto Rican writers like Ana Lydia Vega, we also need to take into account a more virtual conception of community, where the imaginary ethos of crossing is constructed on a compass-less refugee boat lost somewhere between Port au Prince and Miami, or encapsulated in a multilayered literary homage to a repudiated colonial past. With González Viaña the reader remembers as well the multiplicities and confusions of *latinidades* subsumed under a single, inadequate identity marker in the United States. Following Appiah, we might conclude that texts such as these point toward the difficult concept of a nontribal, noncentered fantasy of identity formation, one in which the perspectives of writers from the South looking North as well as from the North looking South are given equal weight—in whatever language(s) they choose to deploy.

chapter four

Arrival: Dorfman, Salazar, Sainz, Rivera-Valdés

AT THE END OF HIS 1995 FILM, *Nueba Yol (A Funny Way to Say New York),* Angel Muñiz's protagonist, Balbuena, a Dominican immigrant to New York City,[1] returns to the island no better off financially than when he left, but with an increased sense of the importance and value of home. This renewed commitment to his country of origin is confirmed with a textbook happy ending to the movie. Balbuena marries his sweetheart in a fancy church ceremony and makes a poignant farewell to his tragically lost first wife at her gravesite. His bride, Nancy, a Dominican woman whom Balbuena meets during his New York misadventures, has shared the heartbreak of trying to make it in the harsh, cold North and fully understands and shares his rededication to his homeland. Prior to his coming to terms about his disillusionment with the American Dream, she had already made her own decision to go back to the Dominican Republic, and her arrival there preceded his own. Their marriage, then, confirms not only Balbuena's commitment to his native land, but also to a choice made in the full knowledge of a seemingly attractive alternative. Implicitly, Nancy and Balbuena's incipient family will be free of the unhealthy stresses that plague the more affluent but deeply fissured and unhappy family of his New York cousin.

Yet, surprisingly enough, two years later, the movie's sequel, *Nueba Yol, Part Three: Bajo la Nueva Ley* opens with the revelation that Balbuena's triumphant return to the Dominican Republic and reunion with Nancy was just that—a dream that sustained him when he was left for dead after a brutal assault in the penultimate scene of the first film. Instead of his Dominican happy ending with Nancy, in the second film Balbuena takes part in a green card marriage in order to secure legal immigrant status and Social Security benefits in the United States: a stark and dystopic contrast with the idyllic conclusion of the first movie.

I won't undertake a fuller analysis of these films in this chapter, but merely suggest that they succinctly point to an easily recognizable trope that contextualizes the reshaping of expectations and redefinition, if not of political citizenship, then of what it means to "assimilate" to the United States, and what are the costs of "belonging" to this culture. All of the texts explored in this chapter have to do with displaced writers who find themselves in the United States and are caught between nostalgia for the homeland left behind and a conflicted sense of belonging to the new country in which they have arrived. Strikingly enough, as in the Dominican films, in all of these texts, the conflict crystallizes around the narrator/protagonist's emotional and sexual relationships with one or more women whose unambiguous national and cultural identity clearly positions her as the desired Other, the concrete correlative of the fantasized nation left behind and/or, alternatively, the imaginative projection of the still-unintelligible new nation: in both cases, the screen against which the narrator's own ambivalences can be more sharply projected. A relationship with this woman, then, in some sense serves as a synecdoche for the protagonist's mastery of both national and familial roles.

Perhaps because the protagonists are all writers, they deliberately assault the expectations of the auto/biographical forms they mimic, eschewing the strictly confessional in favor of a more poetic appropriation of the familiar story of the immigrant experience, exploring the capabilities and dispositions attaching memory to social identity. As David Palumbo-Liu asks, "if social identity and community membership are so attached to common memories . . . is memory dependent upon direct experience, or does a collective memory not rest instead upon a tradition of narration and performance?" (298). In the narratives explored in this chapter, the singular nature of the auto/biographical subject rubs up against the dearth of a familiar collective against which to measure experience, and memory has to be reconfigured in a transnational context. It is in this context of loss and appropriation that the narrations' key female figures serve as anchor and counterpoint.

While geographical displacement is the motivating factor, in these texts of arrival the question of the relation of the individual to specific landscapes is less crucial than the unfolding of such projected new memory spaces. In each case, as in Muñiz's films, the psychological tension between the two geographical spaces is staged with respect to the yearned-for other—the land left behind, the new land opening its arms—but always this longing becomes metaphorically figured in the body of woman. These writers read immigrant space almost obsessively within the most intimate of interpersonal relationships, and understand assimilation less as occupying a specific social or geographical location than as focusing on the (sexual, psychic) possession of a specific woman. At the same time, these women characters often and tellingly appear in these texts as functionally overdetermined while narratively flat. Despite their depiction as the obsessive object of desire and focus of the protagonists' energy, there seems to be little enough narrative motivation for such excessive attention. What at first glance looks like an opportunity for resolution remains stylistically dissonant in context.

In Ariel Dorfman's memoir, *Heading South, Looking North,* this anchoring figure—his wife, Angélica—defines the author's otherwise shaky claim to Chileanness against the almost overwhelming pull of his U.S. identity. For the fictionalized José Eustacio Rivera in Boris Salazar's *La otra selva,* the correlation of two imagined nations corresponds to two female figures: Claire (New York) and Alicia (Colombia), almost too neatly representing the divided claims of his neo-Latino self. Likewise, in Gustavo Sainz's *La novela virtual,* the sexagenerian protagonist, a Mexican novelist teaching in a U.S. university, is torn between the charms of sex with his nubile students in a Vermont summer college and the competing attractions of an online affair with an adoring young Mexican fan named Camila who sends him long e-mail messages throughout the summer. Finally, in Sonia Rivera-Valdés's collection of linked short stories, *Las historias prohibidas de Marta Veneranda,* the narrator gives the old heterosexist story a twist. "La más prohibida" of the tales is less so because of its lesbian relationship (homosexuality is a common feature of many of these stories), but because it describes a successful return with the beloved to the homeland. In all the other tales—Muñiz's, Dorfman's, Sainz's, Salazar's—any return, other than an imaginary voyage to the country of origin, is strictly outside the narrative reach of the texts.

It would be easy to argue that this overlaying of national imaginaries upon a woman's body is a well-established metaphor in Western (including Latin American) fiction; indeed, we could even call it a cliché at this point. To some extent, "the retrospective activity of nation-building in modernity is always predicated upon Woman as trope, displacing historical women" (Alarcón, Kaplan, and Moallem 6). This tropicly conceived Woman as displaced and imagined Other falls into a particular variation on the simplifying model succinctly described by Spivak: "Only the dominant self can be problematic; the self of the Other is authentic without a problem, naturally available to all kinds of complications. This is very frightening" (*Post-Colonial Critic* 66). Woman as trope, unproblematically "authentic": the conjunction of these two lines of thought should remind us that while analysis may focus on the workings of this trope, it would be a mistake to look for evidence of a convincing female character in any of these highly solipsistic texts. What is most striking in the texts studied here is the additional twist involved in the energetic maintenance of this cliché when so much else breaks down in the in-between or transnational space of immigration. More accurately, what we have in each of these fictions is a woman-effect serving as a placeholder for a fundamental catachresis between the impossibility of abandoning the native culture and the inachievability of an imagined full assimilation to the United States. She is a possessable subject/object that cannot be consolidated into something/someone appropriable to the immigrant's own experience. At the same time incomprehensible but graspable, she represents a guaranteed authenticity within reach.

Dorfman provides the easiest point of entry into this cluster of signification, as his work most overtly plays with the frustrated utopic aspirations of his narrated self. While much of Dorfman's work is famously attentive to the international cultural and political scene,[2] his 1998 memoir, *Heading South, Looking North,* along with the Spanish alternate text, *Rumbo al sur, deseando el norte,* dramatizes in a particularly powerful way the theme of cultural difference and cultural identity as played out in the process of writing, and in the subtly but significantly different stories made possible or prevented in the choice of language. Consummately self-conscious about his bilingualism, Dorfman comments in an interview that "my Spanish is haunted by English and vice versa. . . . I want to write for the gringo with a sense of familiarity. After all, I'm also a gringo. . . . But I also want to convey in my writing a sense of alienation, distance, discomfort" (Stavans 308). He writes easily and fluently in both languages, and often translates his work back and forth between them, often using one version to refine the other. Thus, for example, he tells Stavans that in his various renditions of his novel *Máscara,* the play between languages was particularly productive: "*Mascara,* published in 1988, is the first of my novels that I wrote in Spanish, then rewrote in English, only to then use what I had redone in English to change the Spanish version" (305). In all of his self-translated texts, the English and Spanish versions are at least slightly different, as Dorfman takes into account his expectations about the two different bodies of readers.

He contrasts his own situation with that of more established U.S. Latino/as who seem to have achieved a resolution he lacks—or one for which his imagination cannot conjure up a sufficiently motivating audience: "For me the perfect audience would be one made up of some forty to sixty million people as bilingual as I am. I honestly think if I had that audience I would write in an entirely different way. I would write the way I live: switching languages, going in and out, like the Nuyoricans and Chicanos" (305). While it is unclear from this statement if he is suggesting that the Nuyoricans and Chicanos at least potentially have an access he lacks to that large bilingual audience, or that they are privileged to write irrespective of those exigencies, in either case Dorfman's curious statement hints at a peculiar lack that can only be supplemented with extreme difficulty, and only as an unrealized imaginative projection. Later in the same interview, he adds: "as years go by, I feel I belong but that I also don't belong. . . . Often I'm struck by nostalgia and sadness, by the realization that I will always be globetrotting, that I will never call a piece of land my own" (Stavans 310–11). This nostalgia shapes the memoir, with its sequencing of a series of abrupt exiles.

In *Heading South,* Dorfman contemplates his exile from Chile from within the recollection of his journey's mythic dimension: "I was consoling myself with one of the basic myths of the species, a story which every civilization has told itself since the beginning of history: there is a place, one place, where you truly belong, a place that is often but not always the place where you were born, and that place is akin to paradise." In the working out of this myth, the hero loses paradise and the story of civilization becomes that of the hero's journey, of his quest to return to his originary paradisal home (275–76). For Dorfman, his wandering life is preordained to fall short of the full scope of the hero's journey; the paradise lost—alternately imagined as the United States and as Chile—cannot ever be regained. Even when the physical space seems potentially recuperable, a prior innocence has vanished, and the return to paradise is always taken in the consciousness of its earlier loss, and of the long journeying that brought the hero back to a place that is no longer the dreamed-of home. Noncoincidentally, this frame tale is borne out in the choice of subtitle for the English text: *A Bilingual Journey*. The book opens with the trauma of the fall (from grace, as the hero is cast out of Eden), and indeed the metaphor of falling pervades this narrative. Dorfman's family abruptly sets out on each of its North-South moves as if responding to physical laws of force and gravitation, forcibly ejecting them from the current Eden to send them forth on a looping quest for its recovery.

This metaphor of the fall is especially insistent in the English version of the text, where Dorfman manipulates a particularly rich system of signification that does not easily translate into the Spanish version of his memoirs. In Spanish, by way of contrast, the text's subtitle is *Un romance en dos lenguas,* highlighting another kind of quest myth, grounded not in biblical Genesis but in the Spanish tradition of the octasyllabic poetic form used in ballads, of the *novelas de caballerías,* and, in another sense, in the Romantic tradition in all its various senses of the term. Thus, while there are other riches for the Latin American reader, for the gringo, it is the insistent reminder of the fall (from paradise) that serves as Dorfman's dominant myth of the constituting trauma defining and setting in motion his wandering life. In Spanish, the metaphor of the fall recedes to the background.

The first chapter of the memoirs, a kind of prologue, opens with insomnia—"if I can't fall asleep" (6; Spanish: "no puedo dormirme" 12) and the narrator's persistent reliving of September 11, 1973, the day of the bloody coup against Chilean President Salvador Allende, the day Dorfman should have died: "it was warning me of what was about to befall me, to befall all of us" (7; Spanish: "acaecer" 14). In both cases, the English (unlike the Spanish) plays on the word "fall," and anchors the story to the primary mythic structure, preparing the reader for the densely allusive referential system to follow. The second chapter of the narrative confirms this incipient leitmotif as it restarts the memoir at the conventional beginning of autobiography, with the author's birth. The first sentence of this chapter, "I was falling," standing alone as the section's first paragraph, serves both as a description and as a quote, with fuller context given immediately: "I was already in danger. I did not need to be told. . . . But my mother warned me anyway that I was falling, the first words I ever heard in my life. . . . '*Doctor, se cae el niño, se cae el niño,*' she told the doctor that I was falling, the boy was about to fall" (11–12).

The metaphor is picked up and expanded almost as a genealogical imperative. Dorfman describes in similar terms, for example, his father's passion for Russian: "the language that caught him as he fell into the abyss of birth happened to be the very language that he believed was destined to redeem the whole of fallen humanity" (23), using two senses of the verb—the fall into life and language that Dorfman has already established as his particular metaphorical nexus, and the "fallen humanity" of messianic and Marxist teleologies. He repeats the image when commenting on why his parents had to leave Argentina for the United States: "again my father was falling" (24). Expelled from Argentina for his political views, Dorfman's father falls north, tugged by the invisible force lines of gravity and a Guggenheim fellowship. When shortly after the family's arrival in the United States the toddler has to be hospitalized, the narrator comments, "here we go, falling again" (44), as the uncomprehending child finds himself pulled into another language system. At kindergarten age, says Dorfman, "what was falling in my life were London Bridge and Humpty Dumpty who sat on a wall, Humpty Dumpty who had a great fall, and me, I was falling down and laughing and squealing as I ran a ring around a rosy, pocketful of posies, all fall down!" (65)[3] By the time we reach the middle of the book and the first reference to his future wife, the reader is well primed to add another fall, even without Dorfman's prompting: falling in love.

Things in Dorfman's world are constantly threatening to fall down, fall apart; yet threatening is not yet the completion of the action, just as falling is not yet fallen. In the English version of these memoirs, Dorfman takes advantage of the semantic field offered by the more expansive use of the present participle as verb and gerund, and it sometimes seems that everything crucial in the narrator's life is held in suspension, or remains almost painfully dilated on the cusp between an action and its not-yet completion, the markers *-ing* and *-en* attaching to the word *fall-*. The triad of children's rhymes figure a game of falling as practice for life; always menacing at least a symbolic death, a death that in the memoirs too often literally threatens but continues to be deferred. In life, unlike the play of death in "London Bridge," "Humpty Dumpty," or "Ring around the Rosie," Dorfman describes falling, but he is always scooped up, rescued: by language, by love. And yet, at the same time, the bicultural author would be well aware of the historical realities hiding behind seemingly innocent children's rhymes—"Ring around the Rosie," for example, describes the process of the plague that repeatedly swept medieval Europe, the Black Death. "Languages," says the narrator, "do not only expand through conquest: they also grow by offering a safe haven to those who come to them in danger, those who are falling from some place far less safe than a mother's womb" (13). Falling, thus, signals his in-between status, his distance with respect to a mythic site of departure or arrival, and his defiance of death. It also marks his highly contingent access to a simulacrum of the authenticity he seeks.

This access cannot be more than a simulacrum for obvious reasons. Existing in free fall is the opposite of grounded, and throughout the memoir the grounding is provided by Angélica, who occupies completely the space left for Truth, Authenticity, Nation, Love. What is left for the writer is an uncertain process-driven mode of existence and a conviction about the importance of storytelling (another gerund, an *-ing* word pertaining in this narrative to the same English-language semantic field as *falling*). The frustration of Dorfman's yearning for a firm ground is implicit in the need to state his fears upon learning that he will have to leave Chile or face probable death for himself and his family: "I can't stand the idea of being shut out of the country and excluded from witnessing and transmitting its story through my words, that I cannot miss this chance to become totally, definitively, forever Chilean by writing myself into the country and the country into myself" (148). Ironically, Dorfman measures his distance from this desired ground in the intensity of the desire itself, in his awareness that in choosing to write this story of his life he is making a commitment. Writing himself into the country and the country into him will always seem second best, not quite authentic, a storyteller's trick. "It is a comforting idea, that I was spared because I was to be the storyteller," he says in a typical moment of candor. "If it is not true that this was why I was saved, I have tried to make it true. In every story I tell" (39–40).

One of the stories he tells has to do with how someone named Vladimiro, for his parents' admiration of the Russian revolutionary leader, came to be called Eddie by his friends, and now responds to the literary name Ariel (via Shakespeare's *The Tempest* and Rodó's *Ariel*)—the name that also appears on the cover of all his books. As a young boy suffering from a cultural doubleness in New York, he borrowed a character from Mark Twain's *The Prince and the Pauper:* "I told myself that in reality I was Edward the Prince. . . . I decided to force the world to acknowledge, if not my princehood, at least my Edwardliness." The opportunity for the transition, ironically, occurred during the transit back to Latin America, when he introduced himself to his new social set with the impeccably Anglo name: "Many of my friends from Chile still call me Ed or Eddie, and not the Ariel which I was eventually to adopt" (80–81). Dorfman, thus, engages in a continual play of self-fashioning, in some sense refusing to be interpolated into cultural subjecthood on any terms but his own. At the same time, the persistence in renaming himself in response to new cultural circumstances (naming himself against the grain of the culture) hints at both his ungrounded condition—the gesture of defiance—and its eventually self-cancelling nature: to defy one cultural imperative is to fall into another imperative that is equally constraining.

The evolution of the author's given name is paralleled by what Dorfman characterizes as his equally stubborn insistence on a choice of literary language and cultural milieu. In Chile he rejects Hispanophone culture and writes in English; in Berkeley in the 1960s he reverses his earlier decision: "I swore never to write another word in the English language. . . . I willed myself monolingual again" (101). And yet, of course, in all of this determination, this conscious and conscientious staking out of a firm position, Dorfman is also aware that the background to his imaginative retransformations is still a dominant culture into which he is falling, or from which he is falling away.

When the young Dorfman falls in love with his future wife, one of her attractions is that she successfully, to his mind at least, embodies the nation in a full and uncomplicated way not available to him: "I realized that Angélica's connection to Chile was the opposite of mine, that it was not and never could be willed, that she could not discard it as I was in the process of discarding the United States, that it was as much a part of her as her lungs or her skin" (181). Here, Dorfman's sentiments intersect uncannily with the great nineteenth-century Romantic tradition by which Woman becomes reduced to a trope, serving as a man's muse. Following through on the implications, we see how she comes to embody the ideal in herself; hence, in good Romantic fashion, by definition she cannot write, only be written. In one of the most cited and frequently deconstructed versions of this motif, Spanish poet Gustavo Adolfo Bécquer asks in his "Rima XXI":

> ¿Qué es poesía?, dices mientras clavas
> en mi pupila tu pupila azul;
> ¡Qué es poesía! ¿Y tú me lo preguntas?
> Poesía . . . eres tú. (122)
>
> What is poetry, you ask while stabbing
> In my pupil your blue pupil
> What is poetry! And you ask?
> Poetry . . . is you.

Like Bécquer's muse, Angélica does not need to write or even speak about Chile; she *is* Chile—simply, or, as Spivak would say, unproblematically, authentically. Dorfman's "preface by way of a dedication" begins: "Angélica: this book is for you" and ends "*Sin ti, no hubiera sobrevivido.* Without you I wouldn't have survived" (np). Whatever fallings or failings present themselves, Angélica provides the writer with a ground to catch him up, the essential link to home that the rest of his memoirs so ably dissect: "She was worried (and always was and still is) that I was not *ubicado*—that I was unable to place myself, to put myself in the place and the moment as I should" (229). Angélica's concern for her husband's well-being comes through in the details Dorfman uses to hint at the tenor of their relationship. She worries, for instance, about his insistence on jogging (which she sees as a pernicious and dangerous custom picked up in Berkeley) in the early morning Chilean streets. His response confirms that wherever he is located, Dorfman remains irremediably out of place. In the English text, he tells her in Spanish, "*Las calles pertenecen al pueblo*" (229), an unimpeachably leftist Latin American sentiment; in the Spanish version he says, "respondí en inglés con una frase también aprendida en las protestas de Berkeley: —*The streets belong to the people*" (305). In each case, he calls upon the cultural registers of the alternate country to anchor the rightness of his actions. At the same time, this response confirms Angélica's function: to grab hold of her peripatetic husband and *ubicarlo*, creating a link to a series of spatial, linguistic, and cultural referents and bringing him back home. No longer, or not only, a story he tells himself about himself, "The question of language had become ensnared in the question of nationality, and therefore of identity" (47).

Expanding on another metaphor, this one very close to the nineteenth-century nation-building prose so aptly analyzed in Doris Sommer's *Foundational Fictions*, Dorfman describes his love for Angélica/Chile in self-consciously ironic terms, seeing her both as an exoticized object of conquest (for the gringo in him) and as conceptualized through a specifically Latin American male body of metaphors for loving their women: "the woman as earth, the earth goddess to be excavated, a territory to be explored by a pioneer, a land in which to root your manhood like a tree" (178). Through the metaphor of land, she contains the nation, gives her husband access to the entire community: "I could feel the country bringing me back to her for more, my need for the identity she gave me fastening me to her" (179). Only upon realizing that her life will be in danger should he follow his first impulse to remain in the country, does the narrator make the discovery that "I would rather lose Chile than lose Angélica. . . . It was then, I think, that for the first time in my life I separated my wife from the country where she had been born. Ever since I met her, Angélica had been confused, in my mind, with Chile" (177). Nevertheless, while Dorfman distances himself from the metaphors expressing his youthful sexism, he does not stray far from the core concept by which he characterizes his love for Chile, and for the Chile in Angélica that sustains him in his new exile and that grounds and defines his identity as a Latin American, and more specifically *Chilean*, man.

Ironically, while Dorfman imagines himself as a typical Latin male, rooted in an earth-mother nation-woman, Angélica intuitively recognizes the otherness that Dorfman does not want to admit to this particular story, though he does accept its force elsewhere. In an interview with similarly bilingual writer Ilán Stavans, Dorfman muses upon his interlocutor's evocation of Henry James, who describes an individual's first language as his mother tongue and the second as his wife/mistress tongue. He comments, "the fact that Henry James would talk about wives and mistresses is already a very gendered approach to the issue." Tellingly, he then stutters through his own version of these family relationships: "In a way, I think I'm married to both languages. . . . Perhaps I have two mothers. . . . Or is it two mother-wives?" (305). In Dorfman's version, the gendering takes on incestuous overtones. Similarly, in *Heading South* he attempts to resolve the tensions of "my schizophrenic, adulterous existence" (132) with the statement: "I became a bigamist of language . . . I married them both" (270). In marrying both languages, he also and necessarily binds himself to both cultures, and he repeatedly describes this commitment by way of reference to the same gendered metaphor he decries in the earlier author.

Furthermore, Angélica, the Chilean English teacher, is not fooled by his Latin male rhetoric of gender construction. Beyond the pernicious earth-mother-nation system of allusion, this is a cultural formation in which the long-suffering wife often has to graciously support the existence of her counterpart in *la casa chica*: an adulterous relation in fact and not just metaphor. In effect, she calls her husband to task for his adulterous-incestuous metaphorical structure. Angélica also clearly cuts through the wish-fulfillment in another direction as well, seeing the gringo substratum only lightly overlaid with the Latin American surface. She tells her husband that what kept them together when times were bad was her sense that he was a gringo and thus more to be trusted than Chilean men (179). Moreover, unlike Dorfman, who returns to the United States only to yearn for the liberatory possibilities he sees in Latin America, she found in Berkeley relations more "authentic and challenging and democratic than anything she had ever found in hypocritical, repressed, middle-class Chile" (218)—in a sense making her more open to cultural doubleness than her more bilingual husband. Thus, on the one hand, it is very much to Dorfman's credit that he registers in his memoir both his projections upon his wife, and, if only marginally, her resistance to such simplistic categorizations. It is very striking, on the other hand, that despite his rejection of the Jamesian gendered rhetoric, his own meditations begin and end with exactly the same gendered division of labor: rooted woman-wife-nation-language versus male traveling storyteller.

In such passages, and indeed throughout the narrative, Dorfman implicitly falls back into the Jamesian narrative that he otherwise and explicitly ironizes or decries. What Dorfman craves from Angélica is the sense of *ubicación* that she—in a clichéd understanding of femininity—seems to embody, while at the same time, the whole thrust of his work is shaped by the equally cliched ur-masculine concept of the journey and by the willful falling away from such fixed and centering and limiting categories. He wants to participate in that linguistic, cultural, and sexual homeland, but he also wants the joys of incestuous bigamy—the second wife-mother, the mistress culture. In some way, we might say that Dorfman's gendered plot of his round-trip journey between the two poles remains unrealized, for if Angélica anchors one end, he has not yet—in contrast with his fictional counterparts in Salazar and Saínz as we shall see—found a name for the second wife at the other. Perhaps this metaphorical yearning toward the absent Other Woman and the lack of resolution lies behind Dorfman's insistence on the metaphor of falling. It also underscores the blurring of the mother/tongue that catches him up with the wife that reels him back home, as well as with his overdetermined need for confirmation in a guaranteed audience of "forty to sixty million people as bilingual as I am" in order to be able to engage in code switching like the Nuyoricans and Chicanos.

EROTIC-UMBILICAL GEOGRAPHIES

In contrast with Dorfman, both Salazar and Saínz have cast a more overt layer of fiction over their auto/biographical texts, and both have a female object of desire anchoring the two sides of the biculture. Moreover, one of these women is held at a distance, erotically unavailable, while the other is explicitly linked to umbilical imagery (in Salazar's case, the character Alicia has recently given birth; in Sainz's novel, the narrator obsesses about the ring piercing a student's navel). Both are intricately plotted works, metatextual in scope, and deeply invested in the play of multiple voices across a single narrative, a narrative that, moreover, tells of the writing of the novel we are currently reading. New York–based Salazar's *La otra selva* (The Other Jungle) looks back to the recent past, highlighting a key moment conjoining the two Americas in the person of novelist José Eustasio Rivera. Gustavo Saínz, for many years a resident in states ranging from New Mexico to Indiana to Vermont, orients his book to the present and near future, using the computer logs of a fictional "Gustavo Saínz" in *La novela virtual* to superimpose Mexico on the U.S. heartland.

Salazar fills the biographical lacuna in the biography of Colombian author José Eustasio Rivera with a richly imagined account of the last months of his life, and his sudden death, in New York City. The background to this text is therefore straightforwardly biographical. Briefly, Rivera, already celebrated in his home country as a distinguished poet, had shifted genres when he published his most famous work, *La vorágine* (The Whirlpool), the prototypical *novela de la selva,* in 1924. He was working on his second novel, *La mancha negra* (The Black Stain), when he made his trip to New York City in 1928. During the period between April and December of that year, he founded Editorial Andes as a way to promote Latin American literature, signed a contract for the translation of *La vorágine* with Ángel Flores and Earl K. James, published the fifth and corrected edition of that novel, and spent a good deal of time trying to interest filmmakers in the work. This record of intense work came to an abrupt end on December 1 when the writer "moría de muerte misteriosa," according to Isaías Peña. Adding to the mystery, the manuscript for his novel-in-progress was never found (Peña 10–11). Salazar's novel, for its part, is a long riff on this notorious unsolved chapter in Colombian letters. It is written as a detective story intricately woven with a series of voices and textual echoes, as Jonathan Tittler notes in his lucid and helpful commentary on the text:

> In addition to the omniscient voice that narrates the well-known fate of the legendary author, first- and second-person voices give new dimension to the tale: the voice of a private detective who has been contacted by powerful patrons to trail Rivera and defend Colombia's national interests, and that of an American woman whose relation to him is at first linguistic (they agree to exchange Spanish lessons for English) and then turns romantic. . . . Just as the detective becomes inseparable from the author Rivera, the woman becomes inseparable from the author's text. These mergers are reflected in the way the Colombian Amazon interpenetrates the steel-and-concrete jungle of Manhattan. The City in *La otra selva* swallows up the Colombian poet with the same voracious indifference with which nature in Rivera's novel devours Arturo Cova and Alicia. (130–31)

Along with the Spanish student, Claire Weingest, the fictional Rivera also frames his interaction with New York City by reference to possibly apocryphal sightings of Greta Garbo, and meetings with a mysterious Garbo-esque actress introduced to him by a set of shady individuals (including the detective) who convince the Colombian author that they can sell his novel to the big movie producers. Thus, these two women, each exotic in her own right, define New York City for the novelist even as they merge with text and screen images of femininity respectively. For if Claire represents the other language in which Rivera has been immersed, Garbo (or her counterpart, Lupe Velez, or Lupe's textual double) stands in for the U.S. culture's visual correlative. Each an incomplete analogue in and of herself, the two women together comprise the shape of Rivera's anchoring metaphor for Salazar's purposes. These women are perhaps inevitably overwritten in their turn by the encroachment of the metaphorical/textual jungle onto the City, and the voice of *La vorágine*'s Alicia strengthens and becomes more discrete as Salazar's novel approaches its climax.

New York City is in many ways a strange and exotic place in this novel, but Salazar's perspective on it is North American, in strict analogy to the relation of the exotic Amazonian jungle with respect to the implicit position of the earlier Colombian novelist. Thus, in each case the narrative perspective is that of a native of the country who through a series of circumstances is forced to become unexpectedly intimate with that country's hidden heart. The almost inevitable evocation of Conrad's *Heart of Darkness* is very much to the point, and underlining this suggestive analogy, the novel ends with Claire's voice, projecting beyond the ending of Salazar's work to the proposed next stop on Rivera's itinerary: "mañana, muy temprano, él habría enviado su novela a Colombia y tú estarías a su lado, anunciando el comienzo de ese viaje hacia el África con el que ambos habían soñado" [tomorrow, very early, he would have sent his novel to Colombia and you will be at his side, announcing the beginning of that trip toward the Africa that you had both dreamed of] (185). Thus, economically, Salazar links Rivera's Amazon with Conrad's *Heart of Darkness*, both of which can be funneled through the perspective of the New York woman who—like Alicia in Rivera's novel or Kurtz's African mistress in Conrad's—occupies the point through which men's dreams intersect with an overdetermined heterotopic geography.

Because of his attentiveness to this heritage, in Salazar's novel the homeland has both "real" and "exotic" determinants, as does the country of arrival, and quotidian reality often yields up strangenesses that make it even more inaccessible than the supposed jungle that serves as the real's delimiting Other. For Salazar there is always slippage between these two levels: the historical nation and the imaginary one, home and its exotic alibi, memory and fictional invention, the clear and the mysterious, Claire Weingest and Greta Garbo/Lupe Vélez (or Claire/Garbo and Alicia), New York and the Amazon, hardboiled detective fiction and Latin American baroque. The mediating subjectivity juggles these two (or four) chronotopes, imaginatively projecting one on top of the other in a dazzling play of intertextual overlays. Thus, the stereotypically urban U.S. genre of the detective narrative inflects and is infected by the "real maravilloso" (marvelous reality, to use Carpentier's famous term), the baroque style so often associated with the mid-twentieth-century Latin American writers. In a parallel manner, New York for Salazar's Rivera is not only "la otra selva," it is also an intermediate stop in a projected series of such liminal sites ranging from the Colombian Amazon to the African jungle, all of which ambivalently retain echoes of both the paradisical and the hellish. As Salazar's detective says in response to Rivera's query about the improbable doubling of the villainous character, Lesmes, who is extracted from the earlier novel to reappear in this space: "todo es posible en Nueva York" [everything is possible in New York] (152).

One of the novel's leitmotifs is a frequent reference to imagery of paradise, often, as in Dorfman, from the perspective of one who has lost or been expelled from it, and from there alludes to or mourns his fallen state. Thus, for example, at the opening of the novel, set in the last moments before his death on a rainy December morning, Rivera meditates on life and language, evoking his "expuls[ión] del paraíso" [expulsion from Paradise] (11), here associated both with a spiritual state of grace and with his home country of Colombia. The novel then travels back in time to recuperate the lost period in Rivera's life, and the leitmotif repeats with other resonances. At one point a salesman promises him "viajes gratis hacia el paraíso terrenal ('que está tan sólo as dos horas de aquí en la todavía virginal y más pura reserva natural de Long Island, en la preciosa región de los Hamptons . . . '), oportunidades diseñadas para personas como usted, 'totalmente originales en su manera de pensar y vivir' " [free trips to earthly paradise (which is located only two hours from here in the still virginal and pure nature reserve of Long Island, in the beautiful region of the Hamptons] (160–61). Paradise in this second evocation is both a real geographical space and a travel agent's too easily dissected hyperbole, both Colombia and the Hamptons, the perpetually lost homeland and the groomed nature reserve. Yet, at the same time, the uneasy relation between paradise and *selva* returns to haunt the narrative as a metaphor for the author's creative practice.

To a large extent, the function of the female figure in this novel is to mediate between this sense of a paradise lost and paradise yet-to-be-uncovered, to create a point of access to the feared and loved terrain of creativity, the writer's truest jungle. In *La otra selva,* however, this crucial female presence is divided between the tutor, Claire, and the actress, Lupe/Garbo, who stand in this novel as the correlatives for the slowly emerging ur-female figure of Alicia from Rivera's *La vorágine.* Each of these three figures deserves to be studied in turn.

While Claire's role in the novel is much more developed, the figure of the actress is crucial, though essentially both undefined and symbolically overendowed. Importantly, Salazar's novel stresses the mystique of the celebrity rather than any particular woman's specificity. In this fictional account of the attempt to get a film contract for *La vorágine,* the actress who will play Alicia is the most crucial consideration, yet that role is constantly shifting and evolving in the fictional Rivera's mind. The detective observes of the Colombian author that "como todos . . . él también ha deseado la mujer ideal. . . . Como todos . . . cree haberla encontrado y se equivoca. Como todos, la encuentra alguna vez y no se da cuenta" [like everyone . . . he too has desired the ideal woman. . . . Like everyone . . . he thinks he finds her and is mistaken. Like everyone, he finds her sometime and does not realize it] (25). Alicia is that imaginary and idealized woman for the fictional Rivera (though interestingly enough, much of what his alter ego Arturo desires in her is access to his lost enemy). A good deal of Rivera's energy is spent trying to match his mental concept of Alicia with what he fantasizes to be true about the workings of Hollywood, connecting his evolving understanding of his fiction to what he does not fully recognize as Hollywood hype. This mental morass too is a *selva* of sorts. "Esa selva suya es como una mujer" [this jungle of yours is like a woman], says the false Lupe Vélez in an intimate conversation with Rivera (86), and he readily agrees.

What he does not notice, however, is the degree to which he overlays the imagery of the *selva* with the constantly shifting figure of an indiscriminately chosen Hollywood silver screen goddess whom he mistakenly identifies with the figure of the ideal woman.

This tight association of landscape and iconic female figure holds for "la otra selva" as well. Tellingly, the author's first impression of New York substitutes Lady Liberty for the famous screen actress Greta Garbo as the dominant image focusing lines of sight in New York Harbor. As Rivera descends from the boat after his trip from Colombia:

> los ojos de la multitud lo guiaron, sin remedio . . . allí estaba una mujer vestida de azul, los ojos mirando no hacia la multitud, sino hacia la ciudad, hacia los edificios cubiertos de bruma, hacia Nueva York. Ellos la miraban a ella, pero ella no los miraba a ellos . . . . "Es Greta Garbo que regresa de Suecia"—dijo alguien detrás de él. (14)

> the eyes of the crowd guided him, without recourse . . . there was a woman dressed in blue, her eyes looking not toward the crowd, but toward the city, toward the fog-covered buildings, toward New York. They looked at her, but she did not look at them. . . . "It's Greta Garbo, who is coming back from Sweden," someone said behind him.

The impact of this image permanently marks Rivera's stay in New York. His attempts to decipher the city are figured in his imagination through this accidental sighting of the actress. Later experiences in the city find him "siempre mirando hacia la bruma, siempre tratando de encontrar el rostro oculto de Manhattan . . . a Greta, a la enigmática Greta" [always looking toward the fog, always trying to find the hidden face of Manhattan . . . Greta, the enigmatic Greta] (21). To some extent, the famously enigmatic actress fuses with the enigmas of this *otra selva,* defining his experience in the city by her absence and shaping it through the iconic afterimage of her fleeting presence. To some extent, despite elaborate descriptions, no other woman in the novel achieves Garbo's solidity.

More specifically, the question of the actress defines Rivera's efforts in his New York negotiations on the project of filming *La vorágine.* This project was casually suggested in Cali as a simple and straightforward task of learning English, translating the novel, and getting Hollywood to film it—after all, explains Rivera, he was planning on going to La Habana anyway and he could just stop off in New York to take care of this business as well (71). However, achieving this goal looms as a much more complex task once the author reaches this country. Rivera never does make any contacts with the true Hollywood impresarios, though he imagines his meetings are making progress in that direction. More important, though, from his perspective, he never quite resolves what is for him the crucial first step: casting Alicia. Like the mirrors so often reflected in this novel, the images of the female lead are refracted continually, are subject to extreme slippage, and retain a distant quality. Rivera can never quite meet—or even fully imagine—the (any) actual actress or cast her for the role. Thus, Rivera first thinks of silent film great Lillian Gish as the perfect actress for the role of Alicia (73); then Garbo's name enters the conversation (70), convincing him to rethink the project from another perspective. In this line of thinking, if Garbo is the "rostro oculto" of Manhattan, and New York is "la otra selva," the other face of the Amazon, then Garbo by metaphorical transference is the only actress who can perfectly represent Alicia, who increasingly comes to seem the face of the Colombian *selva.* It is just one more additional layer of irony that Greta Garbo, the face of the United States for Salazar's Rivera, is herself an import, as foreign a celebrity as Rivera.

At the same time, it is clear from the context that none of Rivera's acquaintances has the slightest chance of being permitted contact with any of these silver screen stars (or even with their agents), and that Rivera's own preferences are based on very a partial understanding of these women's typical on-screen roles, which he confuses with their most intimate selves. The detective, who is trying to find an excuse to get close to the writer, proposes that Garbo be replaced by Lupe Vélez, the object of his own private obsession, who he describes as "la más pura imagen de la mujer fatal latina" [the purest image of the Latin femme fatale] (80).[4] Rivera allows himself to be convinced by the argument that a Latin woman would more adequately play the role of Alicia than one of the "rubiecillas lánguidas que abundan en las películas gringas" [languid little blondes so abundant in gringo movies] (83). In keeping with the already-established context of the novel, the reader will instantly suspect that while Lupe's talismanic name is evoked, she is unlikely to appear in the novel. Indeed, her place is taken by a Macy's employee named María del Rosario, who the detective describes as follows: "no se llamaba Lupe, claro está. Ni tampoco pudo actuar en ninguna película. . . . Pero era como tú. . . . Alguna vez me dijo . . . —Claro que soy Lupe Vélez, pero sin las borracheras" [her name wasn't Lupe, of course. Nor could she act in any movie. . . . But she was like you. . . . Once someone told me . . . "Of course I'm Lupe Vélez, but without the drunkenness"] (80). As part of his ongoing intrigue, the detective not only suggests Lupe Vélez for the role but indicates that she is dying to play the role of Alicia. He even goes to the effort of setting up a meeting between Rivera and "Lupe" (65) and eventually engineers a letter supposedly from the Mexican actress confirming her interest in doing a film of Rivera's novel after wrapping up her current project (151).

Yet, strangely enough, in the meeting the elaborate scheme falls apart, achieving a kind of "realness" beyond the conspirators' dreams. The Lupe Vélez double, María del Rosario, in the transcursal of the evening eventually seems no longer to be playing a role, but somehow *becomes* the famous actress: "había alcanzado un grado de perfección tal que yo mismo empecé a creerme que la que estaba allí sentada, tomando champagne y preguntándole con voz susurrante al poeta Rivera sobre los portentos de la selva, eras tú, la mismísima Lupe Vélez, y que en este momento algo histórico estaba ocurriendo, algo que trascendía lo que yo me había imaginado" [She had reached a level of perfection such that I myself began to believe that the woman who was seated there, drinking champagne and asking the poet Rivera in a whispery voice about the wonders of the jungle, was you, the very same Lupe Vélez, and that in this moment something historical was happening, something that transcended whatever I had imagined] (86). And yet, of course, we never forget that this realness effect relies upon our acceptance of a body double for a Mexican actress whose career, almost entirely Hollywood based, has until recently been all but completely unknown in the Hispanic world, and whose most well-known roles involve parodying her Mexicanness along the lines of preferred gringo stereotypes. María del Rosario, in other words, is in the context of this novel the double of a ghost nearly as fictive as herself.

In more general terms, this momentary slippage between role and referent is not particular to this scene, though it offers a superb example of Salazar's method. Indeed, one might argue that the whole of the novel is balanced upon such ambivalent exchanges by which fiction contaminates reality and vice versa. Fictional characters enter the biographical frame of the "real" life of José Eustasio Rivera, and the detective/author moves easily among the various levels of narrative, including the self-conscious production of the text we are reading, reminding the reader that despite inclinations to suspend our disbelief, we are irrevocably caught in a world of multiple textualities. Salazar's and Rivera's biographies and novels are equally texts to be mined and placed into dialogue.

Unlike any of the actresses, who engage the novel's most stylized and stereotyped metaphors, Claire Weingest serves as one of the central point-of-view characters in Salazar's novel. She speaks either in first person (as in chapter 4) or more frequently through the distancing of second-person narration (i.e., chapters 6, 8, 18, 20, 24, and 28). She introduces herself in the first instance as a single woman, nearly forty years old, the only granddaughter of a poet and watercolorist named Marie Claire Benoist, an old maid whose solitary occupation is visiting her grandmother in the sanatorium on Sundays. Despite her anxiety about her self-image—"el miedo de aparecer como la solterona 'yankee' con deseos de usar su inagotable tiempo libre al aprendizaje de algún idioma exótico" [the fear of appearing as a Yankee old maid who wants to use her inexhaustible free time to learn some exotic language] (61)—Claire responds to the newspaper advertisement of the Colombian poet offering an exchange of English for Spanish lessons, "con la esperanza de sentirse humana otra vez, con la ilusión de encontrar, del otro lado del periódico, un territorio desconocido, un nuevo mundo" [with the hope of feeling human again, with the illusion of finding, on the other side of the newspaper, an unknown territory, a new world] (38).

But who, asks the narrator, is the "verdadera" Claire Weingest? As a young woman, she had felt obliged by society to encourage a young man to aspire to her hand in marriage, but she found she had no particular affection for her admirer and was vaguely relieved when he left her for another woman. In the aftermath of this failed relationship, "volvías a ser tú misma" [you became yourself again]. Yet this self is both strangely underdetermined and, strikingly enough, highly correlated to the screen images of the same actresses that attract Rivera's interest: "cuando pensabas en ti, no lograbas formarte una imagen clara, definida, o, lo que es peor, tomaste otras imágenes y te ponías los ojos de Mary Pickford o dejabas caer sobre tu cabeza el aura de Lillian Gish" [when you thought about yourself, you were not able to form a clear, defined image, or, what is worse, you took other images and you put Mary Pickford's eyes, or you allowed the aura of Lillian Gish to fall on your head] (47–48). The author details meticulously the process of preparing for her first meeting with Rivera, concluding that "frente al espejo . . . le diste los últimos toques a lo que debía ser el rostro de Claire Weingest" [before the mirror . . . you gave the final touches to what should be the face of Claire Weingest] (53). Here the telltale qualifer "debía ser" foregrounds the artificiality of the proceedings and the fluidity of the "verdadera" Claire; the process of making herself up as she prepares herself for the meeting involves self-construction but not necessarily the introspection fiction readers have traditionally come to expect of prolonged narrative sessions in front of a mirror.

The crucial chapter in the Claire Weingest/José Eustasio Rivera relationship, detailed from Rivera's point of view, occurs in chapter 21, two thirds of the way through the novel. This chapter stands on the threshold between a series of spaces and concepts laid out in binary form. The poet imagines crossing the threshold from Claire's living room to her bedroom, and he theorizes that his English teacher will become/has become some other person in that more intimate space: "le acosaba la idea de que ella era otra persona, distinta a la Claire que él creía conocer y desear" [he was vexed by the idea that she was another person, distinct from the Claire that he believed he knew and desired] (144). It is, perhaps, the poet's own desire, and fear of that desire, that creates the split in Claire's personality and opens up the threshold space. At the same time, the interjection of desire into the placid world of the tutor's living room catalyzes another fear, that of a destiny irremediably linked to death in *la selva.* Thus, Rivera's incipient desire for Claire, hinted at in the half-open door of a bedroom whose threshold he does not cross, is paired with his "temor de estar siendo llevado hacia un lugar que él no deseaba" [fear of being carried toward a place that he did not desire] (146). What he desires is precisely what he fears to desire, in exactly equal proportions. Rivera's *La vorágine* has taught him that to follow up on Claire's proposal to leave New York for somewhere, anywhere, would impose upon him a confrontation with his destiny, with his own death: "él conocía los resultados de esos viajes. El sabía que la muerte era la única compania posible" [he knew the results of these trips. He knew that death is the only possible companion] (145). Later he adds: "no podía aceptar que en la novela de su vida una mujer llegara a proponerle su destino. No quería ser un protagonista a merced del súbito deseo de huir de un personaje femenino que apenas acababa de entrar en escena" [he could not accept that in the novel of his life a woman might arrive to propose his destiny. He did not want to be a protagonist at the mercy of a sudden desire to flee from a female character who barely just entered on the scene] (146). Nevertheless, because "la palabra, él lo sabía muy bien, era femenina" [the word, he knew very well, was feminine] (147), fleeing (a much-used trope in *La vorágine,* which Salazar cleverly reproduces) only brings him back to the jungle and the woman associated with it. Turning his back on Claire means returning to Alicia, whose story remained truncated in the novel of his original Amazonian *selva.* Thus, in this instance, he decides to postpone calling Claire and instead calls on his earlier protagonist, figuring in the text the precise moment before putting pen to paper, the instant before the act of writing occurs: "Ahora, sí, ahora puedes comenzar, Alicia, estoy listo, la vieja pluma en mano, la cabeza lista para aceptarlo todo" [Now, yes, now, you can begin, Alicia, I'm ready, the old pen in hand, the head ready to accept everything] (147). This chapter, then, is poised on a multiple threshold, an agony of indecision involving desire, destiny, and death: between living room and bedroom, Claire and Alicia, *lenguaje* and *palabra,* speaking and writing, *selva* and *selva.*

Thus, Rivera economically sets up a series of binaries attached to the abstracted female figure who comes to represent for him the fabric of life that he longs to seek out, that has been lost to him, that he in some manner wishes to reject but cannot help desiring. He wants to retain his association with the placid English tutor of the front room, but also imagines and desires the potentiality of a bedroom Claire who is entirely different. He desires "la palabra" but rejects destiny and death, two elements that he strongly believes are linked to the feminine. His art, his fatal attraction to "la palabra" leads him inevitably to *la selva* and *la mujer*—any effort to escape this destiny, he notes, betrays his art: "¿Cúantas veces, por haber querido huir de ciertas palabras . . . se había rebajado a la utilización del lenguaje más pesado, más falso, más tramposo . . . ? [How many times, for having wanted to flee from certain words . . . had he lowered himself to the use of heavier, falser, trickier language?] (146). In this way, the abstractions *selva/mujer/palabra/muerte* are inextricably bound together. Rivera's attempts to evade his destiny by creating a superficial and unstable equivalence among images relating Claire's front room/English tutor/language (*el lenguaje*)/life only serves the purpose of bringing him back more forcefully to the original equivalences half seen through the door of Claire's bedroom, the forbidden threshold that once crossed, even in imagination, brings him back to his original jungle, to Alicia, and to death.

Rivera prizes in Claire the "placidez" (placidity) that he finds in her living-room world. She sees Rivera as a Don Quixote and dreams of a future together as traveling companions, but worries that he would not want a woman like her, "una mujer que no lo dejara terminar su obra inmensa y no le permitiera estar a la altura de su desafío" [a woman who will not let him finish his immense work and will not permit him to rise to the height of his challenge] (140). By the end of the novel, however, learning to drive cars and chew gum "le había ayudado a encontrar un nuevo ritmo vital" [had helped him to find a new rhythm in life] (163). Her last chapter finds her making plans to meet the poet on Rockaway beach for a final midnight rendezvous before embarking on a trip to Africa with him the next morning (185). When she is unable to find him, she takes the un-Claire-like step of searching the city, eventually learning that he has been admitted to a hospital in a coma from which he never awakes. It is this abrupt termination of her relationship with Rivera that propels Claire Weingest into the role of biographer: "Ese día comprendió que todo tendría que acumularse hasta que ella misma, muchos años después . . . pudiera escribir estas líneas que ahora tratan de hallar su fin en un pedazo de papel que se llena de trazos, en un banco junto al Hudson, en una tarde de octubre"

[That day she understood that everything would have to accumulate until she herself, many years later . . . would be able to write these lines that are now trying to find their end on the piece of paper that is filling with penstrokes, on a bench near the Hudson, on an October afternoon] (191). The sequence of chapters focused on Claire Weingest, thus, reveal themselves at the very end of the narrative as Claire's own self-writing, her version of these events, which are being written simultaneously with the parallel narrative by the detective, and which both come to an end in the fugitive "now" and the present-tense verbs of the act of writing, years after the events narrated, only a short distance apart in the city of New York.

This focus on the act of writing is explicitly recapitulated from another perspective in chapter 30 with the last words of this novel, those of the detective, who also enters the same "now" of writing, and who furthermore proposes to take his manuscript to Claire, thus joining the two bodies, the two manuscripts together:

> podría escribir la palabra "fin" . . . Prefiero decir que estoy a punto de levantarme de la silla en la que he estado escribiendo durante meses, el manuscrito de hojas amarillas bajo el brazo, dispuesto a salir a la calle para encontrar a la mujer del mechón de pelo rojo . . . y ofrecerle mi versión de lo ocurrido: estas páginas, este cuerpo que ha comenzado a buscar la puerta sin saber qué hay del otro lado. (199)
>
> I could write the word "end" . . . I prefer to say that I am at the point of rising from the chair in which I have been writing for months, the manuscript of yellow pages under my arm, ready to go out into the street to find the woman with the lock of red hair . . . and offer her my version of what happened: these pages, this body which has begun to seek the door without knowing what is on the other side.

Here too, the author plays with the liminal spaces between the act of writing and the gift of the written, the threshold that has not yet, quite, been crossed because the imagined word "fin" has not yet been written, because the word "fin" is another word for the author's anticipated narrative death.

This closing mediation follows directly upon the detective's decision to tell "mi versión de lo sucedido al poeta Rivera" [my version of what happened to the poet Rivera] (197). In the recapitulation of these events, he finds the dying poet and hears Alicia's voice in the foggy room saying, in part, "Déjalos, Arturo, déjalos que busquen su camino. . . . ¡Deja de huir! ¡Enfréntate a mí! . . . Ya no puedes huir, Arturo. Ahora nos pertenecemos, ahora" [Leave them, Arturo, leave them to seek their road. . . . Stop fleeing! Confront me! . . . You can no longer flee, Arturo. We belong to each other now] (198). In the end, thus, the narrator and Claire stand together poised on the threshold of narration in *la otra selva* of New York City, while the dying José Eustasio Rivera/Arturo Cova abandons his typical strategy of flight and crosses the threshold to his original jungle, death, to destiny, to Alicia.

Rivera, speaking in first person in the first pages of the novel as he lays dying, gives his last thoughts to Alicia, with a mysterious comment that takes the whole of this novel to unravel, but in the end is as simple as Flaubert's famous "Madame Bovary, c'est moi" and as difficult as a character's declaration of independence from her author. The fictional Rivera comments: "al menos Alicia había logrado contar parte de su historia, al menos Alicia había podido decir las tantas cosas que no se sabían sobre sus últimos días, al menos ella había logrado hablar con su propia voz. . . . Para él, en cambio . . . su historia estaba siendo escrita por otro" [at least Alicia had been able to tell part of her story, at least Alicia had been able to stay the many things that were not known about her last days, at least she had been able to speak in her own voice. . . . For him, on the other hand, . . . his story was being written by another] (12). Indeed, in this novel several chapters—most important, chapters 16 and 23—speak in Alicia's voice and from her perspective. The first of these sections begins, tellingly, once again in the "now" of an ongoing narrative: "ahora, por fin, decidí comenzar a escribir" (107). Alicia has taken up her pen and is writing after the end of *La vorágine,* from the other side of the experience of childbirth. Her son has been born, and after the traumas of childbirth in primitive surroundings, her body is settling into its new shape. Arturo avoids contact with her too newly maternal body; he also rejects her sexually out of unspoken fear/desire that perhaps that body was not exclusively his during the whole of their time in the *selva.* Says Alicia, "lo único que le produzco es temor (y, a veces me atrevo a pensarlo, asco. . . .)" [the only thing that I produce is fear (and, sometimes I dare to think it, repulsion. . . .)] (113).

In the later chapter, she returns to this theme, waxing a bit more philosophical: "a veces creo que Arturo quiere encontrar en mí las huellas de su enemigo muerto. . . . Es más, ahora que Barrera está muerto . . . Arturo está más solo que nunca. . . . Barrera vive a través de mí, y a través de ese recuerdo sobrevive Arturo" [sometimes I think that Arturo wants to find in me the traces of his dead enemy. . . . More: now that Barrera is dead . . . Arturo is more alone than ever. . . . Barrera lives through me, and through that memory Arturo survives] (157–58). Alicia's own narration never clarifies this point of contention between the two men, which has less to do with her body than Arturo's beliefs. At the same time, Alicia feels that if Arturo felt he knew for sure whether or not Barrera and she had ever had sexual relations, everything would change in their relationship; instead of avoiding sex, he would be trying to win her over so as to continue the battle with his old enemy. Even further: the lack of this definitive knowledge is all that allows Arturo to survive, dependent upon the absolute unknowability of Alicia's past. Nevertheless, Alicia, in either case, is, as she is well aware, relegated to the sidelines of a conflict that at heart has little to do with her other than as an abstract token of exchange between two men, one dead, one fleeing life: "El amor—para los hombres—es un asunto que sólo les concierne a ellos; nosotras sólo contamos como bellos objetos de disputa, como trofeos que pasan de mano en mano hasta perder el valor" [Love—for me—is something that only involves them; we women only count as beautiful objects in dispute, as trophies that pass from hand to hand until they lose their value] (158).

Alicia's clear-eyed understanding of her role as a token object serves as this novel's most straightforward acknowledgment of the mechanisms of control in the masculinist text. By a sleight of hand, suggests Alicia (a character borrowed from Rivera's novel, after all), even when women speak in their own voices, as they do in numerous chapters in Salazar's novel, they do so as characters created by others and for other purposes. They exist to establish a limit space, to conform a textual frame, to allegorize a complex experience of powerlessness in confrontation with a feared and desired other. Thus, *La otra selva* engages with its own conditions of creation on numerous overt levels in the layers of narration and the play of fictional and auto/biographical characters, and engages at least marginally with one other unexpected level as well, in the narrative self-consciousness about the limitations of its perspectives. In this respect, Salazar intimates, the *novela de la selva* has not yet escaped the narrative structures that limit it to an exchange among men, in which the heart of darkness, the female principle, the word must be expelled and abjected only to return as that narrative's most feared and desired unknown.

On its simplest level, *La novela virtual* [The Virtual Novel] chronicles the experiences, ideas, and moods of its protagonist, an anonymous fifty-nine-year-old novelist with a distinct similarity to Gustavo Sainz, who is teaching in an unnamed (but easily identifiable as Middlebury College in Vermont) summer program. He is sponsored by this program partly to complete his new novel, *La novela virtual,* but his energies are also spent on interacting with other artists and literati in the program, examining the customs and culture of the new environment in which he is now immersed, writing to his friends and professional associates, and becoming romantically involved with a Mexican university student attending school in the United States, with whom the narrator engages in progressively more intimate and steamy e-mail exchanges and stream-of-consciousness monologues (though we rarely have any concrete examples of the author's side of this e-mail correspondence). In the course of these meditations, the narrator discloses his own impressions concerning particular novels, often under the guise of a summary of classroom lectures, and at times offers in-depth analyses of certain works, including transcriptions of, and commentaries on, apocryphal stories by his young Mexican girlfriend. The novel also includes, seemingly to underline the point about the transformations of autobiographical form, his Mexican girlfriend's commentary on the three hundred-page manuscript autobiography of her coworker from Jalapa, Nereída. The last chapters of the novel detail the increasingly intense obsession of the older man and the young woman with each other, to the point that the author sets off on a hallucinatory cross-country trip to St. Louis, Missouri, ending with a coy obfuscation of their actual/potential meeting in a St. Louis hotel lobby.

The novel follows two distinct and usually disparate strands. A large part of the novel consists of a highly fragmentary and associative narrative reproducing the meditations of the writer about his admittedly uninteresting, repetitive, innocuous daily activities (preparing coffee, reading books, going to the movies) as well as his musings on high art. This fragmentary, meandering text is interrupted by the more traditional narrative plotting of the e-mail letters from the young Mexican woman revealing the highly colored soap-operatic events in her family life, especially fights with her parents and problems with her boyfriends. In this manner, *La novela virtual* provides, at the same time and in alternating formats, both a difficult but boring experimental text and a highly plotted juicy melodrama.

While there is a clear tension between the two parts of the narrative—the intellectual palaver/implicitly elitist audience/experimental style sits uneasily on the page with its counterpart of melodramatic events/mass media audience/traditional plotting—the novel seems to resolve into, finally, no more and no less than the playing out of the most trite of all back-to-school fall questions. The first chapter queries: "¿y ustedes qué hicieron ese verano?" [What did you do that summer?] (21), and this question serves as a leitmotif throughout the novel, until at the very end, the last line of the narrative reiterates this insistent question with a slight variation: "¿y ustedes qué hicieron el verano pasado?" [And what did you do last summer?] (495). And yet, this banal query, which presupposes a realist, autobiographical narrative as an equally banal response, crashes against the insistent textuality of the work itself where realism, autobiography, and even the concept of "novel" are all to some extent pretexts.

The first clue to addressing this apparent impasse comes from the title itself; this novel offers many possible points of entry, but remains a "novela virtual," never quite actualized despite its almost five hundred pages of text. It is, to follow upon the famous definition given by Roland Barthes in his eponymous nonautobiography, "an endlessly receding project." As Barthes says, "First of all, the work is never anything but the meta-book (the temporary commentary) of a work to come which, *not being written*, becomes this work itself. . . . [T]he work is a (theatrical) *rehearsal*, and this rehearsal . . . is verbose, infinite, interlaced with commentaries, excursuses, shot through with other matters" (174–75). Thus, the "virtual" novel or the meta-autobiography reflects that prior state of creative ferment before the ordering of elements into coherently structured form. The fiction "atrás," as Sainz hints in the subtitle, has to do with the fictionality of creating this rehearsed pre-text of an unwritten work, and the red herring of "What did you do last summer?" serves more as linguistic prompt than an as engine to motivate a spinning out of any traditionally imagined narrative. Sainz's narrator muses:

> pero se trataría de una novela sólo en apariencia
> ¿una autobiografía?
> seguramente
> pero en lo más hondo: allí en donde todos los demás detenían
>   sus palabras: él franquearía todos los umbrales (272)
>
> but it would be a novel only in appearance
> an autobiography?
> certainly
> but at the deepest level: there where all the rest detain their
>   words: he will cross all thresholds

Not only is this an unusual and linguistically focused meta-¿autobiography?, it also has as its explicit project an opening up of the genre: "arriba, adelante" [up, forward] says the subtitle; going beyond previously imagined boundaries, says the narrator. This kind of project is perfectly in accord with the theoretical position already elucidated by Barthes. As Sainz's narrator says at another point, in what could well be a rephrasing of Barthes:

el significado era nuevo o no lo había
una nueva creación o ninguna
novela o nada
La novela virtual
su novela de la suerte que estaba echada
decir una cosa para decir otra (492)

the signification was new or there was none
a new creation or none
novel or nothing
The Virtual Novel
his novel of the dice that was tossed
to say something in order to say something else

From another point of view, the project of a virtual or empty novel exists not as a creative choice but rather as an inevitable necessity. The narrator has made the decision that during his summer in the eastern United States, he will write every day, producing a certain fixed quantity of material that will become the text of his new novel (469). The problem with this project is that he is faced with a paucity of material: "su vida en la que (casi) nada sucedía" [his life in which (almost) nothing happened] (402) means that willy-nilly "no tiene nada de que escribir" [he has nothing to write about] (366). Thus, he fills the pages of his work-in-progress with academic speculations, the minutia of an uneventful intellectual life, and successive false starts toward the fictional project. These associative fragments by definition never cohere, creating a problem for the writer who "siente una como presión, cierta responsabilidad, como si le exigiéramos que nos contara su historia de una manera convencional, lineal, sencilla, periodística" [feels a certain pressure, certain responsibility, as if we had demanded that he tell us his story in a conventional, linear, simple, journalistic manner] (366). At the same time, the writer finds himself ever more seduced by the highly plotted narratives of his e-mail fan, Camila, who shares with him long descriptions of her peripatetic life including difficulties with her parents and her boyfriends/lovers (this part of the novel reads like a 1990s female-focused variation on the 1965 male point of view in *Gazapo*). These "autobiographical" tales, by reason of their method of transmission, are also—and in a literal sense—virtual texts; like clients who log into chat rooms, "Camila" exists only as a coherent narrative construction of a computerized identity.

Informally, we have all heard anecdotes about how the Internet has changed the shape of interpersonal dynamics through role playing in chat rooms, cyber-romance exchanges, and cyber-porn sites. One of the attractions of Web technology for a contemporary writer like Gustavo Sainz is precisely this democratization of fiction effects whereby adults are able to continue playing a grown-up version of make-believe. Camila constantly plays with her name: "Camila Rana," "Camilonga," "Camile des Forets," "Camilanova Bosa Nova," "Camilammermann, K," "Cami Mi Mi La Mi," and so on, and both the famous author and the young woman play at an updated version of the genius and his muse. Chatting online is a game in which anyone can alternate between the role of author and reader; what has been given far less attention is the way in which these games play themselves out theoretically.

Already in the mid-1980s, Arthur Kroker and David Cook were presciently signaling what they called the last and most purely artistic phase of capitalism: the site of power as the process of estheticized recommodification in the computer age. For Kroker and Cook, one of the key phases in this recommodification of capital involves a shift into virtuality, "where we experience pure imagining-systems as real, and where perspective itself is always only fictional because it is perfectly simulational. Estheticized commodification is the region of *virtual* cameras, of *virtual* technology, and of *virtual* perspective–the region, in fact, where the aesthetic symmetries of particle physics become the structural logic of the Real" (20). For Kroker and Cook, these changes loomed on the literary and cultural horizon as the "dark side" of the aesthetic transformation they correctly predicted, a commentary that meshes perfectly with a good deal of the anti-Net hype so familiar to all of us. Worried commentarists fear that electronic dialogue is coming to replace human interaction, that technically savvy children are all too ably maneuvering their ways into unsavory locations, that electronic input (the booming electronic market in, say, Quicktime movies, interactive video striptease, etc.) can have all-too-evident real effects on the bodies sitting at the keyboard, and that assumed virtual identities pose threats to users' perceptions of reality by inappropriately merging categories of fact and fiction. To this "dark side" technological aesthetics, Olalquiaga would add that with the fusing of performance and spectator in virtual space, the "boundaries between what is being watched and who is watching barely exist" (6).

Sainz's novel explicitly inserts itself into the exploration of the effects of this e-revolution on the novelist form, on the writerly identity, and on the rethinking of thematic development. The e-mail transmissions attributed to Camila also comprise a meta-autobiography, although in a different sense from that adduced by Barthes; they offer the computer age's temporary rehearsal of an assumed identity. For the author within Sainz's text, however, Camila's long, interconnected letters also represent a golden opportunity to fill out the growing pages of his novel about nothing with a simple cut-and-paste from a hypereventful narrative; in this sense, antiquity's virtual muse takes on a specific and literalized form. Thus, he notes, "todas las partes de su nuevo relato serían producidas como lados disimétricos/direcciones rotas: cajas cerradas: vasos no comunicantes" [all the parts of his new tale were being produced as dissymmetric sides/broken directions: closed boxes, noncommunicating vessels] (441) combining "su novela Camila" [his Camila novel] (470) or "su novela de Camila/una novela libre de definiciones previas" [his novel about Camila/a novel free of previous definitions] (478) and "su novela académica" [his academic novel] (471).

Unsurprisingly, the author finds himself constantly beginning again; as late as ten pages before the end of the novel he is still typing in "primer capítulo" [first chapter] on his computer screen, staging a mock erasure of the foregoing text, and suggesting a new point of departure to organize the disparate elements of the as-yet unwritten novel (which we, of course, are nearly finished reading). Throughout the long novel, the author continually tries out such clarifying foci in an effort to define this text-in-process; I note just a few of these instances by way of examples: "el amor era pues un elemento constitutivo de la híperprealidad/su novela virtual" [love was then a constitutive element of the hyperreality/his virtual novel] (90), or "su novela de la vigilia/aunque escribir realmente no importaba" [his novel of the vigil/already writing really made no difference] (107), or "la invitación posmoderna . . . /su novela lúdica" [the postmodern invitation . . . /his ludic novel] (186–87), or "¿no podría ser este libro en algún sentido un cocodrilo que intentara devorar nuestros pensamientos?" [couldn't this book be in some sense a crocodile that tries to devour our thoughts?] (224), or "su novela del tiempo perdido/o la del arte de perder el tiempo" [his novel of lost time/or the art of wasting time] (239), or, tellingly, "su novela en blanco" [his blank novel] (359).

Roland Barthes writes: "Fiction would proceed from a new intellectual art. . . . With intellectual things, we produce simultaneously theory, critical combat, and pleasure; we subject the objects of knowledge . . . no longer to an instance of truth, but to a consideration of effects" (90). Donald Shaw, in an article on several post-Boom writers, would seem to add to Barthes's commentary about knowledge, truth, and fictional effects the queries: "Can we, in any sense ever know reality?" and "Can literature ever have a significant social role?" (16). The answer to these questions involves exploring the implications of this still-undertheorized new intellectual art. One response, Barthes's response, might be to reject the presuppositions underlying such questions about reality and signification and suggest that a postmodern art would require a rethinking of the way we produce and understand objects of knowledge or entertainment. Sainz's response is perhaps less radical, for while the technical difficulty of much of this novel suggests an affinity to the Barthesian model, Shaw is quite right in concluding that the Mexican writer's work more properly involves a strained relationship with these key concerns. In typical fashion, Sainz's response to the questions posed by Shaw might be an ambiguous "yes and no" (Shaw 16–17, 19). In fact, Sainz has himself defined his work in general terms as composed of realist narratives—but in the postmodern rather than the nineteenth-century sense of the term, one that understands language as the only reality.

This postmodern project of a linguistically founded realism works only intermittently in Sainz's texts, and remains one of the factors that produces the most narrative tension in his novels. Thus, for example, in earlier books like *Serpiente,* this concept of a new realism has to take cognizance of unsettlingly powerful historical events like Tlatelolco. *La novela virtual,* with its explicitly more banal context, specifically elides such concrete historical embeddedness, and the combination of a novelist's meta-autobiography with that of an electronically constructed individual allows for greater free play of the intellect. Here, more clearly than in the earlier work, Sainz is able to focus—like Barthes—on the linguistic creation of the writer in search of his identity, and on his evolving understanding of the constructedness of this meta-autobiographical effort without abandoning his ongoing commitment to a postmodern exploration of the possibilities of realism in the computer age.[5]

If one point of entry into the novel is given by the exploration of the question of virtuality, an entirely different analysis involves looking more closely at the function of the two crucial women who serve as focal points of the narrative: the lovely "Ombligo Anillado" [Navel Ring]—who seduces the writer with her perfect, postmodernly pierced body—and Camila, his Mexican e-mail love. It is perhaps worth noting that while the author's relationship with the first woman is entirely physical, the course of this second, electronically conducted affair (like those described elsewhere in the recently established subgenre of cybernetic fiction) specifically precludes the actual meeting of the two persons involved.[6] In both cases, the author envelopes his sexual attraction to the women in highly elaborated and even mannerist prose, full of poetic asides and literary comparisons.

The author's literary references and allusions run the range from British metaphysical poets to contemporary Latin American novelists, but the one inescapable figure who provides the clearest key to unraveling this eroto-literary aspect of the novel remains elusive in the text. I am thinking of Vladimir Nabokov and his novel, *Lolita,* which, like

Sainz's novel, details the course of an intergenerational love affair as a way to come to terms with the location of the foreign scholar with respect to U.S. culture. In his afterword to *Lolita,* Nabokov describes the five-year project of writing the novel as his way of becoming an American writer:

> It had taken me some forty years to invent Russia and Western Europe, and now I was faced with the task of inventing America. The obtaining of such local ingredients as would allow me to inject a modicum of "reality" (one of the few words which mean nothing without quotes) into the brew of individual fancy, proved at fifty a much more difficult process. . . . Once or twice I was on the point of burning the unfinished draft . . . when I was stopped by the thought that the ghost of the destroyed book would haunt my files for the rest of my life. (283)

Like Nabokov's Humbert Humbert, Sainz's author is a fiftyish foreign academic working on the U.S. East Coast; like that famous character, he falls in love with a much younger woman (or, in *La novela virtual,* with two young women), and in search of some elusive quality he associates with her, sets off by car across the United States. John Brushwood has spoken of Sainz as an extremely locally grounded author: "El Distrito Federal es su provincia, su terruño, su diario vivir" [the Federal District is his province, his terrain, his daily life] (49); the problem in *La novela virtual* is that after twenty years in the United States, the narrator can no longer define himself by the daily life of Mexico City and yet neither does he identify fully with the kind of rootless U.S. existence so clearly delineated both in his temporary position as summer instructor for an Eastern program and in his final road trip memoirs. At the same time, and paradoxically, his life in Mexico was always already defined by his relation to U.S. culture, and his sense of Mexicanness is traversed by the multiple U.S. identities he carries with him like excess baggage: "lo extraño es que yo soy más americano que la mayoría de los americanos / porque a pesar de vivir en México asimilé la cultura norteamericana. . . . / mírame a mí, soy un escritor mexicano pero en realidad soy múltiple, porque también soy francés, y norteamericano de Chicago, y de L.A., y de New York, y de New Mexico, y de Florida, y de Maine" [the strange thing is that I'm more American than the majority of Americans/because despite living in Mexico I assimilated U.S. culture. . . . / look at me, I am a Mexican writer, but really I am multiple, because I am also French and a North American from Chicago, and from LA and from New York, and from New Mexico, and from Florida, and from Maine] (371–72). He is quintessentially Mexican, a certain kind of middle-class, U.S.-influenced Mexican like Carlos Fuentes, whom he cites approvingly. Like Fuentes, his life is defined by an expatriate, peripatetic existence that incorporates and includes the knowledge that he is more American than the Americans whose culture he has assimilated, and who will never see him as anything other than foreign.

The narrator's very short-lived affair with the woman he identifies only as "la muchacha del Ombligo Anillado" [the girl with the Navel Ring] involves his sexual awareness of her, her seduction of him, his belief that he has fallen deeply in love with her, and her calm and educated dismissal of her time with him as an enjoyable, purely sexual interlude that she has no interest in repeating. Like Nabokov's Lolita, Sainz's slightly older nymphette "era una Seductora Nata" [she was a Born Seductress] and like the earlier novel, one of the titillating attractions of the relationship with her is precisely their age difference: "las grandes historias de seducción eran incestuosas y la de él era incestuosa porque esa chica podría ser su hija" [the great stories of seduction were incestuous and his was incestuous because this girl could be his daughter] (29). It is impossible to tell, of course, what might be the imaginary perspective of this woman identified only as an erogenous body part; as in Nabokov's novel, the girl is less important than the combination of delicately lyric and crassly sexual effects that cohere around her image. Nabokovian also is the association of a search for a national identity with this incestuously inflected sexuality. Interestingly enough, the narrator of *La novela virtual* interrupts his meditations on his desperate love for the girl with a comment that makes these symbolic stakes transparent:

> amor **amor amor**
> te he estado esperando
> aislado en mi soledad
> me siento lleno de cicatrices
> ¿seré un país? ¿me habré vuelto México? (176–77)
>
> love **love love**
> I have been waiting for you
> isolated in my solitude
> I feel full of scars
> am I a country? have I become Mexico?

Here, the narrator's project, and his obsession with the girl, flips dramatically into the narrator's reevaluation of his national identity, as if, in a reversal of the Nabokovian project, a sexual affair with a young American girl opens up the renewed possibility of remaking himself as an archetypally Mexican author, as the narrative embodiment of Mexico itself. At the same time, and as Barthes has so eloquently noted, the narrator's repeated, almost hysterical insistence on his love for this girl points to some other masked need: "'*I love you, I love you!*' Welling up from the body, irrepressible, repeated, does not this whole paroxysm of love's declaration conceal some *lack*?" (112). In this virtual love affair, the site of this profound lack is immediately apparent. Despite the narrator's many and fervent protestations of his love for Ombligo Anillado, the narrative provides no access whatsoever to the beloved Other. She rarely speaks, and then only as ventriloquized by the author's indirect discourse. Naturally she never becomes a fully fledged character. Thus, inevitably, his protestations of devotion fall into a curious void. Ombligo Anillado is nothing more than a dismembered and decorated body part, overdetermined by the narrator's reading of authors like Freud, by his association of her most important (only!) feature with the impenetrably mysterious dream's navel, by his symbolic projection of her as the essence and the lack delimiting his sense of national identity.

This poetic identification is buttressed and given greater complexity by the narrator's allusion to John Donne's famous Elegy 19, "To His Mistress Going to Bed" (1669). Tellingly, the author uses Donne's elegy twice in the course of this novel: once with reference to the failed affair with Ombligo Anillado: "*su América encontrada, Terranova, reino sólo por él poblado*" (117)[7] and later with reference to the projected relationship with Camila: "Su Terranova / su América encontrada / su Machu Picchu" (493).[8] Nabokov called *Lolita* the record of his love affair with the English language (288), a text where a hyperconsciousness of style, structure, and imagery overweigh the notorious depiction of a character's "tepid lust" (284). Here too, in Sainz's novel, lust for a forbidden girl-woman charges the text with an erotics focused on love of language, and, by further extension, the eroticized text reconnects the author with his originary (navel) body, his native (Camila) tongue. Futhermore, through the narrator's own fudging of the virtuality of space, Ombligo Anillado gives him possession of his (United States) "America"; Camila his "América" in the more expansive Latin American usage of the term. The two women together, then, delimit the boundaries and fractures in the narrator's sense of his profound and divided Mexican/American self. Like Donne, like Nabokov, Sainz's novel—to use Nabokov's words—"has no moral in tow. For me a work of fiction exists only insofar as it affords me what I shall bluntly call aesthetic bliss." At the same time, this aesthetic bliss is in fact tempered with another project, that of discovery of the meta-autobiographical self as an immigrant identity. Nabokov continues: "I am trying to be an American writer and claim only the same rights that other American writers enjoy. On the other hand, my creature Humbert is a foreigner and an anarchist, and there are many things, besides nymphets, in which I disagree with him" (286).

While his encounter with Ombligo Anillado brings the narrator to the dream's overdetermined navel in his literary meta-autobiographical self-analysis, his concurrent dialogue with Camila serves as a projected reconnection with a Mexico that, after twenty years in the United States, has become too hypertrophied and overanalyzed, too much a (meta)literary representation. The author's first contact with Camila comes by way of a handwritten fan letter postmarked from Manzanillo. The narrator immediately goes to his computer, types in Camila's e-mail address, and sends her a long letter detailing associatively his list of historical, literary, and cinematographic Camilas in a kind of overeducated intellectual's substitute for a personal response. This initial letter sets the tone for the correspondence that follows: for Camila's own constant playing with name and identity, for what the narrator later calls the "síndrome de Camila" [Camila syndrome] (297), which finds its ideal precursor in Humbert Humbert's lyric/erotic spinning out of Lolita's name in the opening pages of Nabokov's novel: Lolita, Lo, Lola, Dolly, Dolores . . . A desultory exchange of e-mail between the two exiles gradually evolves into an intense obsession. While letters from the young woman start out as a kind of footnote to his day, by the end of the novel the narrator confesses, "ahora no podía empezar el día sin leer algo de Camila / ¡encamílame, Camila!" [now I can't start the day without reading something from Camila/Camila, camillate me] (398).

And yet, of course, Camila too remains essentially a literary abstraction; the Mexico to which she provides access is as literary as the works by Fuentes et al. he quotes in his classroom: "Camila o aquello que representaba / Camila nunca estaba: siempre era pensada / quizás por eso lo seducía" [Camila or whatever she represented/Camila was never there: she was thought/perhaps that was what seduced him] (422), says the author at one point, and toward the end of the novel repeats this equivocal phrase: "su verdad era su necesidad de Camila / o aquello que Camila representaba" [his truth was his need for Camila/ or whatever Camila represented] (484). "Camila," then, is less a person than an objective correlative for another constellation of desires and lacks, one that complements and supplements that lack described by the absent/abstract Ombligo Anillado. Her e-mails at the same time satisfy the author's need for connection with the Mexico that he imagines her representing, and signal the futility of these attempts:

Camila era su punto de inflexión
un collado: nudo: foco: centro
punto de fusión: de condensación: de ebullición
esencia de sensibilidad y máquina deseante (482)

Camila was his inflection point
channel: knot: focus: center
fusion point: of condensation: of ebullience
essence of sensibility and desiring machine

And yet, this center always escapes him, perhaps because, while Camila is the opposite of Ombligo Anillado, she is *exactly* that opposite: all language in contrast to Ombligo's nothing but body:

¿cómo podría haberse comunicado, digamos, con la muchacha
del Ombligo Anillado?
si ella no hablaba (casi) nunca y no volvió a hablar más
de comunicarse comunicarse, sólo comunicaba con Camila
aunque con Camila eran sólo palabras (428)

how could one have communicated, let's say, with the girl with
the Navel Ring?
if she (barely) talked and never talked again
for communicating communicating, he only communicated with
Camila
although with Camila words were all.

The narrator, then, in spinning Camila's language and e-mails into his unwritten novel shapes his life through reference to and in implicit comparison with hers. Her love of his language and his burgeoning love for the woman he imagines behind the computer screen intersect on the page of *La novela virtual*, infect and inflect each other. While the exchange begins with the older man very much in control, displaying his intellectual credentials in the play of her name through history, by the end of the novel, the author is hurtling toward St. Louis in a fever of erotic imaginings. By that time the very essence of his language has been reforged, and he can no longer either speak or think without allusion to her. Nevertheless, the "Camila" that so shapes his experience remains beyond his reach:

camileaba
camilándose
obnubilado por Camila
pero cómo pensar en Camila si le faltaban sus imágenes (474)[9]

This impasse cannot be resolved, for a very good reason. Despite all the play of autobiography and identities national and personal, this novel remains recalcitrant to recuperation by any such theoretical or thematic concerns. Bottom line: it insists stubbornly on its own provisional quality as a set of electronic impulses coded onto an electronic screen. In this manner, *La novela virtual* most clearly delineates its departure from and updating of masterpieces like those of Donne and Nabokov; this is a novel shaped by the computer age and its hybrid English techno-speak.

Julio Ortega has commented that in Sainz's work the "inmersión popular tiene el poder de lo específico, de lo material y sensorial" [popular immersion has the power of the specific, the material, and the sensorial] (674). In this novel, the specific, the material, the sensorial are given only through an insistent reminder of the virtual text's cybernetic nature; the sign itself has become a kind of hypertext, with all its codings and links left intact. The narrator confesses that he is "rey y esclavo de su IBM" [king and slave of his IBM] (355), and much of his fragmentary text consists of the record of his daily interactions with the e-world: e-mail requests for letters of recommendation or support, administrative memos from program coordinators, lesson plans, notations about having responded to e-mails or transcriptions of isolated bits from letters: "cordialmente / *delete* / su nuevo lector y amigo / *delete* / atentamente / *backspace backspace backspace*" [cordially/*delete*/your new reader and friend/*delete*/sincerely/*backspace backspace backspace*] (55).

Camila too is an able traveler in cyberspace. Her e-mails to the writer detail the daily boredom of her tasks as a library employee in her U.S. college, as well as constantly making flattering reminders of her obsession with him: "A veces durante el trabajo pienso en Ud . . . Si estoy buscando cosas en OCAT pongo su nombre y aparecen sus libros . . . Si estoy en INNOVAQ hago lo mismo. . . . Si estoy en OCLC recuerdo algún título de sus libros y lo busco y que lo tienen en WU y digo . . ." [Sometimes at work I think about you . . . If I'm looking up things in OCAT I put in your name and your books appear . . . If I am in INNOVAQ I do the same. . . . If I'm in OCLC I remember the name of one of your books and I look it up and check if they have it in WU and I say. . . .] (199). She chats to him about e-mails from her mother and from her friends in various parts of the world, consults with him about the idea of getting a memory upgrade for her computer, records her delight at the message "YOU HAVE MAIL," especially when the mail is from her beloved author, and she gives him a running commentary on her boss's addiction to e-sex.

In his discussion of *Serpiente,* Sainz tells us that one of the impulses behind that novel was "el deseo de convertirme, yo mismo, en escritura" [the desire to convert myself into writing] (157). In *La novela virtual,* he takes this transformation a step further, making it the pervasive structuring metaphor of the work as well as its thematic ground: "ya no existía como novelista ni como personaje / sino como una terminal de redes de computadores múltiples . . . / y una desk top en su otra mente: o una think pad / un displaywriter system" [he no longer existed as a novelist nor as a character/but only a terminal in a network of multiple computers . . . /and a desktop in his other mind: or a think pad/a displaywriter system] (189–90). Similarly, this reminder of the computer-generated nature of characters is true not only in the obvious case of Camila, but also in his meditation on Ombligo Anillado's body, which is flattened out into the two dimensions of word-processing text: "entre esas líneas luminosas se filtraba un cuerpo todavía adolescente" [between those luminous lines filtered a body that was still adolescent] (63). This insistence on characters that in "reality" (to use Nabokov's quotation marks) come into existence first as text on a screen before solidifying as hardcopy on the readers' printed version pervades the novel. While other markers of contemporary existence appear throughout the text—as when the author meditates on the moments of "*instant replay*" (477) in his life, or complains that key moments remain "fuera de tiempo, sin *rewind*" [out of time, without rewind] (489), it is the computer that serves as the most essential and pervasive referent, both as metaphorical system and as leitmotif.

One final example serves to demonstrate the point: the narrator marks his distraction from one of Camila's e-mails by repetition of a key phrase: "entonces volvió la vista a la pantalla de la computadora / *Please RETURN for more* . . ." [then he returned his gaze to the computer screen/ *Please RETURN for more* . . .] (134). This English phrase is repeated several times during the rest of the chapter, as the narrator's attention wanders back and forth from the e-mail letter (e.g., 140, 141). On the one hand, the phrase reminds us that the novel's action, such as it is, occurs on and around the computer screen, and that pressing a button on the keyboard will link the reader to additional text possibilities in the virtual world. On the other hand, the phrase also has an internal narrative function: the author within the text indeed "returns" again and again for more of Camila's continuing story. The "return" key, however, does more. It speaks directly to the reader about the essentially circular and closed nature of this narrative world where messages fly back and forth in virtual space to appear, as in this narrative, on a single laptop located in a transient scholar's dingy summer lodgings. By extension it serves as a reminder that we are all readers, and writers, engaged in solipsistic mono-dialogues (meta-autobiographies) on/in the computer screen/world.

HOMEWARD BOUND

Like the other authors studied in this chapter, Rivera-Valdés is an immigrant, and she writes about the immigrant condition: the nostalgia, the loneliness, the sense of conflicted belonging. Like those of Dorfman, Salazar, and Saínz, these tales by Rivera-Valdés also take the form of pseudo-autobiographical narratives that find an anchor for their metaphorical structures in female figures who come to stand as correlatives for the lost homeland. As if emulating the author's journeyings, the publishing history of this collection is itself somewhat peripatetic. Sonia Rivera-Valdés is Cuban American, as are most of the characters in these stories. Her book was first published in Colombia, and then reprinted in Cuba after being awarded a "premio extraordinario de literatura hispana en los Estados Unidos" in 1997[10]—where "in the United States" seems to refer to the existential condition of the author and her characters and not the site where the book appeared in print. Maja Horn notes that "sexual desire in Sonia Rivera-Valdés' stories is often explicitly linked with national desire, or desire for the nation" (7).

There is more than one twist, however, in Rivera-Valdes's *Las historias prohibidas de Marta Veneranda* [The Forbidden Stories of Marta Veneranda] that distinguish this book from the others analyzed thus far. First, *Las historias prohibidas* presents itself through a series of eight interconnected "interviews" with New York City Latino/as and a brief scientific introduction defining the methodology for this supposed social science research project ("Nota aclaratoria" [Explanatory Note] supposedly authored by "Marta Veneranda Castillo Ovando, Ph.D."). Thus, like the other texts analyzed in this chapter, it uses an autobiographical matrix, but the genre is quite different, since the author plays off the ethnographic interview rather than the celebrity life story as a basic structuring model. Characters are imaginarily presumed to serve as case studies for a more general social science research investigation rather than existing as extraordinary examples of exemplary lives with a particular resonance for the general public. Second, while in almost every story a female character is endowed with symbolic importance as the representative of the desired culture, in Rivera-Valdés's work, in complete contrast with those studied thus far, the working out of this national/personal relation *never* involves the valorization of a normative heterosexual pairing. Furthermore, unlike the mysterious and enigmatic female characters in these other narratives, in *Las historias prohibidas*, the love interest is far less likely to be a representative of U.S. dominant culture. Instead, she is often an even more recent immigrant than the protagonist of the tale.

The introduction to the book signals its difference in yet another way. Rather than adopting standard Spanish, or worrying about the problem of cultural contamination from English-dominant surroundings, the "editor" notes that "hemos decidido mantener las formas de expresión y giros coloquiales que caracterizan el lenguaje de las comunidades hispanas en Nueva York" [we have decided to retain the forms of expression and colloquial style that characterize the language of the Hispanic communities in New York] (7). While the text is by no means as Spanglishized as this note might suggest, the fact of this footnote's existence hints at the text's interest in engaging with colloquial orality. At the same time, it reminds us that the book's original audiences might be expected to raise some objections to the language of the stories and in this manner serves to preempt criticism.

The premise of the interviews is that each speaker is telling Marta Veneranda—a PhD researcher working under, and at cross-purposes with, distinguished academician Professor Arnold Haley—about his/her most secret or prohibited sexual adventure. The conventions of academic confidentiality "facilitate this converging of the reader with Marta's position in the text. In this intimate tête-à-tête, the reader feels the voyeuristic pleasure of overhearing something deemed private, very secret, and sexually illicit" (Horn 4). Nevertheless, while the apparatus of secrecy deploys at some level, it soon becomes clear that the protagonists know each other, recommend each other to the researcher, and are completely familiar with these supposed secrets. Academic protocols in this manner intersect with Latino/a *chismografía.* Thus, for example, Mayté tells the first story, swearing her interlocutor to secrecy. However, the second story begins with a reference to Mayté, who had recommended this researcher's project, and the context indicates that Mayté's story has been fully dissected in her small community. The narrator begins, "la misma historia de Mayté estaba bastante loca, la verdad. Pero la mía es peor. Se lo juro" [Mayte's own story is pretty crazy, in truth. But mine is worse. I swear it] (27/24), and in the next tale the third storyteller adds: "Mayté es la muchacha periodista que tuvo un romance, si puede llamarse así a aquello, con una prima que vino de Cuba a visitarla. ¿Se acuerda?" [Mayte is that journalist who had a romance, if you can call it that, with a cousin who came from Cuba to visit her. Do you remember?] (35/32–33). In context, this atmosphere of an open secrecy about their sex lives creates an atmosphere of one-upmanship, in which each story, and each storyteller, self-consciously has to work to impress Veneranda and to exceed the revelations of the one before.

The book begins with Mayté's story, following upon her observation that "en Nueva York hay tantos cuentos escabrosos en la vida cotidiana que casi nada parece prohibido" [So many lurid things take place in New York every day that hardly anything seems forbidden] (11/9).

Mayté's comment establishes the context for the whole of the book; New York is an exotic land where taboos lose their force—the land of opportunity given another twist. This first story tells of Mayté's love affair with a Cuban cousin named Laura; the second is about a Cuban man's attraction to obese, bad-smelling women; the third relates the tale of an abused Peruvian woman who (perhaps) turns off the life support on her husband when he is hospitalized and dying; the fourth talks about a gay Cuban man who breaks faith with his lover through his guilty interest in heterosexual pornography; the fifth tells of two Cuban immigrant women in love with each other; in the sixth, the protagonist, yet another Cuban woman, in order to help a female coworker, agrees to have sex with her male boss; and in the seventh, a mature woman, a voyeur of her husband's affair with a younger woman, poisons the man and invites the mistress to move in with her. This catalogue of taboo and prohibited loves culminates in the final story, titled "La más prohibida de todas," and it is this story that is more fully analyzed below.[11]

Choosing prohibited stories, assuming that we will look beyond the seductions of their titillating content, suggests a special urgency on the part of the narrator, a willingness to take risks. Most important, Rivera-Valdés concretizes the relation of body and of desire to the spoken language (the interview form) and to writing (the text before us), and she also reminds us that many of the texts like the ones we have explored so far are bursting with paradox. This seems especially true in the cases of Salazar and Sainz, where symbolic feminization offers a method for confronting the vastness of U.S. political and social power, implying the Other's desirability but also revealing a manageable weakness in which the man still remains on top, though ambiguously, and with considerable discursive contortion. These narrators are demonstrably seduced by U.S. culture into attitudes of assimilation, imitation, imposture, but by retaining the traditional binary masculinist associations about heterosexual couples, the narrators in each case are able to disavow their vulnerabilities, their entanglement in this seductive language and culture that they nevertheless must repudiate in order to retain their narrative potency/virility.

"La más prohibida" is the longest of the stories in Rivera-Valdés's collection; at forty pages, it has something like the weight of a novella. Unlike the other stories, which follow the interview format, where Marta Veneranda exerts full control over the shape of the material, this story is narrated by a self-conscious author named Martirio Fuentes who is assuming considerable authority over the form of her own text: "Espero sacar de esta conversación *mi* propio cuento sobre el episodio, por eso voy a grabar" [I hope to draw out of this conversation my *own* story about this episode, and that's why I'm recording it] (102/93–94). Throughout the narrative that follows, the tension between the interviewer and the interviewee remains patent. For if Marta Veneranda ostensibly performs research functions in order to produce a valid social scientific study, Martirio Fuentes records her story for the fictional possibilities it holds, though she worries a bit about its potential pornographic undertow: "Aquí es donde comienza mi problema con la narración que planeo. Tú conoces mi trabajo literario, jamás he escrito pornografía, pero para que ese cuento sirva es necesario reproducir, al menos parcialmente, el impudor de aquellos diálogos soeces" [Here's where I run into a problem with the story I'm planning to write. I've never written pornography; that's not my line of literary work. But for this story to function, it's essential that I, at least in part, reproduce the shamelessness of that dirty talk] (107/98). Martirio Fuentes, in other words, serves as a clear double of the implied author, both of whom disguise their erotic tales under other literary formulae: high art, raw materials for research.

Horn's reading focuses on the "affair/relationship with another woman who resides in Cuba. Through this relationship they recover and reconnect with the 'lost' Cuban nation" (7). While this is true, Cuba in this story appears in an unusual guise. Martirio's relation to Cuba is one of an always-already originary displacement. She is the daughter of an Andalusian Republican woman, who flees Spain for Cuba after her partner is shot by the opposing forces in the Spanish Civil War. The adolescent girl is sexually precocious and is particularly drawn to affairs with older, married men. Her problem, she comments, is that in her early adventures she had difficulty in figuring out the "guión del día" [script of the day] that her Saturday lovers expected to hear in response to their attempts at seduction, or once she learns the script, she has a mood-destroying tendency to imagine herself writing the encounter at the moment in which she is supposed to be living it instead. In either case, she neglects her "proper" role as the essentially secondary character in the drama of her seduction:

> El fallo conmigo era que les convertía los diálogos en monólogos. Por ejemplo, el intercambio ideal, ya empezando el episodio de la penetración, hubiera sido
>
> —Nada más te voy a meter la puntica, mami, el resto lo voy a dejar afuera, pa' que sufras. . . .
>
> Y el tipo se quedaba quieto. Entonces, yo debía contestar:
>
> —No papi, por favor, enterita la quiero dentro, toda, no ves cómo estoy sufriendo. Papi, papi.
>
> —Es que te va a doler mucho, mami, tú sabes lo grande que la tengo.
>
> —No importa, papito, toda aunque me desbarate. Métemela, que la necesito.

> Y ahí venía el chorro de obscenidades, que probablemente tú conoces. Pero yo no contestaba, aunque en poco tiempo aprendí cuál debía ser mi parte del libreto. (108–09)

> The problem was that I turned dialogues into monologues. An ideal exchange, once arrived at the stage of penetration, would have gone:
>
> "All I'm putting into you is the tip, *mami*, just the tippy-tip. I'm leaving the rest outside, just to make you suffer. . . ."
>
> And the guy would be quiet and hold still. Then I was supposed to answer:
>
> "No, *papi*, please, all of it. I want your whole sweet thing inside me. Don't you see how I'm suffering? *Papi, papi*, please."
>
> "But it will hurt you, *mami*, you know what a tool I've got."
>
> "It doesn't matter, *papi*, baby, I want it all, even if it ruins me. Put it in me, oh I need it now."
>
> And here would come a torrent of obscenities that you probably know. Only I didn't answer, even though I quickly learned how my part of the script was supposed to go. (99–100)

By withholding her part of the heterosexual script, Martirio also establishes her ironic distance from what is happening to her body and maintains a passive, but very effective, control over the affair.

Martirio's first sexually satisfying relation occurs with a young man from India. Unfortunately, her affair with Shrinivas is doomed after only one weekend, as her lover's male partner is due to return to the city (118/109). Later, in New York City, Martirio realizes that "los hombres me interesaron cada vez menos para el romance" [I grew less and less romantically interested in men] (123/114), and she begins a series of relationships with other women. One lover, a psychologist named Ada, teaches her that not all women are equally proficient with the language of intimacy (an insight she also already amply achieved with respect to the male gender through her early experiments). Another lover, Betina, inspires a chapter of one of Martirio's novels. After a seven-year period of celibacy, she meets a much younger Cuban writer, Rocío, who has been invited to read one of her stories in a literary conference. Rocío's background is strikingly similar to Martirio's and they become inseparable during the conference period, though they separate without trauma when Rocío returns to Cuba. Six months later, Martirio leaves the United States for Cuba and reencounters Rocío, whose first words to her are: "Le conté a mi madre que estaba enamorada de ti y necesitaba el apartamento por el fin de semana. Después podemos alquilar un cuarto en la casa de un amigo" [I told my mother I was in love with you and needed the apartment for the weekend. Later we can rent a room in the house of a friend of mine] (139/130). Martirio responds with "le ofrecí desde el primer abrazo lo mejor, las palabras del dueño de la finca de Camagüey, las posiciones de Shrinivas, las pasión de Betina. . . . [E]ra la primera vez que encontraba a alguien que sabía todas las líneas del guión." The story ends: "aquella tarde fue hace tres años. Y en eso estamos" [From our first embrace I offered her my best: the words of the planter from Camagüey, Shirinivas's positions, Bettina's passion. . . . This was the first time I'd ever met anyone who knew all the lines of the script. . . . That afternoon was three years ago. We're still at it today] (140/130–31).

Given the range of sexual adventures outlined in the previous seven stories, there seems nothing per se about Martirio's range of affairs that makes her story "la más prohibida." Indeed, the major difference among them is that Martirio's relationship with Rocío seems contented and ongoing, and that Martirio has no apparent regrets or even second thoughts about having left the United States and returned to Cuba to be with the woman she loves. The taboo that is violated, thus, seems to be the tacit prohibition against returning to the country of origin, and of all the books studied in this chapter, only in Rivera-Valdés's story is this tale of a happy return to the motherland instantiated fully. This story, obviously, is transgressive in another sense, as the Cuban discourse of homosexuality is, as Quiroga reminds us, omnipresent, but only in a negative context (127). Sainz's novelist remains suspended on the U.S. highway system, Salazar's Rivera dies before he can make plans to leave New York, and Dorfman meditates on his lost Chileanness and inability to return in any definitive way to the country he so passionately adopted.

Pointedly, in contrast with Dorfman, Rivera-Valdés's Martirio never engages with history. Or perhaps we might say that history—because it is so obviously discarded—is, to borrow a phrase from Palumbo-Liu, "depleted of any weight, it becomes simply one 'optional' narrative among many" (323). With the exception of the passing reference to the Spanish Civil War, Martirio makes no mention of any political issues whatsoever (this is a point also made by Maja Horn in her analysis of this author, 11–12); her tale is purely one of an emotional attachment between two women who by happenstance meet in one place and casually decide to live in another. There is no hint here of the much-traversed territory related to the Cuban exiles' familiar discourse of explusion from the beloved homeland. Nor is there any repudiation of what is so frequently decried in exile circles as Castro's perversion of authentic Cuban values. At the same time, Martirio's decision involves no reference to any commitment to a leftist political agenda. The absence of this almost inescapable discourse highlights by omission an important taboo against seamless exchanges between Cubans and Cuban Americans. Instead, the focus here is on the politics of the sexualized body and the recuperation from male discourse of the language of and about the woman's body. This story speaks of taking ownership of that language of embodiment, celebrating its coming into its own, and, as Horn reminds us in her discussion of the stories, "hint[ing] at other forms of community for sexual minorities that are not as private and limited to the domestic sphere" (18).

In all of these books, identity rests upon a fundamentally performative basis. It is created in dialogue, and the individual's sense of self develops through interaction with others. Presumably and normatively, identity sediments itself through reiteration and confirmation in a rooted community. In the immigrant situation, however, this communal network of identity creation has been disrupted by the physical relocation of the narrators from Latin American to U.S. cultural spaces. And yet, of course, the need for identity affirmation remains and becomes, if anything, even more critical. Interestingly enough, in each of these cases, the textualized immigrant seeks out a woman who can be allegorically endowed with a projected and overdetermined cultural content and who serves as the projected interlocuter for this identitarian dialogue. This projection of meaning on an allegorized other *does* create a mechanism for a continued performance of identity. At the same time, this is in nearly every case a false dialogue, one that evens out the immigrant's frustrations with his lack of power but distorts the potential for a richer interaction and displays the fragility of the performative textual artifice. Thus it is no wonder that so many of these tales end inconclusively: with death (Salazar), irresolution (Sainz), fallen status (Dorfman). It is a truism that the United States is characterized by a refusal to open to otherness, as evidenced in a much-documented and commented sociopolitical tendency to remain willfully and almost preternaturally ill-informed about other cultures/countries. Ironically, texts such as these foreground a parallel move, in constructing the domination of specific national cultures by means of the seduction of a woman identified with that national space, but represented almost invariably in stereotypical terms.

The insistence with which this dyad presents itself suggests a crisis in control over the allegory, a potential breakup of the unitary male voice and, as Rivera-Valdés's story hints, a capacity to change the shape of desire and its affiliations. Palumbo-Liu speaks of the "stalled rhythm of social integration" (345) in ethnicized U.S. communities, where atemporal understandings of the cultural nation come into conflict with the historical now of present contingencies. Literary texts such as these more sharply delimit the semiotic terrains and contested arenas of these stalled rhythms.

They offer a challenge to conventional ways of thinking about the immigrant experience and provide a space for a type of interrogation difficult to articulate in other social sites, helping us rethink relations among gender, national affiliations, and desires and enabling a more critical examination of their construction and consequences.

chapter five

Language Games: Hinojosa-Smith, Prida, Braschi

IN HIS 1994 ARTICLE, "Dialogical Strategies, Monological Goals," Bruce-Novoa identifies a crucial paradox in the construction of ethnicity in the United States. In the process of adaptation to the United States, he suggests, the immigrant struggles mightily to maintain contact with the originating nation, through increasingly ritualized interaction with elements of "the now distant 'authentic culture' ": food, language, material objects, social customs, festivals. These fiercely maintained and highly symbolic relations to specific cultural remnants define the ethnic identity as well as the individual's claim to authenticity, serve as codes for social interaction, and act as survival strategies to counteract perceived threats from outside. Ironically, says Bruce-Novoa, "The fact that [these cultural remnants] are remembered, practiced, or consumed with such intense need and pleasure as different from the surrounding society makes them no longer [authentic] national traits but U.S. traits, their particular value and significance determined by this country and not the country of the group's origin" (228). As Bruce-Novoa intuits, it is precisely their nature as isolated remnants and their highly valorized status that make them peculiarly a U.S. construction, and no longer unremarkable traits embedded in the immediacy of a rich home culture. Inevitably, these remnants are now abstracted, nostalgically recalled, ineluctably distant. Thus, the more the immigrant struggles to carve out a space for authentic cultural difference, the more this construction serves to define a quintessentially U.S. ethnicity. The more the immigrant self-consciously strives to maintain cultural authenticity, the more inauthentic, the more U.S. ethnic, s/he becomes.

This situation is not unique to the U.S. immigrant experience. Todorov makes a similar point from a slightly different perspective when he comments on his double identity as French and Bulgarian, where the implicit contamination of one identity by another makes the whole of his existence moot: "My twin affiliation produces but one effect: in my own eyes it renders inauthentic each of my two modes of discourse, since each can correspond to but half my being. . . . And so it is that once again I am locked in an oppressive silence. . . . It was impossible to create a whole being out of my two halves" (211–12). Ruben Navarrete, Jr. adds a complicating element to this already fraught scenario in his description of the typical encounters between two Latinos of different backgrounds and their seemingly inevitable jockeying for the moral high ground: "the rules of the game were simple. . . . The difference is noted. It might be a difference in skin color, Spanish-speaking ability, religion, even political affiliation. At first glance, it appears unlikely that both people can be authentic. The difference dictates that one must be a real Mexican, the other a fraud. The objective of the game becomes for the contestants to each assert his or her own legitimacy by attacking the ethnic credibility of their opponent. *More ethnic than thou*" (443). These almost ritual expressions of difference, suggests Navarrete, are so hotly contested, and the outcome so ambiguous, that they resolve little except for the recognition of anxiety itself, repressed and continually returning. The scenario does not settle the question of the relative authenticity of the competing Latino experiences; instead, all it does is confirm the effectiveness of the model that has convinced large numbers of people that there are recognizable criteria to define an indisputable purity or truth of ethnic identity, and that these criteria can be used to establish the definitive superiority of an authentic self with respect to a less-authentic other.

Todorov, Navarrete, and Bruce-Novoa signal a deeply troubling quality of the modern ethnic/immigrant imaginary, quite different from the celebrated cosmopolitanism of the omnivorous postmodern subject. In identifying with and residing between two nations, identity seems to slip inexorably into the shadow of the inauthentic, felt as a loss of voice, a loss in moral authority, and even a loss of self. In this reading, the authentic being, like the authentic culture, seems curiously marked by a tight imbrication in a nostalgic and Manichean perception of an impossibly distant alternative national identity. In this way, ethnicity, identity, authenticity are closely tied together and tightly linked to specific understandings of space. This now-distant monological space, moreover, imaginarily becomes the only space where the individual can have access to a full and true voice. And yet, of course, this national space is only imaginarily monological, only a projected rather than an actual monolithic culture, a decisive factor ignored by an uncomplicated and unreflective virtual participation in what often comes down to the patriotic myths promoted by the nation-state (Mexico, United States, France, Bulgaria) about itself and its citizens.

Juan Perea notes that this felt division is perversely reinforced by U.S. legislation, specifically Title VII of the 1964 Civil Rights Act, which prohibits discrimination by reason of national origin. As Perea astutely argues, because of its focus on a difference defined by national origin, the concept forces plaintiffs in discrimination cases "to define themselves as outsiders, belonging to some other country or place of birth and, correspondingly, outside the scope of American identity" (593). Latino/as, thus, are constructed —and even to some extent construct themselves—as foreign. They are invisible to the body politic even as they assert their rights to full participation, become symbolically deported (in Perea's terms) from the borders of the United States. To be an authentic ethnic somehow means to be always already inauthentic, to belong to no space, to have no legitimate voice. Arteaga would concur, and he proposes a thought experiment to drive home his point. Asking us to think about the ideological stakes in the supposedly objective record of U.S. history, he reminds us, "history is not written chronologically but, rather, from East to West so that Spanish is encountered . . . during the Western expansion late in U.S. history; it appears *historically* after English. Spanish is made alien, an immigrant language" (25).

Two queries immediately present themselves, and the discussion of their implications will be the burden of this chapter's analysis of aggressively performative bilingual/bicultural texts by Rolando Hinojosa-Smith (Texan, *Mi querido Rafa*), Dolores Prida (Cuban American, *Coser y cantar*), and Gianinna Braschi (Puerto Rican, *Yo-Yo Boing!*). I am, admittedly artificially, defining these strategies with respect to a theoretical stance toward emphasizing imbrication in space or privileging the spinning out of voice over time. These are the opening questions: (1) What do we mean when we talk about authenticity, and how does it relate to the placedness of highly performative texts? While this concern engages all the authors examined in this study, it can be most fruitfully explored through the analysis of the determinedly sited texts by Hinojosa Smith and Prida. (2) What would happen if we were to imaginarily decouple ethnicity from place? With Braschi, identity becomes fluid and contextual, and temporal vectors assume priority over spatial ones. Perhaps overly schematically, we might say that these two sets of authors describe two different strategies for confronting the apparent dilemma posed by the authenticity paradox and addressing monological expectations.

Lionel Trilling's classic *Sincerity and Authenticity* serves as a helpful point of departure for the first question, despite that critic's current unpopularity in many contemporary literary critical circles. We need to take into account, of course, the caveat that his Arnoldian-inspired meditations on the nature of sincerity and authenticity echo a clearly Victorian frame of mind;[1] nevertheless, his discussion of the ethical stakes in the decline of appeals to sincerity in the twentieth century and the increasing popularity of the alternative concept of "authenticity" remain astonishingly applicable to the very different circumstances of the bicultural writer. Trilling begins his analysis by recalling the tremendous evocative power of the creative appeal to authenticity, "which implies the downward movement through all the cultural superstructures to some place where all movement ends, and begins" (12)—one example would be as the injunction to aspiring authors to write from the heart. Authenticity, then, is a word we use for a quality that is granitic, highly valuable, exceptional in its particularity: "hard, dense, weighty, perdurable" says Trilling in a typical, and much repeated, set of metaphors (94). The authentic has the generative and creative force of being able to cut through falsification and mere fantasy; it represents as well a counterforce to both disorder and to the totalitarian imposition of order by violence. To be authentic is to have a certain moral weight and force; its implicit contrast is with experience that does not have this ontological weight and is, therefore, flighty, unanchored, inauthentic.

Nevertheless, this seemingly innocent appeal to the heart also and inevitably implicates a heart of darkness. Not only is the term polemical, inevitably opening up issues of anxiety about the credibility of one's own individual existence—"the authentic work of art instructs us in our inauthenticity and adjures us to overcome it" (100)— Trilling also recalls the explicitly violent cast of the original Greek etymology, which adds another layer of complexity: "*Authenteo:* to have full power over; also, to commit a murder. *Authentes*: not only a master and a doer, but also a perpetrator, a murderer, even a self-murderer" (131). Thus, almost as a countermeasure to his own Arnoldian impulses, Trilling traces the most subtle and explosive implications of the concept through the dialectic of Eros and Thanatos in Freud, and the often bitter misanthropism of Nietzsche's will to power. In Trilling's reading, the main burden of Freud's work is to substitute belief in the sustaining authenticity of human existence for God, keeping the world from becoming weightless, and thus confirming "an authenticating imperative, irrational and beyond the reach of reason" (158). In Nietzsche's case, Trilling argues that for the German philosopher, art rather than morality is our true metaphysical destiny (33). In all these cases—Freud's, Nietzsche's, Trilling's own—the appeal to weight and depth anchor the critique; yet he never loses sight of the original ambiguity of the concept, that to have power over oneself also threatens self-murder. In Freud the ego is checked by the id, and Eros dances with Thanatos; in Nietzsche, the will to power is hidden under an ironic mask. Indeed, in Trilling's analysis, weight is countered by irony, and it is the ironic posture in and of itself that nevertheless makes a strong appeal to the authentic, while skirting the borderlines of madness, or more specifically schizophrenia, which is a divided self's strategy for responding to the imposition of inauthenticity.

Todorov too matches his yearning for authenticity with a discussion of schizophrenia, warning that the "new *doxa* of widespread polyphony, . . . that unconditional endorsement of mixing" (204) requires more complication than most critics wish to allow it. For Todorov, "unbounded polyphony . . . leads to schizophrenia, taken in its commonly understood sense of split personality, mental incoherence, and attendant distress. Doublethink too is a kind of madness, since it implies a decision to accept incoherence or even contradictions" (206). His perspective is honed by his eastern European origins and his experience of a totalitarian government which, he suggests, almost inevitably creates a kind of madness in its citizens, a condition that is only intensified by the subsequent biculturality of his later life. He concludes his article by reminding his reader of the painful divisions in his own life and his own techniques for managing them: "I believe I saw silence and insanity looming on the horizon of boundless polyphony, and I found them oppressive, which is doubtless why I prefer the bounds of dialogue." For Todorov, this boundedness involves an articulation between cultures rather than an imaginary—and entirely utopic—reversibility of his two languages (214). Still in Todorov, and unlike Trilling, the monocultural individual has access to an uncomplicated simplicity of authentic being—the darker side for the French-Bulgarian thinker resides in the split between two cultures rather than the violent underside inherent in the concept itself.

Likewise, in his seminal *Asian/American,* David Palumbo-Liu dedicates considerable space to the discussion of the use of psychologizing discourse in general, and the trope of schizophrenia more specifically, to explore the politics of ethnic identity and to unpack attempts at fuzzing the lines between creativity and pathology. Taking his lead from Althusser and Jameson, he is attentive to the "symptomatics" of narrative, especially in the "schizophrenic text" of modernity that is put under even more extreme pressure in the bicultural narrative of the hyphenated U.S. citizen. Says Palumbo-Liu: "I want to draw forth three key issues from this debate: first, the tension between the psychologistic reading and a pragmatic and ethical one; second, the importance attached by all parties to some sense of 'national' or racial character; and finally, to the fact that this 'character' is adaptive to specific historical contingencies." It is, argues Palumbo-Liu, still extraordinarily difficult to separate a heroic, schizoid creativity from an unproductive pathological condition that has been internalized and taken as real, and it remains unclear what politics can be deployed to prevent the slide between creativity and pathology (302–03). Extending his concept, we might perhaps conclude that the persistent concern about authenticity, especially in its typically oversimplified form, is itself a pathological symptom. Here too, some resolution is required. What Trilling reveals as the dark underside of a valued quality, and Todorov attempts to resolve through dialoguism, Palumbo-Liu explores as a dialectic. Especially interesting with respect to Trilling's emphasis on a necessary weight to anchor metaphysical claims is his deployment of the tropes of floating and the drive to secure, which he is careful to resist:

> The precise nature of "dual" personality cannot be grasped without a specific sense of the forces that create the schism, the assumptions that underlie the imputed *separateness* of the two realms of experience, and the nature of the "wholeness" sought. Rather than assuming simply a free-floating land of neurosis and schizophrenia, we should see the separation of "Asia," "America," and "Asian America" as *itself* a psychic rationalization that, in seeking to simplify complex forms of identification and disidentification, blinds us both to the precise politics of separation, and concomitantly, to their grounds for interpenetration. The question behind cultural nationalism is therefore not the availability of a "nation" to secure "culture," but rather the historical materiality of a culture produced in a psychic space wherein a particular and contingent formation of the nation appears *in relation* to multiple identifications which are themselves driven by specific contingencies. (308)

Extrapolating from psychic to literary spaces, we could further argue that the rifts and discontinuities in a work of art make themselves available to study in a parallel manner. Some of these rifts are defined spatially—the text occupies a position in a particular cultural space and evokes the occupation of other spaces: nations, local geographies, specific sites of enunciation. In the texts under analysis in this chapter, one of the strategies for refusal of a secure culture involves the use of significant and untranslated stretches of discourse in two languages, refusing universalist monocultural presumptions, rejecting the supposed inevitability of monolingualism as the critical condition for defining an intellectual's or an artist's occupation of national academic space and, in the U.S. cultural context, interrogating the unquestioned assumptions about Anglo-American social and linguistic practices.

Thus, for example, Argentine-U.S. philosopher María Lugones writes long sections of her article "Hablando cara a cara/Speaking Face to Face" in untranslated Spanish, accompanied by an explanatory footnote: "If you do not read Spanish, see footnote below. *Porque si compartes mis lenguas, entonces comprendes todos los niveles de mi intención.* And if you do not understand my many tongues, you begin to understand why I speak them. . . . It is here to be appreciated or missed and both the appreciation and the missing are significant. . . . To play in this way is then an act of resistance as well as an act of self-affirmation" (46).[2] In this manner, Lugones amplifies the spaces of inquiry by mixing languages and combining oral with academic styles. It also seems that despite dominant culture rhetoric to the contrary, her partial exclusion of the monolingual once again, as Bruce-Novoa suggests and Gómez Peña confirms, encodes a quality that is particularly typical of the United States: "the objective was to make the audience members or the readers experience how it feels to be partially excluded, to be minorities in their own city, foreigners in their own country. . . . [W]e felt that partial exclusion was a quintessential contemporary experience, a quintessential American experience. . . . This is a very different proposition from that of the first generation of Chicano and Nuyorican writers who were using bilingualism and Spanish to map a binary cartography, in which Spanish and Spanglish meant 'us' and English meant 'you' " (Gómez Peña and Mendieta 550–51). For Lugones as for Gómez Peña, the aggressive bilingualism of their writings/performances poses a direct challenge to the supposed coherence of Western modes of knowledge, with its presumed universal codes, which are as a consequence and necessarily reformed and adapted to other circumstances even within the supposedly bounded national discourse. For these thinkers and performers, the locutionary and the local constantly infect and inflect each other. Since neither the philosopher nor the performance artist limit their critique to a U.S.-centric perspective, it is also pertinent to inquire about other audiences as well. Thus, for instance, in a broader, pan-American context, it would be important to think about the specific enunciatory sites and audiences defined in and by this kind of work—for example, would Lugones or Gómez Peña be able to present the same "quintessentially American" performances in, respectively, Buenos Aires or Mexico City, and what effect would be achieved?

In all the authors under analysis in this chapter, mixing Spanish and English, or deploying Spanglish, destabilizes, and the audience most destabilized in these texts is explicitly or implicitly the U.S.-dominant culture monolingual, who serves as an unstated point of reference for the openly transgressive textual discourse. Beginning in

Spanish also serves, as I indicated above and is literally the case in Lugones's article, as a clearing of the voice within a very specifically defined context. In that context, the bilingual reader is empowered, and the monolingual reader of either language is asked to meditate on the effect of skipping and stuttering through a text that at best can only be half understood. Thus, this chapter needs to open with a warning: there can be no translations for these heavily, aggressively, formally Spanglish performances.

To some extent, coming from within a Spanish-dominant milieu, English serves the same function in Ana Lydia Vega's much-cited short story, "Pollito Chicken." Says Vega, "There is no such thing as the universal: there is no universal literature, no universal culture. . . . What is termed 'universal' is the dominant culture's regionality" (Hernández 56). Because of its continuing colonial status under the hemisphere's undisputed imperial power, Puerto Rico often seems marginal to discussions about the Caribbean—as Vega notes in an interview, even Cuba, with all its political and social complexities, is more easily decipherable (Hernández 56). For Vega herself, this consciousness of her nation's complicated history and peculiar contemporary status is intensified by her own belated and secondary relation to literature in Spanish. Like many Puerto Ricans of her generation, when heavy pressure from the U.S. government forced children into English-only schools, Vega's early literary studies were first subject to the circumstances of schooling in English; later by her career as professor of French. Thus, she reminds us, her relation to Spanish has always been mediated by the oral rather than the written.

The question of language emphatically remains a burning political issue in Puerto Rico, and in this story Vega takes on the question of straddling two languages and two cultures in a particularly powerful way. While her protagonist is often mistaken for a Nuyorican in analyses of the story, Vega has reminded her readers that she explicitly describes her as a first-generation immigrant to New York. At the same time, for the author of the story, her own experience of living in the United States for an extended period honed her perceptions, in a way that echoes the ironic narrative voice, bringing Puerto Rico into sharper focus by the fact of a temporary distance from her homeland. She says that her "sense of nationalism was rekindled by our Nuyorican experience" (58). It is precisely this bifocal reality that Vega attempts to capture in her ironic story of Suzie's Caribbean adventures.

"Pollito Chicken" begins with what is actually a coda, when a self-described Republican assimilationist immigrant returns to her job in New York after what she imagines as an exotic Caribbean getaway vacation in Puerto Rico, her country of origin. Here's how the story opens:

"I really had a wonderful time, dijo Suzie Bermiúdez a su jefe tan pronto puso un spike-heel en la oficina" (75). Even more so than Lugones's article, Vega's story is only accessible to bilinguals, privileging readers who share the same uncomfortable position of in-betweenness as her protagonist. Yet, unlike Lugones, where the bilanguage wraps *la lectora enterada* in a double comfort of domestic support and sharp academic analysis, in Vega's case the jarring quality of her story's highly stylized code switching enters with the tap of a spike heel, efficiently and uncomfortably jostling together cultural and gender politics in unexpected ways.

In this story, the exposed xenophobic regionality of the U.S. dominant rubs uncomfortably against the complexities of Puerto Rico's vexed relation to its double colonial heritage, including Puerto Rican gender and political stereotypes. For instance, Suzie has to decide, upon reaching Puerto Rico, whether to stay at the popular and ironically named tourist hotel El Conquistador or to visit her grandmother in Lares (noncoincidentally the site of the aborted 1868 independence effort against the Spanish). Suzie's apparent choices often take the shape of a hard dose of reality, which she tries to defer with appeals to an Anglocentric vision of the exotic Other. The white culture's exotic imaginary, however, continually betrays her as, for example, when in a shudder of erotic daydreams, she imagines herself into the white woman's fantasy of having a black Haitian man "efectuar unos primitive Voodoo rites sobre su naked body," and finds herself settling instead for the sexual attentions of a kinky-haired Puerto Rican bartender (78–79). Most pointedly, the dramatic rhythms of the spoken tongue highlight discontinuities between the "breathtaking poster" image of happy colonization and the *independentista* shout in Puerto Rican dialect that ends the story—"¡VIVA PUELTO RICO LIBREEEEEEEEEEEEEEEE!" (79)—while it forces an ironic rereading of its opening line.

Suzie reenters corporate U.S. space with her clichéd remark about a having a "wonderful" time, in retrospect repressing her newfound *independentista* convictions. She has, by her actions while in her homeland, parodically at least, taken part in "the downward movement through all the cultural superstructures" described by Trilling and reached the authentic core of herself beneath the assimilationist trappings. It is impossible to say with any certainty whether her cheery greeting to her boss reflects self-preservation in the corporate setting or self-murder in the ethnic perspective, though I like to think that the aggressivity of her spike heel offers hope. At the same time, her boss responds with the equally clichéd "San Juan is wonderful" while repressing, "I wonder why you spics don't stay home and enjoy it," a heavy-handedly xenophobic comment that nevertheless accurately defines a familiar dominant culture subtext. Here, as throughout the story, Vega's language is sharp and double edged; in each case the appeal to "wonder" encodes both a public/spoken and a private/unspoken script. Furthermore, the English word "wonder" or "wonderful" has no exact equivalent in Spanish ("maravilloso" accesses a somewhat different psychic/emotional spectrum), certainly none that would allow for the repetition/echo in the two clichéd phrases of the employee and her boss.

The highly stylized code switching in this story in no way emulates everyday speech; the overloading of meaning gives the text a feel and intensity equivalent to poetry. Yet at the same time, in this story as in all her work Vega manages to overlay this deeply artificial language onto a recognizable and believable orality. Her work is double voiced in more than the obvious way, taking advantage of the reaches of her bilanguage and implicitly reflecting on code switching in common usage versus literary texts.

Since the performance of orality is so crucial not only to Vega, but to all the authors being studied in this chapter, it behooves me to take a step back and say a few words about forms of bilingualism and code switching.

Scholars have increasingly focused on the distinction between subtractive and additive forms of bilingualism as lived in the U.S. context. For the bilingual Latino, bilingualism tends to be perceived as subtractive, in that it detracts from social status, whereas for the educated non-Latino, learning Spanish is additive in value. The poor immigrant speaker is subject to discrimination since lack of fluency in English tends to be taken for general ignorance, while for people from higher socioeconomic classes who are fluent in English, knowing a bit of Spanish becomes an advantage and an asset (Callahan 420–21). Equally important, in the United States, Spanish has been stigmatized as a language of the poor, and even if such were not the case, more cachet accrues to academic study of language than knowledge of a language through immersion in one's own cultural heritage. Villanueva describes the difference this way: "the bilingualism of Chicanos is more existential, while Eliot's and Pound's is more referential. . . . Missing in their bilingualism (multilingualism in some instances) is the immediate context of, and their everyday relationship to, the cultures implied in the languages they quote" (709). This immediate and everyday relationship to Spanish has a different weight than an immediate and everyday relationship to English; curiously enough, the secondhand knowledge is preferred. If we look to the other side of the border, in Spanish-speaking Latin America, English is generally a status marker and increases cultural capital, parallel to academic study of a second language in the United

States. An unresolved dissonance arises, however, when fluent English speakers from the presumed lower classes (Chicanos, returning Nuyoricans) complicate this scenario, suggesting that in both cases the assignment of value follows analogous class-based mores.

In this context of weighted and differentially valorized types of bilingualism, the use of Spanish in U.S.-based literary texts and English in Latin American ones always carries political freight with enormous implied meaningfulness both to the author and the reader. "Al hablar en Spanglish, siento una especie de liberación interna" [On speaking Spanglish, I feel a kind of internal liberation], says Ilán Stavans to María Barbero (September 9, 2000, e-mail circulated on Internet). In the same interview, the Judeo-Mexican-American scholar comments acerbically on the pretensions of the Real Academia Española, which often exaggerates its importance and its influence: "El paternalismo trepidante, en anhelo imperial que no cesa, siguen causando estragos" [The shaky paternalism, the unceasing imperial desire continue to cause havoc], and in another, related interview he adds, "el que en España se festeje esta diseminación del español como un triunfo resulta cómico. Al fin y al cabo, muy pocos entre la población hispánica sienten algo —una deuda, un cordón umbilical—hacia España. La gente ni siquiera sabe que existe una Real Academia de la Lengua Española" [the fact that in Spain they celebrate this dissemination of Spanish as a triumph turns out to be comic. After all, very few members of the Hispanic population feel anything—a debt, an umbilical cord—toward Spain. People don't even know that a Royal Academy of the Spanish Language exists]. Most significantly, says Stavans, "vale la pena señalar que el spanglish, aunque se le escucha a diario en las calles de las ciudades norteamericanas, es también un fenómeno de España y América Latina" [it's worthwhile to note that Spanglish, although it is heard daily in the streets of U.S. cities, is also a phenomenon in Spain and Latin America] (<http://www.cuadernoscervantes.com>). Thus, for example, "McOndo" writers like Chilean Alberto Fuguet have served as lightning rods for extremely virulent reviewers, who accuse him of selling out to U.S. cultural imperialism because of the heavy deployment of the images and language derived from U.S. mass culture in his novels. On the U.S. side, to greater or lesser degree, textual use of code switching is typical of almost all Latino texts, also with a mixed reception, often dependent upon presumptions about the inclusion or exclusion of specific potential audiences.

Up until very recently, in U.S. publications Spanish usage was severely limited, often by editorial fiat, on the theory that the English-speaking reader has an extremely low tolerance for non-English words. Thus, Spanish tended to be accompanied by glossaries and/or often awkward translations, as in this relatively early example: "Basta! cried Lupe, meaning Enough!" (Barrio 115). Many Latino/a narratives continue to use Spanish sparingly and highly symbolically, often to textualize references to language impoverishment or loss. For many writers, typically formulaic or tag phrases serve to identify a particular speech context or to sustain character: home, street, workplace, group solidarity, generational context. Nevertheless, readers have proven to be far more flexible than mid-twentieth-century editors imagined, and U.S. Spanish today flourishes not only in texts by bilingual Latino/as, but also in general in those narratives located in territories crossed by multiple languages. Thus, for example, in the novels making up Cormac McCarthy's bestselling, well-received Border Trilogy, hardscrabble Anglo Texas cowboys quite naturally expect to be equally fluent in Spanish and English. All three of these books, while aimed at an English-speaking audience, frequently feature untranslated sections in Spanish, often with a wink to the bilingual reader:

> Bueno, he said, We can speak english.
> Como le convenga, said John Grady. (*All the Pretty Horses* 113)

Other critics have noted that the underlying structure of these novels remains very close to the racial mythologies of the traditional Western (Sugg 119); this criticism is certainly well taken. I am less interested, however, in recalling the permutations of the Anglocentric foundational romance than in signaling the weaving of languages and the linguistic slippage that occurs in these novels, most often in the respectful exchanges between one of McCarthy's culturally ambivalent Anglo heroes and Spanish-speaking Texan or Mexican authority figures. Early in *The Crossing*, for example, there is a chapter in which Billy Parham consults with an old man about wolf trapping; the old man's comments and instructions all appear in untranslated Spanish:

> He said that Echols had caught all the wolves.
>
> El señor Sanders me dice que el señor Echols es medio lobo el mismo. Me dice que él conoce lo que sabe el lobo antes de que lo sepa el lobo. But the old man said that no man knew what the wolf knew. . . . El lobo es una cosa incognosible, he said. Lo que se tiene en la trampa no es mas que dientes y forro. El lobo propio no se puede conocer. Lobo o lo que sabe el lobo. Tan como preguntar lo que saben las piedras. Los arboles. El mundo. . . . Me entiendes?
>
> The boy didnt know if he understood or not. (45)

Here, as in the previous example, the bilingual reader has access to the textual play, the bilingually encoded humor of the exchange, in a way that reminds us of Lugones's admonition that the Spanish in her text is there to be understood or missed, and that both the understanding and the lack are meaningful.

McCarthy's code switching activates the bilingual reader in a way that early texts such as Ray Barrio's *Plum Plum Pickers* could not; Ana Lydia's "Pollito Chicken" requires even more of her audience and points to the body of texts that will be the core of this chapter. Her aggressive Spanglish, like theirs, excludes the monolingual reader of either language. This more aggressive bilingualism opens up opportunities for creative experimentation, multiple associations, expanded possibilities of wordplay, multilingual puns. In addition, says Villanueva, referring implicitly to writers like Hinojosa-Smith, Prida, Braschi, and Vega: "the use of Spanish drive[s] home a point of cultural, sociological and political import in a spirit of defiance against the English-only policies (usually expressed with disdain) of the public schools; the established linguistic requirements of academia; and the prevalent and seemingly arrogant ethnocentric Anglo-culture-only attitude in general" (697–98).

Bruce-Novoa comments: "the readers to whom the text directs itself are, if not in fact at least ideally, products and producers of a mixture of Spanish and English which ultimately is the essence of the group's cultural definition" (237). Most typically, such code switching echoes everyday usage and serves the kinds of purposes Villanueva has helpfully outlined, and which are equally applicable to Alberto Fuguet and Rolando Hinojosa-Smith: "(1) to be more vividly direct in conveying untranslatable concepts; (2) to underscore a sensory state, a psychological or emotional attitude thought best described by a connotatively charged word or idiom; (3) to render a cultural experience identifiably native to either group; and (4) to establish an intimacy between speaker and listener" (Villanueva 693).

Our writers, then, have/cause language trouble. Unsatisfied with a single tongue, they trouble language through elegant, aggressive, delicate, humorous deployment of code switching. They have double trouble with languages' excesses and insufficiencies, and suffer, enjoy, question, deplore the possibilities of doubleness in identity or voice. They uncover the (Anglo-European, Arnoldian-Victorian) cultural and linguistic biases lingering in presuppositions about, say, authenticity or schizophrenia, and ask us to rethink these powerful concept metaphors. In a complimentary reference to Samuel Beckett's turn away from his native Irish English to writing in French, Spivak adjures: "It is not possible to remain within the mire of a language. [In order to write] one must clear one's throat, if you're taking the voice metaphor, clear a space, step away, spit out the mother tongue" ("Bonding" 278–79).[3] Beckett, and Spivak too, perhaps, felt that they had to choose—French or English, Bengali or English. The writers under analysis here also privilege the powerful spatial metaphor—clearing a space, taking a step, stepping away—or the alternative temporal one—clearing one's throat, spitting out mother and acquired tongues—but they do so without feeling an imperative to choose.

STEPPING AWAY: HINOJOSA-SMITH AND PRIDA

To begin with: stepping away for the bilingual writer involves a two-step. Rolando Hinojosa-Smith publishes two versions of many of his novels: a Spanish-dominant bilingual version and an all-English alternative. Thus, *Mi querido Rafa*'s companion text, *Dear Rafe,* roughly follows the original, but is not a strict translation; the author adds and subtracts from the text to create a what he calls a "rendition" tailored to his presumed audience. Dolores Prida—to choose texts only from her most widely circulated collection—writes plays in English (*Beautiful Señoritas, Savings*), Spanish (*Pantallas),* Spanish-heavy Spanglish (*Botánica*), as well as the fully bilingual *Coser y cantar,* which "must NEVER be performed in just one language" (49). For both of these writers, the bilingual text is activated in the context of an extremely well-defined, clearly delimited place. In *Coser y cantar,* that place is most obviously the performance space itself, and within the dramatic imaginary, the refuge/safe space of the character's New York apartment. For Hinojosa-Smith, the narrative space of all his novels is the fictional Belken County in the south Texas Valley, a place where languages and affiliations humorously and promiscuously intermingle.

In an important pan-American discussion of border literature, David E. Johnson uses Rolando Hinojosa-Smith as an important foil to Borges and Paz in elaborating the cultural strategies for reaching and sometimes stepping across the border between English-speaking and Spanish-speaking America. In contrast with the common perception that there is one essentialized national identity for each side of the border, Johnson talks about Hinojosa's "construction of a country that takes place twice, always in translation" and calls his work "the border of American literature and, perhaps, the principle of any possible hemispheric (pan-American) literary production, if not, in fact, that of globality in general" (130). He continues, "what if, for example, there were a body of texts, a *corpus,* for which it was impossible to decide *on any grounds* its place within any national literature? Such an example would explode the limits of national literature. . . . We could name this example 'Hinojosa,' but we won't know in what language we pronounce the name or to what side, if any, it belongs" (148). Hinojosa, as Johnson reminds us, begins from a deceptively simple premise: "everything will be in its place and every place will be determined by language, even if by 'language' is meant the mixture of tongues" (150). In practice, this means that Hinojosa-Smith's novels become unintelligible within the traditional constructs of U.S. and Spanish American understandings of proper and authentic national literatures, based on a one-nation, one-language model, while curiously, at the same time, they more accurately than monolingual narratives capture something like the authentic flavor of south Texas orality, where the mixture of tongues defines ordinary experience. Furthermore, argues Johnson, there is an even more troubling instability. Within the body of Hinojosa's own works, the duplication of titles means that there is more than one "original" text, both occupying the same narrative space in the multinovel world of the *Klail City Death Trip* series. Thus, while seemingly substitutable, *Mi querido Rafa* and *Dear Rafe* are not the same text (152); the renditions appeal to different audiences and have somewhat varying content—some details are omitted or added, characters don't say the same things or say them in the same way, the narrative shape reforms itself slightly.

Firmly rooted in south Texas Valley, Rolando Hinojosa-Smith populates his novels with people who are equally rooted and whose histories in the area date back to long before the Anglo migrations; then he overlays this rooted *mexicano* population with an increasing influx of Midwestern Anglos. Ramón Saldívar calls Rolando Hinojosa-Smith's work "a living chronicle," an ongoing and evolving "border ballad" (132), a "multileveled geopolitical topography" (137). Karem adds: "one of the outstanding qualities of Hinojosa's fiction is its commitment to bilingualism and biculturalism, its insistence on exploring Valley culture from the perspectives of both Chicanos and Anglos, whether they are oppressors or oppressed. This breadth of cultural engagement is rare in the fiction of the Americas and even scarcer in its criticism" (107)—or, as one of the characters in *Mi querido Rafa* comments generously, "a veces los bolillos son más personas que uno" (101).

In his "Prólogo" to *Rafa,* the narrator/ethnographer/reporter "P. Galindo" (he calls himself "el escritor" or, more typically, "el esc.") surveys this sociolinguistic terrain with a touch of impatience toward expected readerly inflexibility about the text's insistent use of a colloquial Spanglish: "¿Sería mucho pedir que no se sorprendieran cuando los Anglos Texanos hablen inglés? Es su idioma natural y casero; se sabe que unos cuantos hablan español y cuando así suceda, el español saldrá por delante. Si se hablan ambos idiomas así saldrán también. También es natural que la raza del Valle hable más en español. Ahora, si la raza sale en inglés, así se reportará" (8). In the English rendition of this commentary, perhaps to make up for the lack of Spanish in the text, there are telling differences in Galindo's emphasis, including a more overt reminder of promiscuous linguistic and genealogical mixing: "Belken County *mexicanos,* aside from their Northern Mexican Spanish language, speak English, by and large; the Belken County Anglo Texans, aside from their predominantly Midwestern American English, also speak Spanish, by and large. Proximity creates psychological bonds and proximity also breeds children, as we've been told" (8).

Hinojosa-Smith has emphasized many times in his essays the importance of this fictional site in south Texas: "for the writer—this writer—a sense of place was not a matter of importance; it became essential. . . . I could see this Valley, this border, and I drew a map, and this, too, was another key" ("Sense of Place" 21, 23). Somewhat more abstractly, the author elsewhere says of another of his novels, in terms equally applicable to *Rafa,* that "instead of a flat picture, or a horizontal one, *Rites and Witnesses,* attempts to recover a vertical plane" ("Baroque" 26). In both cases, the visual, geographical referent is paramount. Repeated metaphors in his discussions of his project include maps, lines, surfaces, configurations, refraction, vistas, points of perception. The first edition of *Estampas del valle* includes an overlay of mental and fictional geographical maps of Belken County. Indeed, implicit maps and genealogical charts are important to other Hinojosa-Smith works, as physical location with respect to other characters is always highly significant and, in traditional small-town fashion, a good deal is adduced about characters from the evidence of their extended families.

José David Saldívar cites Hinojosa in an interview: "My novels don't end, . . . and you never know what is going to happen to these people later on. . . . I pick them up at different stages of their lives because that's how you run across people" (68). As Ramón Saldívar has observed, for this author narrative unity often follows the syntax of genealogical patterns (140). Jehú in one of his early letters in *Rafa* sets the scene: "somos del Valle, casi todos nos conocemos y de una manera u otra mucha raza está emparentada (malgré nous)" (24). Galindo, after tracing particularly complicated family relationships in a conversation with Noddy Perkins, asks the reader, "¿Habrá razón alguna para darle importancia (debida/indebida) a los susodichos enlaces?" (78). Later, the narrator falls into the temptation himself in prefatory note to another interview, this one with Rufino Fischer Gutiérrez: "RFG tambíen es Cano, es decir, es Gutiérrez por su padre, Fischer por su madre, y dos veces Cano: por su abuelo paterno, el primer Rufino Cano Guzmán, y por su abuela materna, doña Florentina Anzaldúa Cano" (82). RFG himself adduces personality based on genealogy, recalling the long-standing confict between the Buenrostro and the Leguizamón families and clearly indicating his take on which family has the moral high ground: "por boca de Jehú supimos que ese Escobar es Leguizamón-Leyva y allí vimos la jugada de Arnold Perkins" (83).

While knotty and multiply intersecting, these baroque small-town relationships also follow a well-known hierarchy that runs from the well-to-do whites who control (or think they control) politics and business in the region to the fruit tramps and poor whites who occupy the social ladder's bottom rungs. In that scale, as Galindo comments, "nosotros no contamos" (66). Ironically, of course, the English-only Anglos are prematurely comforted by their supposed superiority. When the white social hierarchy intersects with the *mexicano*'s genealogical tracings, the influence of, for example, the Leguizamón tribe is as unmistakable as it is unavoidable. *La raza*—Galindo, Jehú, et al.—always know more than the whites despite the apparent power-money differentials, though by the mid-1950s period referenced in this novel they are beginning to suspect that "la bolillada sabe más de nosotros de lo que sospechamos. Se parecen a los viejitos . . . son bilingües aunque hay mucho secreto en eso" (20). Ironically too, the Anglo politicians are well aware of the *mexicano* voting block and the potential Valley voters who have historically ignored the citizenship implications of the 1848 Treaty of Guadalupe Hidalgo. Jehú writes: "Ahí está el radio otra vez: no te digo, they're flooding all the stations. On both sides of the River, natch" (40).

Following the prologue, *Mi querido Rafa* has two parts. At the core are twenty-two letters (twenty-three in the English version) from Jehú Malacara to his cousin Rafa Buenrostro, who is recuperating from an operation at the William Barrett Veteran's Administration Hospital.[4] Jehú's letters are gossipy, focusing centrally on the political shenanigans of local businessmen in a recent election campaign. Following the letters are a series of commentaries on the events gathered by "P. Galindo" from both Anglo and *mexicano* participants and observers, along with his brief commentaries on these conversations, and his conclusions about the events surrounding Jehú's dealings with the Klail City First National Bank as an up-and-coming loan officer. Jehú finds himself dragged into the political campaign, and is fired (and later rehired) at the bank under mysterious circumstances. Galindo's task is not so much to resolve this mystery as to record the comments and perspectives of local townsfolk who may or may not know anything about the particulars of the case.

The title of this novel can be misleading: Rafa Buenrostro, a recurring character in many of Hinojosa-Smith's works, has only the most peripheral role in this one. He is out of town in the veteran's hospital during all of the events described, and—almost axiomatically in this world—once out of Belken/Klail, the character effectively removes himself from the available fictional universe. Thus, the novel includes neither his responses to Jehú's letters nor any commentaries with Galindo. At the same time, his presence can be inferred from the tone of the text. For the first half of the novel, as the recipient of the letters, Rafa serves as the reader's proxy, both defining the social space for us and implicitly shaping as well the form and content of his cousin's letters. The second half of the novel is inflected by Galindo's reading of this collection of letters and his desire to fill in the blanks. Rafa is implicated in another sense to the degree that his past history with Leguizamón, as detailed in other books in the series, serves as an important chapter in the long-standing Buenrostro-Leguizamón feud and, in this highly genealogically conscious world, that conflict has a bearing on this tale by virtue of the fact that Jehú Malacara is his first cousin.

Bruce-Novoa emphasizes the deceptive simplicity underlying the commitment to orality in Hinojosa-Smith's complexly woven narrative structures. As he says, "you feel as if you are eavesdropping on a conversation at a bar" ("Righting" 82); at the same time, the reader also becomes aware of the artfulness of the Texan's literary style. In *Rafa*, P. Galindo serves as the central narrative organizer. Through the apparatus of prologue and conclusion to the book, along with the prefaces and comments on each contributor's material, Galindo seems to be positioning himself as an unofficial local ethnographer who delights in a pseudo-scientific participant-observer style of recording his materials before editing them for publication. Then too, the pseudo-ethnographic continually slides into the narrator's delight in the intrinsic interest of the tale and, perhaps even more so, in the idiosyncrasies of his neighbors: "el esc. en lo que pudo, trató de evitar, a veces con cierto éxito, trató de evitar, se decía, la sátira y el sarcasmo" (90). The writings are pieced-together fragments, barely fleshed out with the editor's brief comments. His project is necessarily inconclusive; as Galindo says in one of his direct addresses to the reader, "de eso se trata, de apuntar todo para que el lector llegue a sus propias conclusiones sin que el esc. lo lleve apersogado" (57). Even for the reader of the whole Klail series, gaps always remain and, in the case of *Rafa*, this irremediable lack of further information is ostensibly due to Galindo's own ill health. Like Rafa Buenrostro, he also finds himself in William Barrett rather than Klail, in his case suffering incurable liver and lung problems that measure his life expectancy in months. Thus, *Rafa* is both a testament of sorts and, at the same time, a storyteller's last effort, à la Scheherazade, to stave off death through narrative. In this way, the twin roles of barroom gossip and scientific observer overlap with a kind of terminal poignancy, suggesting that one of the hidden scripts for this novel is

Galindo's own autobiographical account of the waning months of his life.

There is, of course, a second major tale-teller in this novel—Jehú Malacara himself, whose letters make up the first half of the book. Jehú's epistolary style sparkles with a self-deprecatory wit. He too spins out gossip to wile away hospital tedium, but in his case his storytelling is on his cousin's behalf rather than his own. If Galindo is writing to hold off death, Jehú's trajectory more closely concerns itself with a writing into (another) life; after all, the novel ends with Jehú's disappearance (readers of the series will soon learn he went to Austin) from a career that initially seemed attractive but most certainly was heading toward a disappointing dead end. Galindo's story and Jehú's story, then, are chiasmatic in effect.

More important, though, neither Galindo's nor Jehú's stories are precisely the point of this novel, in the same way that Rafa too is marginal to the tale. Despite the doubled apparatus of storytelling (epistolary and ethnographic), the novel is not so much about creating narrative suspense and telling a rousing good tale as it is about constructing a specific relation to the south Texas space through the patterns of voice and usage, highlighting the seductively attractive linguistic richness of the area. Hinojosa-Smith says of his work:

> When the characters stayed in the Spanish-speaking milieu or society, the Spanish language worked well, and then it was in the natural order of things that English made its entrance when the characters strayed or found themselves in Anglo institutions; in cases where both cultures would come into contact, both languages were used, and I would employ both, and where one and only one would do, I would follow that as well; what dominated, then, was the place, at first. Later on I discovered that generational and class differences also dictated not only usage but which language as well. ("Sense of Place" 23)

In this text, the reader too takes on a specific profile. This is most obvious in the letters, where Rafa is constructed through Jehú's comments on their shared youth, just as Jehú's style implicitly responds to that common history. Galindo too defines his reader, if not so purposefully by name, at least persistently, in his frequent recognition of his audience, whether in indirect dialogue—"El esc. está de acuerdo con el lector" (59), overt appeals—"El lector está libre de aceptar o rechazar lo que diga Emilio Tamez" (110), or commentaries that implicate the reader in an implicit manner—"el esc. interrumpe para informar que el informante habla de sí en tercera persona. Siempre" (103) or "El esc.

cree innecesario el hacer sus acostumbrados comentarios.... El esc. tampoco ha de sobajarse a la ironía en este caso" (108). Furthermore, as Johnson reminds us, the reader's options open even more vertiginously when we take into account that there are two renditions of the text, so that the reader can choose to read either of the two original texts: *Mi querido Rafa* or *Dear Rafe.* Johnson asks, "the question of bilingualism in the *Klail City Death Trip* is precisely the question of reading: How do you, we, read this text, this double and doubling narrative?" The reader's decision of which to read, he concludes, "inscribes American literature within the space of an unacquitable debt to an other" (152).

At another level, Hinojosa-Smith challenges the dominant paradigms of representation that circumscribe and define the Latino/a text. All too often, the "authentic" Latino/a experience has been limited to certain subject matters (gangs, migrant farm workers) and specific thematic content (experience of oppression, love of family), sprinkled with a judicious use of local color (a few key words in Spanish to give flavor to the narrative). Here is where Hinojosa-Smith's work is most astonishing. Not only does he abjure the easy ethnic-identified topics, but, like Ana Lydia Vega, he makes his most striking innovations on the formal level, even while his work seems entirely uninvested in the high-art pyrotechnics of adopting an obscure or technically difficult form. *Mi querido Rafa* relies for its effect almost entirely on an extraordinary degree of verisimilitude in the author's nontraditional use of vernacular rhythms, on the virtuoso capturing of the grain of voice in the particularities of speech, the use of dialect, the code switching between languages in a manner entirely appropriate to his compelling and idiosyncratic cast of characters. This is a novel written in fragments that does not feel postmodernly fragmentary. If Hinojosa-Smith's fine-tuned sense of narrative space creates the opening for bilingualism in the text, it is also true that the bilingualism and code switching are constitutive of a particular site in which such exchanges can naturally occur.

Which language is chosen and how it is used always appeals to a larger social and political context; thus, Galindo and Jehú consistently remark it in their commentaries on other members of their community. When Leguizamón, a force in the *mexicano* community, enters the Anglo world of the bank, he shifts language without ceding any of his formidable authority. Says Jehú: "te juro que ésta debe ser la primera vez que oigo a Himself hablar en inglés; se defiende, I'll say that" (22). Since Leguizamón in Spanish always uses the first person pronoun, and makes sure the listener/reader is aware of his power and influence—for example, "YO [sic], en gran parte, le conseguí el puesto a Jehú" (107)—it is entirely appropriate that Jehú, when describing his old nemesis's

English abilities, defines him by the key word "Himself." On the other hand, Conrado Aldama mistakenly imagines that his excellent English will give him a higher status in the community—instead, it opens him to ridicule. He's a "Col., U.S. Army Ret." and "a éste sí que se le 'olvidó' el español." When Olivia joins Jehú and Ira, she indirectly and ironically reminds Aldama as well as Ira Escobar of where the lines are drawn in Klail: "Somos cuatro raza juntos. I think it wise to disperse; we're too good a target" (27).

Roger Terry, an Anglo who speaks Spanish, is considered an "amigo de la raza" (12), whereas Ira Escobar, despite his heritage, is cordially disliked for his pro-Anglo political positions. At the same time, the powerful Anglo political machine hopes to convince the local *mexicanos* to vote for Escobar because of his ethnicity, and Noddy Perkins supports him because supposedly he (Noddy, Ira) "quiere a la raza" (16). Unfortunately, says Jehú, the *raza* tend to fall for this trick every time. Galindo too makes point about emphasizing language use. He cites whites who speak Spanish; for example, unpretentious Esther Bewley, who "aprendió español en los ranchos y en los campos" (105). In her mostly mostly English interview, she breaks into Spanish with Galindo to better describe her dislike of Perkins' maneuvering: "But that *other* one. ¿Sabe qué? Yo hablo mejor español que él and *he* went to *big* Texas A&M" (106).

Ira's wife, Becky, tellingly, speaks an "español algo mocho, y ella prefiere el inglés" (72) and Jehú adds that "cuando habla inglés hasta suena como bolilla, no del Valle, pero de esas de East Texas" (23). Sammie Jo Perkins, a more favorably drawn character, "habla bastante español aunque aquí se demuestre muy poco," and clever, funny Olivia San Esteban switches languages in blocks. Her interview begins in Spanish for two paragraphs, changes to English for the next five, then, ostensibly in a second interview later in the same day, comes entirely in Spanish (68–69).

Not only are Olivia and Jehú an on-again, off-again couple, but they are also the two most clear-eyed commentators on the foibles of their community. Noncoincidentally, they are also the most eloquent and adept code switchers. While Galindo's interviews offer Hinojosa-Smith an opportunity to display his virtuoso ear for individual voices, with Jehú's letters the reader enters into Hinojosa's world at its best, the witty and deceptively fluid linguistic terrain of the U.S. picaro. In his letters to Rafa, Jehú's code switching sounds entirely natural; yet it responds to very precisely applied expectations. Talk about the bank tends to be in English, as that is the dominant language of that space; talk about the community is in Spanish. Where the two worlds meet, often in Jehú's persona, language itself follows the letter writer into an interstitial position: "no veía que vela tenía yo en ese happy entierro pero allí andaba & ever watchful" (34). Likewise with other characters who seem to fall outside community mores: "La consentida es la Sammie Jo: two marriages, no kids, pero eso tú ya lo sabes" (14). Jehú's language in these letters is entirely comfortable with itself, and the complexity of its construction tends to be obscured by its ostensible wholeness, the obvious completeness of the map he composes.

And yet, here we are brought up short once again, for the novel *Mi querido Rafa* is a fragmentary one, a very partial record of a short period of time and a still-unresolved mystery. The bits and pieces of this tale are only very tentatively brought together in some provisional order by P. Galindo, but the certainty of his proximate death leaves him very little time for editorial polishing. Thus, the reader falls almost unresistingly into the seductive trap of Klail's small-town storytelling, only to realize that this most delicious gossip is almost entirely an excuse that offers a consummate artist the opportunity to polish his skill. The singular sense of place and the always doubled sense of language rub against each other in a chronotope that is also a locus for provisional solidarities.

Of all the authors under analysis in this chapter, it is Dolores Prida who provides the most straightforward depiction of the bilingual dilemma in her *Coser y cantar*, a popular and frequently performed play (it is, for example, a staple production for New York City's Repertorio Español). As in all her works, in this one-act play Prida explores the conjunctions between gender and biculturalism; here, as elsewhere, she focuses on the challenges confronting the hyphenated American woman. Prida divides the set for the play into two mirror-image rooms, one stereotypically Caribbean Latina, the other stereotypically white middle class, each inhabited by one side of a single character, and speaking to that personality fragment's concerns, fears, and hopes. In a prefatory note to the play script, Prida warns, "This piece is really one long monologue. The two women are one and are playing a verbal, emotional game of ping pong. Throughout the action, except in the final confrontation, ELLA and SHE never look at each other, acting independently, pretending the other one does not really exist, although each continuously trespasses on the other's thoughts, feelings and behavior" (49). The back-and-forth conflictual exchanges between Ella and She, between the two languages and the dramatized elements representing the two cultures, are cemented in the claustrophobia of the apartment space, from which there is no exit. Thus, the limitations of the crowded apartment, doubly inhabited by the seemingly irreconcilable sides of the divided self, answer to a particular spatial arrangement that is bound up in the immobility foisted on the woman by her sense of dislocation from her home culture and not-quite arrival in the United States.

The most important leitmotif in this play is that of the (real?, metaphysical?, ontological?) map that will ostensibly allow the character to reintegrate her split identity, to leave the room, to navigate her new reality. Most typically, this search for the map is conducted at Ella's instigation, in her much messier side of the room. Early in the play, Ella begins to search among the clutter in her half of the space: "¿Dónde habré puesto el mapa? Juraría que estaba debajo del Santo" (53), a hunt that takes on an increasingly frenetic energy as the play goes on: "Tengo que encontrar ese mapa" (61). Finally, the search comes to culmination as the two women look at each other directly for the first time at the very end of the play, as they jointly shudder in fear over the gunshots outside their window and utter the last line of the play, spoken simultaneously: "El mapa"/"Where's the map?" (67). The answer to this question necessarily lies with the audience, outside the boundary of the performance space, but the weight given to its symbolic importance brings us back sharply to the women in the staged room.

While the consciousness of duality is common enough to give rise to the cliché "being of two minds" about something when full conviction is lacking, in Prida's case, the mind is divided along linguistic lines, fracturing language against the push and pull of sharply contrary psychic demands: a yearning to turn inward and re-create the homeland versus the desire to integrate oneself into U.S. society through assimilation to assumed dominant culture values. Prida's doubled character, thus, finds herself literally in a threshold situation, signaled in the play by the invisible barrier splitting the room, by the doorway she cannot cross into the U.S. public space, and by the window that separates the warring self from the violence she intuits/imagines/sees on the street outside. The imagined attacks come at all levels: ranging from physical danger to environmental threats to assaults on her sense of identity: "No one is safe out there. No one, not even those who speak good English. Not even those who know who they are" (51). Later, She asks again: "Are we safe? Yes, we are safe. We're safe here . . . No, we're not! They can shoot through the window" (54). This doubt about the integrity of her dramatic space of refuge continues to the end of the play, where, speaking simultaneously, Ella cries, "¡Yo no salgo de aquí" at the same time as She demands, "Let's get out of here!" (67). At different points in the play, the need to leave the room becomes imperative. The woman speaks of going out jogging, of becoming involved in activist causes: "Salvar a El Salvador/Go to the march at the U.N." (52). The bottom line, though, is that while the character can imagine other spaces—not only a life lived fully in the bustling metropolis of New

York, but also the remembered attractions of blue seas and tropical beaches or a romantic interlude in Athens, for instance—she cannot motivate herself to actually cross the threshold into the threateningly foreign public sphere outside the window of her New York apartment.

Unsurprisingly, one important side of this dual personality continually threatens to tip the character into an ultimately nonproductive nostalgia, living in an imagined past of a Caribbean idyll rather than engaging productively with the present and future:

> SHE: . . . that feeling of belonging, of being home despite . . .
>
> . . . .
>
> ELLA: ¡Ay, siento que me viene un ataque de nostalgia!
>
> SHE: Let's wallow!
>
> ELLA: ¡Ay, sí, un disquito! . . . ¡Aaay, esta nostalgia me ha dado un hambre!
>
> SHE: That's the problem with nostalgia—it's usually loaded with calories! (62–63)

Nostalgia, suggests Prida in this and other passages, is seductive, but also unfulfilling. In this exchange between Ella and She, the latter's ironic commentary defuses a reactionary sentiment with humor, but reminds the audience that the character Ella/She is at a crossroads of sorts. Neither the wallowing in nostalgia nor the rootless dedication to U.S.-defined causes serves as a panacea to assuage the character's besetting spiritual and moral hunger.

The subtitle to *Coser y cantar* is a "one-act bilingual fantasy for two women," and without providing a solution to the ongoing struggle to come to terms with her New York existence, suggests bracing doses of specifically feminine fantasy to counteract the character's delicious but unsatisfying dips into nostalgia. When Ella decides to give herself the "Usted y sus fantasías" quiz found in her copy of *Vanidades* (57), Ella contrasts her own "fantasías heróicas" (58), in which she imagines herself in the role of Joan of Arc, with what that character considers She's trivial and too-explicit "fantasías eróticas" about a Greek lover in Athens. They accuse each other: "You are too romantic/¡y tú eres muy promiscua!" (59). The character remains split between the soft-porn romantic tales of Corín Tellado (57) with their reassuringly inevitable heterosexual happy endings, and the fashionable urban angst of her new homeland, where the heterosexual pairings hit comic snags: "tu problema es que ves demasiadas películas de Woody Allen, y ya te crees una neoyorquina neurótica" (66). Ella/She is an immigrant everywoman who plays out an internal debate as a dialogue between competing idealized images of the self from within a refuge/safe house of her mind. The parameters drawn for the performance, however, also shift between the Caribbean sensual (but romantic rather than erotic) woman and, as Ella suggests with her reference to Woody Allen, the New York neurotic. The refuge, appropriately enough, is also a trap.

One of the central conflicts in the play between the two sides of the divided self involves terms that would be extremely familiar to Bruce-Novoa. What is at stake is the status of memory, and of the symbolic artifacts (here, stage props) that anchor a particular ideal construction of identity as real or authentic. Of course, the dramatic event itself highlights the performative nature of both these identities-in-process, which can only insist upon their strength in the context of a fundamental insecurity as represented by their own recognizably clichéd styles and by the dis-recognition of the equal and opposite other. Ella proclaims her priority over her New York–spawned alter ego: "Yo tengo mis recuerdos. . . . Yo tengo solidez. Tengo unas raíces, algo de que agarrarme. Pero tú . . . ¿tú de que te agarras?" (66), while She accuses her counterpart: "I think you *don't want* to remember your dreams. You always want to be going somewhere but now you're stuck here with me, because outside it's raining blood and you have been to all the places you can possibly ever go to!" (61). For Ella/She, the homing desire is split into two equally powerful tropes: the extremely powerful acculturating impulse directed future forward and centering on New York, and the equally compelling myth locked into an idealized past that looms just beyond the horizon as a dream of lost perfection. "Do you know what regret means?" (55) asks She at one point. With this question, Prida suggests that the negotiation involved in the bicultural identity is not just performative, but also includes a fundamental norming impulse; the value judgment implied in having or not having regrets suggests the parameters of an individually policed regulatory mechanism.

This mechanism, in *Coser y cantar* as in all Prida's best-known works, operates most notably through the register of gender. The play's title picks up on a familiar cliché about the unreflective ease of a woman's (presumably happily-ever-after heterosexually coupled) life. At a crucial moment in the play, Ella picks up on this old saying and turns it around: "Mi mamá me dijo una vez que la vida, sobre todo la vida de una mujer, era coser y cantar. Y yo me lo creí. Pero ahora me doy cuenta que la vida . . . es en realidad, comer y cagar . . . ¡en otras palabras, la misma mierda!" (57). The line is played for humor, and always gets laughs in production. More important, the shift in Ella's perspective reflects a change in her understanding of which she is not yet aware. Her *choteo* is typically Caribbean, but the arc of her humorous aside reminds the audience that Ella, as well as She, is already in and of herself a divided being. The woman's life was never just "coser y cantar," but it is only from the perspective of her present existence that she has been able to critique, at the same time as she nostalgically evokes, that past understanding. The bicultural identity, hints Prida, is always being produced by contact and mixture, and unlike the superficiality of "coser y cantar," which is dainty and feminine and almost disembodied, the more earthy "comer y cagar" involves concretely taking something into the body—and then expelling some unwanted remainder, which nevertheless persists, smelling up the room, as a reminder of both the imagined past and the invented present.

And yet, at same time that Prida underscores her character's nostalgia for a lost wholeness and sense of belonging, her still-unresolved search for cohesiveness in this new situation, her intuition that at bottom it's all a pile of shit, the playwright in other contexts stresses that her work underlines the advantages of duality: "Biculturalism is a positive energy. . . . We are the truest Americans because we combine the two Americas" (Feliciano 116). Ultimately, the character needs to find a place for the past, to incorporate and understand it in the context of her current experience and her conflicted sense of not quite belonging, but without slipping into unproductive melancholia. Alberto Sandoval makes a similar point in his study of this play, reading beyond the ending to the larger implication that *Coser y cantar* is itself the road map that the character so urgently seeks: "At this crux, Anglo laws of assimilation collide with her Latina cultural survival instincts of dissociation. . . . For this reason, Ella must re-construct a new subjectivity—a bilingual/bicultural self in constant making—who refuses to be decentered, discontinuous, displaced at the margin" ("Dolores Prida" 237).

Importantly, given the play's almost mathematically precise half-English, half-Spanish text, Prida insists that the play is not solely aimed at bilingual audiences, noting that "I get better reviews for my plays in Spanish, even from English-speaking critics" who are unable to follow the dialogue in Spanish (Feliciano 114). With respect to *Coser y cantar,* she reflects that in her conception of the drama, "language is the third character. If you do this play in one language it doesn't work. . . . Monolingual people who see *Coser* may get only half the story, but they'll get an inkling of the other half. Or else they just won't get it." In this sense, once again, Prida's position sounds strikingly similar to that of Lugones and Gómez Peña. That monolingual audiences from either Spanish or English are invited to experience the play and undergo a sense of partial exclusion is very much to the point, creating a different but not invalid response. In fact, to some extent the play is predicated on the existence of such an audience, if not always in the safe space of the theater, then certainly outside its doors. At the same time, says Prida, "Latinos have another way of looking at the world and *Coser* explores those differences. We will always remain outside of both Spanish and English monolingual cultures, never fully understood by either one" (Feliciano 115). It is important to recognize in this comment a particular and powerful kind of agency that Prida ascribes to Latino/as to the exclusion of either of their intersecting monocultures. The monocultural individual is severely limited in this context; she cannot understand more than her own narrow vision of the world; biculturals understand all three: Spanish, English, and the hybrid bicultural identity.

"Theatre is not literature; theatre is to be 'done,' not read, seen, not imagined," says Prida in a testimonial note ("Show" 183). Prida's comment raises the always knotty problem in the performing genres about what is seen and who is seeing it. In New York City, where Prida's plays are continually part of the repertoire in Spanish-language theater, the traditional mainstream theatergoing audience is largely white. When her recent play, "Four Guys Named José . . . and una mujer named María" opened off-Broadway, rather than in one of her traditional nonprofit venues, producer Dasha Epstein was aware of the marketing challenge Prida's work poses, which she construed as luring diverse Latino/a groups to this musical review. To this end, the producer came up with a unique approach; she convinced her godson, Enrique Iglesias, to lend his name to the project "as a producer in name only." The ploy worked, and during the play's run (September 2000–March 2001) attendance by Puerto Rican, Dominican, Mexican, and Cuban-Americans gradually and steadily built, alongside a 20 to 30 percent white audience (Navarro).

Still, Prida's work naturally speaks in different ways to her divided audience. While she states on the one hand that "an Hispanic playwright writes American plays about other Americans who are also Hispanic. The language is not important," on the other hand, Prida has very specific and critical messages she wants sent, about, for instance, the woman's struggle with cultural pressures to assimilate in *Coser y cantar.* Too often, she fears, the more subtle conflicts in her work result in its being shunted aside by the white establishment, where axiomatically what sells to a white audience are the more negative stereotypes about Latino/as: drug dealers, gang members, welfare mothers. "Write about oppression in the South Bronx and people don't want to hear about it," she says. "They don't want to know about problems around the corner" (Feliciano 118). Almost automatically, these problems become flattened out since the characters in her work must have identifiable qualities to reach at least three potential audiences: Latin American, U.S. dominant culture, and bicultural, bilingual Latino/a.

Thus, Prida's short monologue in two voices, which moves dialectically between two personifications of a divided self, also moves between the two recognizable stereotypes of the traditional Latina:

romantic, emotional, superstitious, and overweight but concerned with looking her best for a man, and the assimilated modern U.S. woman, who is openly sexual, rational, drawn to activist causes, and diet obsessed. The simple, claustrophobic set and the two women occupying that space for the time of the performance, therefore, pose a somewhat larger conundrum than I first suggested with my comment about the straightforwardness of the argument in this text. Just as the two voices weave together into the true character of the play—an abstract quality that Prida calls "language"—they can only do so in the consciousness of a triple audience that is differentially included in and excluded from full participation. Indeed, the full enjoyment of the play requires the (at least imaginary) participation of monolingual English, monolingual Spanish, and bilingual audience members. Here too the unintelligibility of the language(s) for a large portion of the potential audience plays off against the overly intelligible bodies and props that dangerously skirt on cliché.

CLEARING THE VOICE: BRASCHI

Prida's "emotional game of ping pong" echoes with on some level with Braschi's "yo yo" in their mutual appeal to a trope that captures the restless movement of the "I" between two poles. Both resist the pressure to flatten out complexities of an existence that remains stubbornly multiple. Both function best in a performatively savvy awareness of the unspoken potential in the clash of voices, whether on the page or in the theater, though the Puerto Rican poet, in contrast with the Cuban American playwright, "doesn't play the assimilation blues" (Sommer and Vega-Merino 18). In this sense, writers as seemingly straightforward as Prida and as obstinately opaque as Braschi come together in a shared understanding of the jazzy musicality of the spoken word, and differ enormously in their fundamental approaches to aesthetic and epistemological impulses. Where it remains possible to read Prida, for example, allegorically, Braschi's very different aesthetics foreclose the option of reading her work in that mode.

"When cultures confront one another in this contested space of media interpretation and recontextualization, new opportunities arise for . . . 'reciprocal translation' " (18) says Rodowick hopefully, in an introduction to a special topic focus on "mobile citizens, media states" in the January 2002 issue of the *PMLA*. The burden of Rodowick's comments in this context is to bridge to Gómez Peña from his discussion of Chamber's enlarged concept of translation as decoupled from geography. Chambers works with translation in terms of transit, transition, and the transitory, where language rather than geography defines a sense of home; Gómez Peña with an always estranged and defamiliarizing reading of deterritorialization. Later in the same cluster of articles, Foster's analysis of Guillermo Gómez Peña's performances and texts raises a cognate issue, by emphasizing that the work of the Mexican American cultural artist "embod[ies] a concept of spatial relations defined in terms of motion, flux, and relationality, qualities more typically associated in Western philosophical modernity with temporal experience" (46). Tangentially, then, Foster picks up the question of a potential "reciprocal translation," which is always fraught in Latino/a bicultural texts, as there is a generally well-founded suspicion that the reciprocity somehow always seems to occur as framed through the terms of discourse set up by the dominant critical epistemology. This knowledge system shapes claims about translation through too-easily assimilable understandings of transparency and betrayal. In Foster's reading of Gómez Peña, much of the importance of that performer's work involves reframing agency around the staged resistance to understood norms of clear communication, around refusals to speak such that speech/silence/babble becomes a way around the containments of monological national discourse as well as a way to trouble claims about the possibility of translation of any sort, one-way or reciprocal.

Common to all these scholars is a speculation about a basic reorganization of critical axes from something like the cluster space/identity/authenticity to one that emphasizes time/contingency/performance—perhaps even larger-than-life performance. Over and over again, we see in these writers an effort to disconnect identity from space, privileging instead the concepts of motion and flux. Paul Virilio, one of the leading scholars of contemporary information-age angst, in his *Information Bomb* tendentiously argues that "we are not seeing an 'end of history,' but we are seeing an end of geography. . . . [P]olitical frontiers were themselves to shift from the real space of geopolitics to the 'real time' of the chronopolitics of the transmission of images and sounds" (9, 13). In his reading, modern globalization demonstrates not just economic and ecological effects but also what he calls "the pollution of distances and delays which make up the world of concrete experience" (116). What Virilio describes, often with a warning as to its potential negative effect, Braschi celebrates—or mostly celebrates. Hers is an extreme case for dislocated narratives of this type: highly mobile, transnational or cosmopolitan, detached from spatial coordinates and favoring a layering of voices in pseudo–real time.

The inevitable fate of images in such a context, says Virilio, following Bachelard, is enlargement (13). Almost unavoidably, then, when we turn to from Hinojosa-Smith and Prida to exploring the implications of the mock-autobiographic mode favored by authors like Braschi, the "I" looms large in this speeded-up, postmodern song of the self. It is no coincidence that the second and longest of the three sections in *Yo-Yo Boing!* is titled "Blow-Up," echoing not only the process of photographic enlargement but also that of a violent explosion. From another perspective, this enlarged picture of the self meshes neatly with a deeply layered and highly allusive international literary and cultural history that includes Italian Michelangelo Antonioni's famous 1966 film, *Blow-up* as well as Argentine Julio Cortázar's story, "Las babas del diablo," on which the film was based. In both these earlier works, and implicitly in the Puerto Rican's novel as well, the plot turns on the enlargement of a particular chance photograph that powers the absurdist thriller as well as the magical realist story. Braschi's brash (auto)biographical novel-poem, by appropriating this title, clearly sets itself in dialogue and on a par with these canonical twentieth-century greats. In her work, as in the earlier models to which she alludes, technology and timing open up onto chance revelations, albeit ambivalently framed and ambiguously interpreted ones.

Generally speaking, in Braschi, in contrast with Hinojosa-Smith and Prida, the anchored claims of space give way to economies of speed. Decoupling ethnicity from the specificities of local geography attenuates the familiar discourse of authenticity even more insistently, and in ways that are not available to the already problematized interrogations of the Texan and the Cuban American. Braschi reminds the reader of her work's nature as a critical practice or trope, always a (self-consciously, ironically) staged performance of a discursive fiction rather than the thing, "authenticity" itself. No longer is it so much that the question of identity is at stake in the narrative, but rather that of an agency unmoored from the grounding discourse of identity, of agency conceived as performance—constructed and staged. This performance is of an enlarged but also fragmented self/image. Visweswaran, in another context, calls this modality the "deliberate concatenation of the partial account with the partial(ly revealed)identity," and she continues, "For this reason, I attempt a move from the history of the fragment (or partial account) to its epistemology" (91). In other words, the anthropologist, like the poet-memorialist Giannina Braschi, wants to go beyond a reading of the fragmented agent in a familiar epistemological structure into an organization of knowledge that is itself fluid, situated, relational. Says Braschi, "lo importante es que ninguno tenga una frontera," and because borders involve "enredaderas que nos creen ataduras a la tierra, yo siempre miro el horizonte más allá del mar" (202–03).

In all of these culture critics, the focus comes to rest on the constantly changing "now." Curiously enough, this move was anticipated by Trilling, and he explores its implications in an unlikely site, through his discussion of Jane Austen's *Mansfield Park*, a classic nineteenth-century postage-stamp novel of country-house manners. He says in the conclusion of his analysis that the striking originality of the novel has something to do with the fact that

> [i]t is antipathetic to the temporality of the dialectical mode; the only moment of judgment it acknowledges is *now*: it is in the exigent present that things are what they really are, not in the unfolding future. A work of art informed by so claustral a view might well distress our minds, might well give rise to anxiety. And not least because we understand it to be saying that even the reality of the reader himself is not, as he might wish to think, what it may become, but ineluctably what it is now. This is a dark thought . . . one that detaches us from the predilections of our culture. (79–80)

Certainly Trilling's "dark" perspective on the restriction of reality to the now has been revisited and revised in recent analyses where anchoring in the moment has been freed from geography as has come to be understood in terms of its more expansive potential. Rather than a dark and claustral limitation, the exploration of the now offers contemporary readers the deracinated ecstasies of the almost unlimited information highway. Thus, for example, Virilio proclaims: "Henceforth, *here no longer exists: everything is now.* The end of our history has not happened, but we do have the programmed end of the *hic et nunc* and the *in situ*" (*Information* 116). The burden of Virilio's observation is that the "here" and "the site" require rethinking when parsed against the power of the now, with its access to velocities of change, and that this rethinking has explosive potential. Thus, for example, while like Prida's, Braschi's work is presumably sited in New York City, in this book the spatial referent is mediated by a sensibility akin to Virilio's; it is both highly specific and metaphorically, temporally, and even geographically unanchored:

> —New York es una lata de resonancias y una lata de atardeceres y sonidos—resounding—resounding—resounding.
>
> . . .
>
> —It's the last great European city. And the first great American city.
>
> —And the capital of Puerto Rico.
>
> —On the verge of collapsing.
>
> —This city has always been apocalyptic. (128–29)

New York in this context is not an actual site, but rather a fictional construct that serves as a kind of floating signifier to measure the contemporary moment, collapsing past and future, ends and beginnings, Europe and the United States, North and South. New York also, as Julio Ortega reminds us in a 2001 article in the Spanish newspaper *El país,* offers one of the most dynamic and swiftly evolving spaces for a rich and profoundly international Spanish:

> Hoy existen en Estados Unidos no sólo las entonaciones nacionales de 20 países en los que se habla el español, sino las versiones léxicas regionales, los giros y decires de distintas épocas, las normas interpoladas y las sumas híbridas, a tal punto que deben haberse generado matrices de la diversidad, esto es, modelos de habla que organizan las diferencias. Es lo que ocurre con el habla española de Manhattan, de entonación general dominicana, cuyo carácter aglutinante es capaz de incorporar porteño bonaerense y criollo chalaco de Perú. (np)

While Juan Flores, among others would argue strongly that the predominant cultural strain against which the newer Latino/as measure themselves continues to be Puerto Rican (still the largest group, as well as the most settled) rather than Dominican, Ortega's point about the richness and dynamism of Spanish in New York City is well taken.

Of course, even in Virilio the "now" can only be measured against the reminders of the past and the place that have been rejected or reformulated; that which no longer exists still sets the parameters for contemporary work. In Braschi this difficult access to the now is most often figured in performative riffs on an ironically cited literary history which is also a specific kind of formal meditation articulated through a tight focus on a single character. For instance, at one point the narrator comments cryptically, as if she is unable to figure either past or present in suitably literary form: "I don't know where my carpe diem is. . . . And ubi sunt regrets: *where is it?* I'm here" (135). The "here," however, is a highly provisional one, always in motion. Echoing early twentieth-century Spanish poet Antonio Machado, Giannina Braschi—like her predecessor—also proclaims her intention to "hacer el camino al andar," paying homage to and parodically troping a sensibility akin to Trilling's. And yet, in doing so, she recuperates the insistence on movement while giving the controlling anxiety a contemporary twist: "hacia adelante nadie sabe a dónde vamos . . . y hemos perdido de vista lo que dejamos atrás" (202), she writes, and, "puedo seguir hablando porque el agua sigue corriendo y yo sigo caminando . . . : por qué yo—ahora—y no ayer. Por qué yo en este momento—y no en otro momento. . . . Y por qué ahora—y no antes—soy yo, la que ahora y no antes tiene razón en inculparse" (196). What are parsed here are the shifting and incompatible allegiances of a fictional character as she moves through a fluid cityscape, an "exigent present" to use Trilling's words, that offers the contemporary poet a mode of be-ing through the ephemeral rhythms of speech. Maria Mercedes Carrión speaks of Braschi's "lettered world view" in her article on the Puerto Rican poet's earlier work, *Imperio de los sueños,* and she adds in terms that are applicable to the later work as well, "this poetic voice realizes as well that reading has now turned into an empire of dreams in which writing and letters tell their own stories" (168). The stories, like the reading and the writing, are always provisional.

Braschi's narrator gives us a clue as to the nature of this text when she comments, "Wouldn't it be wonderful to write a book all your life—a book that's about your life with all the elements of a biography—but it's not an autobiography. Not a Dream Play. Not a novel. Not a poem" (178). In another modality, says reviewer Persephone Braham: "*Yo-Yo Boing!* is not really a novel. In fact, much of it seems more biographical than fictional. . . . Various passages imply that the text might better be read as poetry, as a musical composition, or as drama but as Jean Franco's jacket blurb suggests, perhaps the most adequate label for it would be performance" (np). The text itself is restless, refusing to settle down. Here too, we intuit the clash between biography and performance—or the recognition that in some sense all biography is necessarily performative in nature and social situational in form.

Since Braschi is well known as an excellent reader/performer of her work, for a certain audience the text will always be overlaid by a persona who appears in public, dressed in a particular way, and speaking performatively of a character whose life and works coincide with the author's own. Perhaps one way to think of this book is as a performance text akin to the published scripts of analogous performance texts by John Leguizamo, Alina Troyano (Carmelita Tropicana), or Guillermo Gómez Peña, where the various voices resolve into a series of roles played by a single individual, and where the geographies alluded to are always excessive, invented, provisional. In this sense, the two dust-jacket photographs of the author echo the role played by still photographs in the texts of fellow performance artists. In this case, she presents herself to us in costume for her performance: painted and stern on the front cover, mischievously smiling on the back—two characters from the repertoire.

Yet if Braschi's is an autobiographically based performance, even in this context of highly self-referential performance art it is a biography and a performance of a very peculiar sort, one that constantly circles around the negation of the character that it is beginning to define. Despite its many references (real or fictional) to the life of the author, one of the interlocutors warns that "a nadie le interesa tu biografía personal" (69), and any expectations of insight into the poetic persona are continually frustrated by the narrator's fragmenting and contradictory voices. Furthermore, the book is also a very literary one, difficult to conceive as a fully staged event except on the stage of the imagination, as a kind of cocktail chitchat in her head among personality fragments. The middle section of the novel most saliently highlights this clever, cutting dialogue interspersed with occasional short meditative or transitional material. In addition, long passages at the beginning and end of the novel take the shape of densely allusive and highly poetic streams of consciousness: "me miro en los espejos y descubro a otra persona que me está mirando a mí. Pero quién soy yo si yo no me descubro en ninguna de las dos personas que se están mirando . . . ya olvidé quién soy y vuelvo a ser el olvido que olvida que se olvidó quién era yo. Ya soy la que soy sin ser quien fui" (196–97).

This is, as noted above, a novel in three parts. The first and third parts ("Close-Up" and "Black-Out"), each eleven pages long, are written entirely in stream of consciousness and in Spanish; reviewers have by and large considered these sections the most successful writing in the book for their finely tuned perceptions and tight composition. It is a difficult feat to sustain, however, and the looser, longer, far more raucous second part of the book opens up the solipsistic gaze to a (perhaps imaginary) dialogism. The middle section of the text, "Blow-Up," which includes the remaining 150 pages or so of the novel, is a pastiche of fragmentary bits of mostly academic conversation and citations of past conversations, song lyrics, bits of poems and nursery rhymes, and so forth. Thus, the briefer lyrically contexualizing comments in Spanish frame the enlargement of the long middle section, such that for the bulk of the text the reader of this novel/poem is flooded with bits of trivial information, often apparently contradictory. Much of this section is structured around highly self-referentially fictional exchanges among a small group of intellectuals, many of them based on identifiable scholars, but in context all spun out as refractions of a single narrative entity. Almost by narrative necessity, it is based in the imaginary axis created by New York City that includes both San Juan and Paris. Characters come and go unpredictably and often interchangeably, there are unresolvable dissonances in the unrelenting stream of conversation that makes up the bulk of the text, the plot takes unexpected turns and swerves, and the reader comes to the inescapable conclusion that in this hyperreferential literary world, accumulation serves the ironic function of stripping away narrative pretense: more is definitely less.

At the same time, clusters of references seem to point us in specific directions. The narrator comments that the shape of her text has been influenced by cartoons and computers and fashion shows—an eclectic mix, but all designating framed and layered productions of one sort or another. Film is another favored genre, and references cover the whole of the second half of the twentieth century, from Fellini and Antonioni to Hollywood to *The Crying Game*, generally pointing up the importance of the mutable and multiply perceived physical body as an image existing in virtual space. Music provides yet another set of cultural references. A character describing the fictive work-in-progress explains that "this is a musical composition" (152). Indeed, Braschi mixes opera, salsa, rock, and Mexican folk songs with Barbra Streisand, Frank Sinatra, and *The Sound of Music*, working to capture not only the promiscuously defined cultural referent, but the very sound and rhythm of these different musical genres. In her evocations of musical form, the narrator again takes on all the roles: producer, director, audience: "Cantar . . . con el tono exacto del color de la música. . . . Tenía que aguantar la nota, . . . tenía que dirigirla con la batuta, y a la vez resistir con distancia su invasión, y controlar su emoción, y ser productor, el motor, la velocidad, y a la vez la oreja que escucha el desarrollo. . . . (29). Her poetic allusions (another form of music) include Dickinson, Eliot, and Williams along with Darío, Neruda, and Vallejo, and, from the other side of the ocean, Baudelaire and Rimbaud. What the narrator seems to look for in music/poetry is a quality both temporal and tonal: "I can't fit life into a rhyme scheme. . . . I'm feeling my own rhythm. The velocity of cars—the engines of our time—concords, faxes, guns, and subways. . . . I do not write little poems. I write big books" (141).

While the author may write big books in terms of the traditional expectations about the poetic genre, she is as concerned about the microlevel of her work as the most highly elaborated lyricist. Braschi's attention to tone and rhythm, to the music of her text is extreme. Over and over, her character asks herself variations on the question, "what do I aspire to be: to be inspired" (36), and the dialogic voices respond: "tú no ves que te estoy inspirando" (56), and "how can I inspire you. How can you—**moooooooooo**—inspire me" (109). The theme of inspiration/aspiration (breathing in and out, producing sonic effects) also picks up on an even more subtle play of tone and sound pervasive throughout the work. Early in the text, the narrator makes a game of repetition from the sound of the letter O, a tonal theme that she follows through bilingually as a leitmotif in the whole of the text, as the exclamation "¡OH! ¡OH!" from the end of the first section (the sound of the vowel, the shape of the mouth, the exhalation of breath, the opening and closing of the eyes—"ojos" [30–31]) mutates finally into the title of this work, "YO YO" (95), passing through the phonetic range of sounds represented by the letter O in Spanish and English—

"Oh, no, no Olmo-Olmo. . . . I told you. I don't know if I can do the job. . . . I rolled my tongue again—**oops**—frenó en el paladar" (94–95). The different shapes of English and Spanish, the sensual range of the vowel in its different linguistic permutations, create another possibility for enlargement, for blowing up in its double sense. And, at the same time, the Spanish chain—oh oh—ojo—oh, no, no—yo yo—finds itself stuttering short, braking/breaking against the English phonemic variety represented by the same graphic symbol: you—moo—oops—told—don't—know—do—job—roll—tongue, such that the two languages jostle against each other, complement each other, cancel each other out.

In this small example, we see close up the process of writing, "giving birth through your mouth, through your tongue, to another fragment" (58). For Braschi, this process of alternating close-ups with blowups and blackouts necessarily involves a duplicitous gesture of apparently laying bare the poetic self. The narrator is playful, however, mock-coyly skirting the issue. She comments, for example, at one point that "every day students come to me to bear their souls," and another/same voice joins in: "You bore your soul to us. You lifted your skirt and you said:—Mírame, linda. Mírame a mí" (154). Here, the word "bare" itself is not used, but rather evoked in a sexual gesture, playing at boredom and the homology of bear-bare: blacking out the word as the *narrador* pretends to offer a close-up of her most intimate self, boring her students and the ambiguous "us."

Despite the apparent plethora of characters—lovers, friends, colleagues—who people the central part of this narrative, again and again Braschi hints that her interlocutor is a constructed and highly literary version of herself, doubled in the mirror, refracted in the written text, the "us" of her own reflections. The *narrador* admits cheerfully to her "unabashed narcissism" (173; the writers of the introduction call it her "sometimes overbearing narcissism" [14]), which nevertheless takes an unusual form of poetic license, allowing, for instance, "parnasiana" and "lesbiana" to operate together as substitutable categories (164), and both to define the solipsistic meditations of our narrator–point-of-view character as she tries on different gender and sex roles. Indeed, throughout this narrative, one of the touchstones concerns the very different exchanges provoked by the male interlocutor, who is incapable of full partnership with the poet-*narrador*, and the refracted woman-self, who allows the narrator the illusion of distancing herself from her text and then encountering it again as a lover. The earlier case responds to the opening pages of the middle section of the novel, in which the narrator and her putative male lover enact the final stages of an unproductive, one-way courtship. "Blow-Up" begins aggressively, with a domestic squabble: "—Ábrela tú.—¿Por qué yo? Tú tienes las keys" (36), and continues to trace the dissolution of the floundering partnership. The *narrador* complains, "Why do you insist on bringing me breakfast in bed when you can never satisfy me. . . . Para qué me invitas a comer y me dejas con hambre, insatisfecha" (39, 41). Not only is this male companion inadequate to her needs, throughout the entire section male characters tend in general to provoke a Bloomian anxiety of influence. They knowingly or unwittingly deprive her spiritually, or, in the incorporated version of the poetic process deployed most commonly as a character in the second part of the work, they try their best, but leave her sexually and physically hungry.

On the one hand, the male character seems to figure access to the Anglo-American world, as in "my book needs your English" (44), and the narrator responds to this pressure by acting to establish distance. The character is not mollified: "now you want to kill me off. Esto es lo que me jode de ti, siempre cambiando el plot" (46). On the other hand, the writer's sexual attraction to other women is figured through literary images and poetic representations, including textual refractions of the self. Satisfaction seems more within reach, anxieties ameliorated. Ultimately, however, the lesbian suggestiveness becomes a tease of sorts: the narrator can find pleasure in her own body, but the projective distantiation of self and alter ego into a viable lesbian couple never quite materializes. Thus, the "Mírame linda, Mírame a mí" of the exposed woman in the passage cited above gives her audience insight into her poetry, her soul, rather than the implicitly more crass genitalia that are never quite bared to her lover's eyes. The more shocking and vulgar address—"Cachapera, ven acá, mírate a ti misma en mis ojos" (170)—plays the same function, suggesting a powerful sexual charge, but resolving ultimately into a soulfelt gaze rather than the sexuality hinted at in "cachapera." In the final analysis, the sensual-sexual play of genders/genres, whether lesbian or heteronormative, cannot be resolved except in abstract form: "eres la más grande de todas las mujeres, eres el hombre más bello de todos los hombres, eres mi poesía" (191). Once again, the act of seeing oneself in the other's eyes, like the experience of reading poetry, images a sensuality accessed through the eye and ear, metaphorically seemingly to interpellate the body, but not quite.

What kind of knowledge is Braschi admitting or producing in these slippery tropic forms? There is a compelling confessional quality in the early pages of this novel's first section, the apparent stripping bare of the self in its most intimate activities, and this metaphor is carried through playfully in other parts of the novel as well—but what does this activity compel? We might posit that, like any canny performer or strip teaseartist, the narrative voices in this text stage certain aspects of revelatory practice, not showing all despite the uncovering gesure, intentionally leaving us unsatisfied. Doris Sommer and Alexandra Vega-Merino's introduction seems to point to this reticence, even as it underscores the richness of Braschi's range of reference and the Babelish confusion she sometimes stirs up: "the book refuses to decide between performing in English and revelling in Spanish" (11). The performing, the reveling, and the refusing all define typical rhetorical strategies in this text. It is playful and stagey, an autobiographically inspired text but not an exposé; it never tells us all, though it often seems to tell us too much, dizzying the reader with a plethora of often banal details seemingly chosen for their sonic qualities rather than to forward plot, revelation, readerly satisfaction.

Sommer and Vega-Merino note that in this book "sometimes the esthetic effects seem to be more off-putting than engaging. . . . *Yo Yo Boing!* flaunts its unfinished business" (16). Along similar lines, in her review, Braham describes the book as blend of engaging and frustrating, intelligent and sophomoric, ambitious and banal: "This is a rigorously self-revelatory but undisciplined book by a talented bilinguist. While Braschi proves that poesy need not depend exclusively on a code of universals, nor narrative on plot (nor literature on monolingualism), she mixes in one genre too many, trapping her potentially fascinating examination of the creative process inside a biography" (np). Certainly Braschi is aware of, and even celebrates, the uneven texture of her work. As she notes in a brief, manifesto-like statement, "toda mi obra es una sola—y la llamo el manifiesto de los huevos poéticos—se hace mostrando los huevos, metiendo la pata, pisseando aquí y pisseando allá" ("Pelos" 50). In this brief comment, Braschi captures and plays with the multiple significations of the word "huevos" to hint at the layered quality she intentionally strives at: her work is ballsy ("mostrar huevos"), involves a specifically feminine creative act ("poner huevos"), is chock-full of poetic flaws ("meter la pata"), and likely to piss some people off as she passes by.

Braschi is frustrating. She is also, I suspect, deeply intellectually engaged by the problem I identified earlier in this chapter as a tension around the question of "authentic" latinidad in relation to the notorious and symptomatic metaphorical pathologizing of the bicultural individual through the use of the term "schizophrenic." Typically, Braschi would like to eschew both terms, if not the implication of their ideological force, although at one key point in her dialogic exchanges, the schizophrenic comes forcefully into play in a discussion of the poet/narrator's literary style:

—Se cree que todo es diálogos. . . .

—Y los personajes tuyos se te escapan.

—Es una alegoría de los perdidos. . . .

—Esquizo-realismo.

—Mi escuela no se llamaba esquizo-realismo. Se llamaba Taller del Cuento.

—Esquizo-realismo.

—Dale con esquizo-realismo.

—Es que me parece más original. Lo único que no me gusta es la alusión a la psicología. (162)

Here, the "schizophrenic" describes a particular kind of stylistic or genre choice, comically analogous to "Taller del Cuento." At the same time, the figure of allegory—always problematic in Braschi—also reconnects with realism of a particular sort, and the putative allegorical schizo-realism helps respond to the critical concerns about a text bridging novel and autobiography, prose and poetry, mediating observations like "Space is what images are about, ordering boarders" (137) and "This is the divorce of true minds" (158). Nancy Gray Díaz says that "Braschi retains for us an anxiety of identity combined with a joy in the release from the stasis and fixedness of identity. . . . The poem is movement, body, thus also action and agency" (336). To some extent, in the confusion of these boarders/borders Braschi commits herself and her reader to a state of indeterminacy, to the looking-glass worlds of computers and television, where the grounding contextualization is always what is least available to analysis.

At the same time, the poetic voice here is determinedly Puerto Rican *and* broadly American, born in the United States and denying neither of her cultural heritages. When at a particular moment in the ongoing dialogues her conversation partner of the moment accuses her of selling out her identity to try to become American, she responds, "no tengo que llegar a ser lo que soy" (167). If the fragmentation of character in the dialogic format hints at the inevitable divisions in the self, the overriding ethos of this volume is of unity within a dialogic frame rather than any pathologizing discourse. Braschi's narrator ultimately and emphatically stresses the "yo soy," in the moment of that plenitude, rather than either multiplicity or a sense of (deferred) becoming. This conclusion is borne out by the final section of the novel, in which the mirrored "I" finally resolves itself in a conversation among equals—Giannina, Hamlet, and Zarathustra—each carrying a corpse, but each continuing on his/her own road. Giannina argues passionately: "estoy en mí misma con lo que soy por dentro. Con lo que tengo por dentro. . . . No me importan los vejigantes ni las quimeras" (204).

And yet, of course, being a Puerto Rican American presents specific challenges. A bit earlier in the second-section dialogue referred to above, the narrator comments, in an exchange with her poetic alter ego, "tenemos que empezar a romper las murallas entre nuestras dos Américas. Y nosotros—tú y yo—tenemos que ser las portavoces, somos bilingües"; to which her (male?) interloctutor responds, "no podemos ser embajadores porque no tenemos un país. Debido a que Puerto Rico no es un país . . . yo no puedo establecerme como gran poeta." The narrator angrily rejects this reasoning as specious and self-serving: "Si yo no soy gran poeta, no le voy a echar la culpa a mi pueblo porque es una colonia. No, yo tengo la culpa" (167). Here, as elsewhere, Braschi dramatizes something similar to the more-Latino-than-thou concerns noted in the opening pages of this chapter, marking intelligently the intersection of freedom and guilt—the perverse freedom from guilt that comes with the weight of oppression, the burden of that unearned freedom, the loss of freedom and self implied by carrying around unproductive dead weights.

One of the ways by which Braschi begins to break down walls in her two Americas, her two "yo"s, is through her use of Spanglish. Though recognizably Nuyorican in its basic rhythmic structures, nevertheless, as the authors of the introduction to the text remind us, "Braschi's crossovers and puns are not part of a common, shared, established, and ready-made Spanglish. . . . Instead they aspire to a signature originality, like poetry does" (16). From a purist's perspective, her Spanish is contaminated and her English often intentionally awkward, as for example in the following elocutions: "I think we should dedicate to the structure," "I swear on my father's lungs," "you'll be . . . revolting all my gavetas with your hot hands" (44–45), "I don't treason the people I love" (65), and "I can't treason you" (103). She enjoys taking well-known poetic lines and pronouncements from canonical poets and displacing them by translating them into the opposite language, often leaving hints of their origin in the slight hitch to the rhythm and word choice: "Lo que madura se pudre. Prefiero ser verde" or "I would like to walk inexhaustible, walk tireless, walk indefatigable" (131).

Braschi not only writes in this highly stylized, aggressive form of code switching, she also takes the opportunity within the body of the text to foreclose criticism by co-opting the critics' voices. "You must realize you're limiting your audience by writing in both languages. To know a language is to know a culture. You neither respect one nor the other," says one interlocutor (142). Another attacks from the Spanish-speaking Latino/a side: "Todo que me leíste el otro día. Este está lleno de inglés. Quiero más español. Claro, la mezcla de lenguas es un problema de tu clase social. Yo no tengo ese problema. Tú discutes en inglés la parte filosófica, y le dejas al español la expresión de los sentimientos. Van a asociarlo con el estereotipo que tienen del hispano" (161). There is no possible resolution to this ideological problem. The long second section, "Blow-Up," can only define its parameters and register the enlargement of the personality fragments who represent the various positions in the dilated "now" of their exploded subjectivity.

The first section, "Close-Up," opens the textual frame with narcissism and enlargement of a different sort. The narrative persona begins by recapitulating her progress into the consciousness of self. The first line of the text is: "comienza por ponerse en cuatro patas, gatea como una niña," and details her first efforts at learning to control body and breath. She brings the reader close to her bodily functions, lovingly describing the sight, smell, and feel of all her eliminations: urinating, contemplating menstrual blood, playing with her excrement, luxuriously squeezing pimples and blackheads, pulling out offending facial hairs. This is the body as manifestly ordinary, held in thrall to the daily necessities of unpoetic, unadorned life. Finally, after an almost painfully long session in the bathroom, the narrator describes the process of putting on her makeup, readying herself for the rest of the narrative, using her face as a canvas or a screen, turning herself into a clown—"un payaso. Toda pintarreteada de blanco, con dos sombras oscuras en los ojos, y dos ciruelas en los cachetes, y los labios listos para darle un beso a un cerezo" (26), projecting an image for public consumption. In this lovingly detailed progress from naive self-absorption to the self-conscious creation of a particular public image, Braschi's narrator equivocally defines the distance between literary and literal, providing the context against which we will measure the passionate confrontations of the second part. The body pitilessly delineated in the opening pages is, ineluctably, a literary body; the self in the mirror offers an unreal double of an imagined self.

The final section of the text, "Black-Out," comes back once more to this bondage to daily necessity, now theorizing the mirror as trap, and focusing on the purposeful movement of the postlapsarian subject. "I'm frontal to my death" (146), says the narrator at one point in the text, and in this final section of a scripted dialogue with Zarathustra and Hamlet, "Giannina" comes closest to a meditation on mortality. Here she keeps in constant motion: "darle otra vuelta a la manzana," which in a play on words is also "la manzana de Adán" (195). Thus, her moving forward brings her always back to the same place, to the same corpse she carries with her, the same knowledge of life, which is also an awareness of her own future death. The book pauses at a crossroads of sorts—"Fui yendo de mí misma para no volver a encontrarme conmigo misma" (196), and cannot come to a more definitive closure because life itself has not yet ended.

This is a human condition, but it is also specifically a Puerto Rican one, her trips around the block echoing the circular migration patterns that often define the Caribbean identity. Where Hinojosa-Smith and Prida come back to the consolations of space as an anchor for the individual character, in Braschi's case, "la única manera en que me siento bien es en el eterno dinamismo de mi ser errante" (200). Braschi can provoke a kind of motion sickness in her readers, a disturbance in our perception of reality; she "trans-locate[s] the limits of this map of cultural and national identity," says Carrión (171). Necessarily, her migrant voice(s) explode traditional concepts about cultural and pyschic space and have a profound effect on geographical figurations and the troping of homespace in the narrative. A Paul Virilio comment offers a compelling way to pull together some of these varied strands. Citing Bill Clinton's 1997 inaugural address, he asks what the president means by "the American Century": "What is it to be, then? An Americanization of the world or the disorders of a pseudo-third worldism extending to assume planetary proportions? And what is an American century anyway? And what, we may ask, is America?" (*Information* 19).

chapter six

Conclusion: Hemispheric American Studies

CONCHA ALBORG (SPAIN), in *Beyond Jet-Lag*, speaks to the increased field offered by having two languages to choose from in her creative work. Like many of the other first-generation writers to whom I have been alluding throughout this book, Alborg describes a sense of never quite arriving, while definitely having left, of remaining in a floating in-between space. Her metaphor, one famously common to many Caribbean writers, is the airplane: "Sometimes I think that I belong flying over the Atlantic, either not quite in Spain yet, but anticipating . . . the trip. Or coming back relieved that I don't have to live there anymore. . . . I want to be American when I'm here, Spanish when I get there. Actually, it works just the opposite and I know it" (7). Alborg's solution is to write about half of the stories in this volume in Spanish and the other half in English. The context determines the language. Thus, her stories about Madrid, the Caribbean, a trip to Nicaragua, an interview with Hispanic writers, a conversation with a U.S.-Venezuelan friend, a visit to a *peluquería* all take place in Spanish. On the other hand, her stories about a trip to the Chicago Art Museum, about a social event in the United States, about her U.S. neighbor all are written in English. These are situational choices, based on the language appropriate to the space in which the story is set, and to that space's cultural expectations.

At the same time, Alborg's knowledge of her own inescapable bifocality, originally described with the metaphor of the airplane and conditioned by her wry recognition of always being slightly out of place, inflects all of these stories. Whether Spanish or English, the other language and other identity ineluctably run under the chosen main voice. Thus, for example, she explains at the beginning of one of the English-language stories, "This is one of those stories that I must write in English, because how would I explain in Spanish what a senior prom is?" (67). Similarly, a later story begins, "The concept of the girl next door doesn't exist in Spanish: someone who represents the goodness, the familiarity of the all-American female. . . . How different it is in French, for example, where 'femme à coté' is rather a temptation" (93). In both these cases, the explanation—why English?—comes from a sense of a lack or deficiency in Spanish to define a cultural nuance as well as an implicit dialogue originally begun in the opposite language from the one used in the story. The projection across languages and cultures is clear. English better captures the concept of the prom, or the sleepover, or the girl next door; yet Alborg feels the urgency to explain these cultural phenomena in a way that is only required for someone coming from, or projecting to, an audience in that other cultural space. In a parallel fashion, from other side, in the Spanish-language story "Alter ego" Alborg writes, "A veces me pregunto cómo hubiese sido mi vida si yo no hubiera emigrado a este país" [sometimes I ask myself what my life would have been like it I hadn't emigrated to this country] (30), where the imagined alter ego's Spanish life is indelibly inflected by the distancing experience of having lived for many years in the United States, and the expression of this concern is anchored linguistically in a double use of the subjunctive mode, a verbal form unavailable to the English speaker.

The crossover between cultures and languages, suggests Alborg, like many of the other authors studied in this book, operates in two directions, not just in the direction of English, but also and at the same time retaining the capacity to move back into the Spanish symbolic orders and inflect and reflect upon those cultural forms as well. Something is always being produced in cultural contact, a mixture, a doubleness, that is often read as performative. This doubleness may pose a challenge to the narrator and her characters; it does not always mean trouble (Butler), schizophrenia (Palumbo-Liu), loss. It may, in fact, be the source of surprisingly valuable insights. It could be a desirable position. Along such lines, Doris Sommer asks, "if you could cure your double consciousness . . . would you want to? Almost everyone else I have asked has answered no" (305).

Authors, texts, and ideas have always moved across international borders; yet to the degree that they confound monolingual and nationally based literary projects, such crossings and meditations have been insufficiently studied even by an academic audience that prides itself on its border-crossing analytic abilities. Ironically, then, we can trace a kind of unconscious critical resistance to the very writers who seem to incarnate the site of the internationalized critical community in their writing, who speak from within the often contradictory spaces of a transborder consciousness, who most strikingly embody the more pertinent observations on transnational cultures in the very weave of their literary works. In this respect, suggests Mike Davis in his articulation of what he calls "the crossover aesthetic," "Latinos are already deeply American, they derive from a North/South divide that is yielding a new geography, and they are thoroughly engaged in the project of further defining what Americanness means" (xvii). Likewise, I would add that they are deeply Latin American, with all the complications deriving from the always already and nearly inevitable presence of the United States in the deepest cultural matrices of their countries of origin.

American dreams, both North and South, are tracked and transmitted in multiple and nuanced ways in these changing relationships. Palumbo-Liu says it well: "as the context for cultural production is dramatically shifted out of a simply articulated local space and placed instead within the nexus of forces that exceed the immediate influences of the local, 'culture' takes place on a shifting terrain that is increasingly contextualized within a dialectal reformulation of local and global" (269). Octavio Paz, in a speech given in Miami in 1987, makes a parallel commentary, focusing his discussion on the breakdown of the old, assumed American symmetry: English in the North, Spanish in the South, and noting the growing bilingualism of many parts of the United States. He also reminded his audience that many canonical works and authors associated with the Hispanic tradition need to be reread biculturally; Federico García Lorca's *Poeta en Nueva York* is a prime example for him, as is Juan Ramón Jiménez's *Espacio* [Space], written in an acute awareness of his surroundings in Coral Gables ("Literatura hispana" 54–55).

In recent years there has been an increasingly urgent call to rethink the United States' relation to America writ large, as well as to the nation's understanding of itself. Alfred Arteaga writes trenchantly: "the presence of an alternative, extant, and *literate* linguistic tradition causes a crisis for Anglo America; not only does it preclude the status for English as sole, unchallenged mode for civilized American discourse, but it also undermines several myths that are at the very heart of the self-image propagated by Anglo America" (22). Almost a decade later, Kirsten Silva Gruesz defines the project of her book, *Ambassadors of Culture,* as "to push Anglophone readers into grappling seriously with Spanish as an essential literary language of the United States." She adds later, echoing Arteaga's challenge, "the challenge posed by the changing demographics of the United States is not so much to accommodate Latinos to an existing national tradition, but to reconfigure that tradition to acknowledge the continuous presence of Latinos within and around it" (xvi, 10).

There is no doubt that much needs to be done. It has been widely noted, for example, that the lack of attention to intellectual work in Spanish often walks hand in hand with a denigration of the language in which that work is articulated. The first step, then, for many scholar-activists is to counter the persistent prejudice in the United States that displays itself in the imbalance of authority between speakers using English and Spanish. Describing that damaging disparity, Laura Callahan writes incisively: "the popular belief persists according to which speaking Spanish is a disadvantage for poor, immigrant children, but an asset for children from a higher socioeconomic class" (420)—though the language's use is often defined in totally instrumental terms. This is a perception that Mike Davis, among others, also echoes in even more pointedly ideological terms: "the ultimate betrayal of Latino children is the demagoguery that asserts that their main 'handicap' is speaking Spanish. Whereas the rest of the world recognizes that bilingualism is an invaluable comparative advantage in a globalized economy, Spanish skills . . . are treated as a learning disability" (119). The effects of this practice have widespread repercussions; as Mary Louise Pratt argues, this disenfranchisement of Spanish also disenfranchises English "by taking English for granted as if it were a fact of nature rather than a human and social creation that needs to be cared for and cared about" ("What's Foreign" 1285). There is something strange, obviously, in the discourse of plurality occurring in the context of monolingualism, creating an odd continuity across realms that are familiar and alien.[1] It is as if extreme rigor and extreme naïveté in the analysis of texts from widely differing languages and cultural traditions are two faces of the same phenomenon.

A related, if not exactly congruent, argument would address the role of U.S.-Spanish and Spanglish texts in Spanish and Latin American studies departments both in the United States and in Latin America. At the very least, the bilingual writer should find a natural community in the bilingual readers from these academic homes, which are structurally marked by the constant realignments of crossing between cultural and linguistic boundaries. Emily Apter talks about "translational transnationalism as a conceptual counterweight to cosmopolitan literariness," adding that "though we are still far from experiencing postnational culture, there are signs everywhere that national identities in the marketplace of international aesthetics may be increasingly difficult to decipher" from a monocultural, monolingual perspective (70). For Apter, following Balibar, "transnationalism" is an activist term, allowing for access, cultural reciprocity; the modifier "translational" evokes the exchanges that occur when languages cross national borders. In the Spanish-language academic setting, scholars and students can fruitfully explore how identity reshapes discursivity, and the reverse: that is, how different discursive universes refashion identitarian claims.

The Conference on the Relation between English and Foreign Languages in the Academy, held at New York University in April 2002, brought together some of the United States' most distinguished scholars to think precisely about the policy and intellectual consequences of these pedagogically driven problems. Over and over, participants urged a recognition that Spanish is in fact the United States' second national language (Alonso 1138; Pratt, "What's Foreign" 1283; Stanton 1267); at the same time, many of them commented on the increasing phenomenon of English departments taking on and fiercely guarding the rights to all literatures written in all languages of the world, including Spanish (and taught in translation, of course) (Bartholomae 1272, Greene 1242, Stanton 1269). Ironically, this academic colonization by English is taking place at the same time that scholars find themselves increasingly uncomfortable with a theoretical position based on Western premises. No wonder there is a widespread sense in many literary circles these days that despite many and manifold advances, current work in the field has reached a crisis point, which is sometimes defined as a limit, sometimes as a state of exhaustion. Ian Baucom calls it a time "of speculative chaos," which he defines as "a moment in which . . . one dominant center of speculation has entered a phase of decline but no new center has as yet established itself as hegemonic" (167).

Certainly, the dwindling authority of the cosmopolitan perspective or Eurocentric normativism that once served as an unquestioning basis for literary talk goes hand in hand, as numerous scholars have confirmed, with the decline of the nation-state, the increasing awareness of international flows of capital and people, the heightening of rapid communication and sharing of popular culture through telecommunications networks and mass media, and, in the academic world, the increasing diversity of the student and professorial bodies that has inevitably led to shredding old verities about universal cultural standards. Globalization, it seems, inevitably changes the relationship of both Western and non-Western self and other that have in the past generally defined discourse communities and set those limits, now understood as artificial, that privilege certain kinds of speech and certain types of speakers.

As I have been arguing throughout this book, one aspect of this huge and much-discussed problem surrounding the widespread sense of exhaustion involving this particular intellectual enterprise in the humanities would focus on some of the key issues as they reflect on new Latin American immigrants to the United States. What Rachel Lee so acutely perceives about the place of women of color in the U.S. women's studies curriculum serves as a useful analogy for the uneasy role that U.S. Latin Americans play in the U.S. American studies context. Lee writes: "Women of color thus are peculiarly positioned in our contemporary moment, hailed as a phantasmatic 'pure space' outside domination but within women's studies. They have the dubious distinction of being celebrated for not speaking and not occupying. . . . Simultaneously, they are expected to act as a palliative agent, assuaging women's studies' anxieties over its uncertain ends and objects" (97). Lee's use of the word "phantasmatic" strikes me as particularly apt, evoking a ghostly but persistent quality, haunting the literary historical scaffolding while old solidities imaginatively remain intact. Once this phantasmatic presence is welcomed into the "pure space," other changes necessarily follow. As Kutzinski notes, "that imaginative writers tend not to respect national boundaries in this hemisphere and in others, has added to many academic Americanists' confusion about borders, and may well be a reason why a US-centric field like American Studies is so unduly worried about the so-called hegemony of literature and literary studies." This primary concern is curiously paired with its contradictory other side: a worry about how to mitigate the adulteration migrant writers could potentially enact on that space (56–57). Border crossing is one of the preferred metaphors of recent theory; it seems, though, that—following Kutzinski's metaphor—most border-crossing writers have yet to be given their naturalization papers and full citizenship in the republic of letters.

Like Lee's woman of color in gender studies, the new Latino/as help focus a critique of knowledge and of cultural practices in a site of contested meanings. It is no coincidence, furthermore, that meanings have been contested and doubt raised in these specific academic locations precisely because of the historical juncture that has placed certain individuals in positions to raise questions and to influence the rethinking of founding assumptions of the literary field. Thus, among other influences, new diasporic communities interrupt old, ongoing conversations in the United States about the relation between nation and identity, about colored bodies and minority spaces, about hemispheric consciousness and the United States' role in an increasingly globalized world, about the way theory and literary practice are imagined and validated in traditional academic settings.

I would like to suggest that traditional "hispanismo" in both the United States and Latin America needs to rethink itself from top to bottom so as to take up the responsibility of moving in the direction of addressing more rigorously the cultural project represented in the challenges posed by U.S. "latinidad." In his recent *Local Histories/Global Designs,* Walter Mignolo makes a radical proposition about the future of academic work, suggesting that if the ideal concept of the university in the past was grounded in the values of reason, culture, excellence, and expertise, the university of the future "shall be envisioned in which the humanities will be rearticulated on *a critique of knowledge and cultural practices*" (xii). Mignolo, I believe, is working out of a crucial awareness derived from this time of epistemological crisis, a realization that what we traditionally call "knowledge" involves a sort of willing complicity of scholars in which certain kinds of cultural inscriptions are selected from a complex social field and given privileged status. For Mignolo, as for many other contemporary scholars, it is precisely this privilege that is a matter for concern, for all too often hierarchies of status feed into and confirm already existing stereotypes. Thus, Mignolo—who as an Argentine-American explicitly claims his bifocal bilocation as a border crosser between Latin American and U.S. structures of knowledge and power—offers a somewhat uneasy solution to the problem of a lack of a strong theoretical center in contemporary literary studies. He locates himself firmly on the dash between Argentine and American, on the slash that separates the local and the global in his book's title, suggesting a fruitful collision/collusion of conflicting knowledge claims.

The problem remains of how to reread the paradigm from the perspective of a locus of enunciation outside that of the Western subject. Colombian philosopher Santiago Castro-Gómez comments that the "herencia [colonial] sigue reproduciéndose en el modo como la discursividad de las ciencias sociales y humanas se vincula a la producción de imágenes sobre . . . 'Latinoamérica,' administradas desde la racionalidad burocrática de las universidades . . ." [colonial heritage continues to reproduce itself in the manner by which discursivity in the social sciences and humanities is connected to the production of images about 'Latin America' managed from the bureaucratic rationality of universities], often, he suggests, in U.S. universities with agendas and ideologies that enter into direct conflict with Latin American interests. Even when these U.S. interests are discounted, Castro-Gómez continues: "las narrativas anticolonialistas jamás se preguntaron por el *status epistemológico* de su propio discurso" [anticolonial narratives never ask themselves about the epistemological status of their own discourse] (188–89), creating a blind spot by which the non-European other is inevitably framed and analyzed through the filter of Eurocentric discourse. Not only, then, are scholars like Mignolo and Castro-Gómez calling for a more careful and thorough analysis of the relations between imperial history and knowledge construction; they also call for the recognition of alternative theoretical knowledge from Latin America about Latin America. Even more radically, in relation to Western institutional settings, they identify the need for an outside critique of Eurocentric knowledge systems, a paradigm shift that will allow for a distanced observation beyond that obtaining when Europeans observe themselves (observing the other).

In the abstract, this sounds like an appealing, if destabilizing, resolution to the problem. Other concerns crop up almost immediately, however. John Beverley asks: "I would like to ask what it means today to articulate pedagogically the identity 'American' in the context of the rapid Hispanization—in both demographic and cultural-linguistic terms—of US society . . ." (162). The implicit challenge in these commentaries goes beyond modifying existing curricula and introducing texts, to changing ways of thinking in the academic sites where authority is vested in particular disciplinary and departmental divisions of labor. Giles Gunn would agree, and he also adds the crucial recognition of an ongoing discussion that has too often been muted partly because it is lost in the halls between English and Spanish departments. We need to remember, he notes, that "the literatures of the Americas have been in continuous conversation" or "mutual interrogation" from the very first postcolonial exchanges—obvious examples include Franklin on Sarmiento, Darío on Whitman, Lowry on Lispector, García Márquez on Morrison (17). Beverley speaks from a Latin Americanist perspective; Giles Gunn from an English and global studies one. All concur in a broad-based critique of a studies program organized around imaginarily posited national languages in favor of a larger pan-American context for scholarly inquiry.

Furthermore, the Hispanization of the United States means that U.S. literature in both Spanish and English needs resituation in a hemispheric context. In terms of traditional institutional structures, this presents a serious problem since, to recur once more to de Certeau's proposition with which I opened this book, the accepted story that underlies methodologies and theoretical arguments is naturally complicitous with current disciplinary structures, providing us with a place to think from but also limiting us in trying to resituate alternative forms of understanding. One sort of problem faces English departments, where the U.S. American studies focus is an important field, since a broader and more accurate understanding of even U.S. American studies (a hemispherically cognizant variation is still an unrealized dream) will have to recognize that "all national traditions are plural rather than singular" (Giles Gunn 18), going very much against the grain of the traditional model of studies, which has been "national literatures defined in relation to historically homogeneous cultures" (21).[2] From the Spanish department side, there is a parallel shift that needs to occur. U.S. literature is not and never has been solely an English-language project, and Spanish is becoming very much a postnational representation, especially when Spanish in the United States is taken into account. In the more fluid division of structures of knowledge, departments given names of languages (Spanish, French, English, and so on) cannot speak so much in terms of an imaginary consolidation of national literatures, but rather as describing the language in which a given work of literature is written.

To remedy this existing lack of a fully realized curricular project, we need to take account of the severely underaddressed challenge presented by the new Latino/as writing in Spanish. Walter Mignolo asks: "From 'where' will I rethink? . . . Would it be possible to build on a foundation that is not the foundation that allowed for the justification of national imperial languages and their complicity with knowledge?" He answers his questions with the appeal to "begin to think from border languages instead of from national languages" (256). Such an effort will inevitably give rise to a new epistemology, a new way to think about knowledge claims, about the disciplinary boundaries in current higher education, and about the stories we tell ourselves that set public policy. In the current institutional weighting of values, Hispanism in general is to literary studies as Latino/a studies is to English—less prestigious, less white; still marginal, but demographically threatening. A new rethinking of the old theoretical biases would take advantage of the natural, and curiously unexploited alliance between Hispanism and Latino/a studies, energizing the scholarly field at large by giving us all new ways to talk, and an expanded body of important works to help us find new and less biased stories to tell.

Notes

CHAPTER 1. INTRODUCTION

1. One example among many of the attention to the Latin Boom following the first release of 2000 census information would be the *Time* magazine special issue "Welcome to Amexica" (June 11, 2001). The issue's special section, titled "La nueva frontera/the new frontier," has articles on Laredo, illegal immigration, gringo retirement in Mexico, Mexican politics, Latino/a pop music, and a feature by María Hinojosa titled "Living la vida latina." News reports from as far away as Spain and Argentina reported on the "latinomania" of the United States at the turn of the millennium (see, e.g., Ambitoweb).

2. These numbers will make the United States the second-largest Spanish-speaking country in the world, after Mexico. Additional census statistics of interest: the 2000 survey identified more than 31.1 million foreign-born Americans (about 12% of the country's population). More come from Mexico than any other country (25% of all foreign-born residents) and another 25% come from other Latin American countries (a total of 16.1 million). About 13.3 million immigrants came to the United States between 1990 and 2000. Approximately 28 million of the 35.3 million in the 2000 count speak Spanish at home. One fifth of this country's schoolchildren speak a language other than English, and seven in ten of these children speak Spanish (for more information see Armas and <http://www.census.gov>).

3. A cogent supporting note comes from a six-volume Mexican study of the representation of Mexico in films made in other countries between 1906 and 1988. The vast majority of these are U.S. movies, although there are also films focusing on Mexico produced in Spain, Great Britain, the former Soviet republics, Germany, France, and Italy. The authors warn that their concluding filmography is necessarily partial; nevertheless it boasts 4,267 entries (García Riera).

4. I'm thinking here of apocalyptic scenarios such as that outlined by J. Hillis Miller, for whom the interest in European theory is part and parcel of a single crisis: "In spite of the inertia that will keep what we have called literary study going for a few more years, the handwriting is on the wall. Literary study's time is up. . . . The development of strong new theoretical reflection about literature, among other topics, by Bakhtin, Benjamin, Blanchot, Barthes, Foucault, Derrida, de Man, Jameson, and all the rest of that bunch (we know their

names) was in part a response to the dislocation of literature that was already taking place even before World War II" (59–60). For Miller, interestingly enough, the most hopeful response to this difficult crisis is to study American literature in its multilingual complexity, as a branch of comparative literature (65).

5. Armijo notes that "varios amigos han comentado que es muy probable que el antecesor de *Se habla español* sea otra antología, *McOndo*, publicado por Grijalbo en 1996. . . . Concebido en el frío brutal de Iowa, *McOndo* busca cómo medir la influencia de Estados Unidos en Latinoamérica—el caso inverso de *Se habla español*" [several friends have commented that it is very probable that the antecedent to *Se habla español* is another anthology, *McOndo*, published by Grijalbo in 1996. . . . Conceived in the brutal cold of Iowa, *McOndo* seeks to mediate the influence of the United States in Latin America—the inverse case of *Se habla español*] (9). Gustavo Faverón Patriau, in his review of this book for *El comercio* (Lima), also speaks of *Se habla español* as a sequel to *McOndo*, commenting that the earlier volume opens with a manifesto-like proposal for a new generation of Latin American writers, while the more recent anthology, also coedited by Alberto Fuguet, emphasizes the U.S. experience that shapes the authors in the new collection (ms. copy of review, June 2001).

6. Braschi's aggressive Spanglish defies translation into either language, partly because of the inevitable flattening out of its biculturality. Like Dolores Prida's play *Coser y cantar* discussed in a later chapter, all such performative texts implicitly come with a warning label: "This play must NEVER be performed in just one language" (Prida, *Beautiful* 49). An English approximation for Braschi's rant here would be, "Where's the cover for my water bottle? Don't you know that germs get in, it loses its fizz, and I don't like water to smell like your chicken curry sandwich, this isn't any good anymore . . ."

Here and throughout the pages that follow in this book, I provide English translations in the main body of the text for critical work and for texts that less problematically use one language or another. I provide loose renditions in footnote form for those quotes where bilinguality is essential.

7. I acknowledge here the essential work of and Frances Aparicio and Suzanne Chávez Silverman in thinking through similar issues, especially in *Tropicalizations.*

CHAPTER 2. ORIGINS

1. Kirsten Silva Gruesz cites slightly different population numbers, indicating that in 1825 six cities in the Americas had a population of over 100,000: Philadelphia, New York, Mexico City, Havana, Rio de Janeiro, and Bahia (23).

2. On Iturbide, see González Acosta 202; on Morelos, Lafaye 123; on Bolívar, Richardson 262.

3. These contemporary commentaries add nuance to the often-cited stereotype of the "black legend" of Spaniards and Spanish Americans as "cruel, duplicitous, arrogant, bestial, hypocritical, oversexed, Antichristian, and *ethnic*. . . . From these formative moments, Anglo-America has harbored an abiding suspicion of all things Hispanic. The ethno-essentializing spirit thrived

after Independence . . . mapp[ing] all too easily onto Creole and mestizo culture in the New [World]" (Griffin 95, 103).

4. Spanish quotations in the text are followed by the English translation in brackets. Pages are given in parentheses, with the Spanish page number first, followed by the English page number for published translations, and separated by a slash. This protocol is followed throughout the book where existing translations exist. The absence of this second page number means that translations are my own.

5. For some of the scattered references to Stavely imprints, see <http://www.episcopalian.org/gambierevangelicals/PChase/Reminiscences1/Remin_19.htm>, <cervantesvirtual.com/servlet/SirveObras/115396562437657615721604/254s.htm>, the introduction to *Jicoténcal,* and Web sites cataloguing Philadelphia rare books. The debate about the authorship of *Jicoténcal* remains unresolved, and the final determination is not crucial to this analysis. Cortina and Leal, in their introduction to a new edition of the text, argue strongly for an attribution to Spanish/Cuban priest Félix Varela, who arrived in the United States in 1823 and spent most of 1824 at 224 Spruce Street in Philadelphia, before moving to New York City in late 1824. González Acosta disagrees and strongly supports the candidacy of Cuban/Mexican poet José María Heredia, who also lived in Philadelphia in 1824 before moving to Mexico in August 1825. Varela, obviously, has a stronger claim to a proto-Latino identity, whereas Heredia was more of a temporary visitor. Heredia and Varela were friends and frequented the same social circles in Philadelphia and New York, which included other liberal Latin American thinkers and like-minded U.S. writers such as William Cullen Bryant. Young Robert Montgomery Bird was a fluent Spanish speaker and Philadelphia native. He was eighteen in mid-1824, and was preparing for medical school at the University of Pennsylvania by studying with Dr. Joseph Parrish and working in a druggist's shop. I have been unable to find any direct link among these figures, although there is some reason for imagining they might have interacted with each other; they lived only a few blocks apart, and Bird was known for his interest in and interactions with the Latin American exile community. Williams, for example, comments briefly on a loosely organized group of Philadelphian Hispanists whose membership included Bird (*Spanish Background* 221).

6. The review of *Jicoténcal* in *The United States Review and Literary Gazette* is anonymous; Williams identifies the author as William Cullen Bryant (*Spanish Background* II, 132).

7. Wainwright describes Bird as "without doubt Philadelphia's ablest literary figure" (291) and Dahl calls him "the foremost literary man of Philadelphia" (26).

8. The very few critical studies of these novels typically describe the characters as pertaining to the stereotype of the "noble savage." I would argue that this characterization is inaccurate to the degree that the noble Indians in these books belong to what are depicted as recognized, highly civilized, and complex cultures, rather than a noble state of nature. Indeed, the critical apparatus that deploys the figure of the noble savage belongs more recognizably to the U.S. cultural setting, where the inevitable passing of primitive indigenous tribes is

seen as the sad but necessary cost of achieving a more advanced civilization. This interpretation by no means obtains in Mexico, where the colonial genocide is encoded as a limit event or founding trauma instantiating a process of national identification. González Acosta takes a somewhat different perspective, arguing that *Jicoténcal*'s emphasis on the indigenous hero serves in the Cuban context as a displacement from the more locally vexed question of the Afro-Cuban. For evidence, he points to Heredia's poem "En el teocalli de Cholula," Gertrudis Gómez de Avellaneda's novel *Guatimozín,* and Gabriel de Concepción Valdés' "Xicotencal" (229). A fuller consideration of these ethnic displacements is beyond the scope of this study.

9. *Jicoténcal* makes extensive use of de Solís, and Bird cites from de Solís, Bernal Díaz de Castillo, Clavijero, Robertson, and others. In the introduction to the 1847 edition of *Calavar,* Bird states directly that his novels were "written with an attempt at the strictest possible historical accuracy compatible with the requisitions of romance." Bird's notebooks apparently give evidence of his wide-ranging curiosity. One of his contemporaries, James Rees, commented that he was "more familiar with the history of South America and Spanish North America than any other man in the country" (Dahl 74–75).

10. This claiming of divergent intellectual heritages is quite rich. On the Yankee's side, most of the historians he cites are Spanish chroniclers, but Francisco Javier Clavijero (*Historia antigua de México* 1780) in his pro-independence-slanted texts explicitly identifies himself as a *Mexican* and also describes indigenous figures as "Mexicans" in his story of the conquest. Spaniards are consistently called "foreigners" (Lafaye 107–09). On the other hand, the *cura* cites both the textual authority of and his direct family descendence from [Juan de Alva] Ixtlilxochitl, historically, a full-blooded Indian, a descendent of the kings of Texcoco, and friend of and informant for Jesuit colonial historian Sigüenza y Góngora (1645–1700). In the absence of heirs, Ixtlilxochitl gifted Sigüenza y Góngora with all his chronicles and other materials (Paz, "Foreword" xviii). Bird's invention of the last blood heir to the indigenous colonial chronicler and his mysterious "lost" texts could well be a reference to the codexes given to the Spanish-Mexican writer (*Calavar* I, 19). An Ixtlilxochitl also makes a cameo appearance in *Infidel* as the king of Texcoco and Cortés's godson (I, 79). In contrast, *Infidel* is closely associated with Bernal Díaz de Castillo, who frequently appears in the novel, writing in a diary or telling his stories around a campfire; one of the footnotes to the novel includes the tongue-in-cheek comment that "the historical reader will find that the worthy Bernal has incorporated many of these judicious sentiments in the work he was then composing, and some almost word for word" (I, 39).

11. To summarize briefly in current terms: Lafaye begins his 1974 book on New Spain with a few stark schematics: there were an estimated 1,500,000 people living in the valley of Mexico in 1519. Spanish rule was by no means accepted at any time in the colonial period; there was a major uprising against Spain on average once every fifteen years, along with many more minor rebellions. One greatly debilitating factor for indigenous resistance was disease; the region suffered from eight major epidemics in colonial times, the first of which, in 1545, killed 800,000 people (xxx).

12. With the exception of Teutila, a fictional addition of the author's, the other characters in the novel, both Spanish and indigenous, have historically documented lives, though not in exactly the terms that this author describes them.

13. Bird seems to have combined two separate historical figures: the "Genealogy of Mexico" describes them as follows: "**Lerma, Fernando de**—As the Conquistadors were retreating from Tenochtitlan (Mexico City) Cortés went back to try and save his men from drowning in the waters that surround the city. The Mexica recognizing Cortés made an attempt to pull him into their canoes. It was Cristoval de Olea who threw himself on the attackers and paid with his life falling at Cortes' side. Lerma was said to have joined Olea but he survived. He ended up losing the use of his hand as a result. An allied Tlascalan chief fought over the wounded body of Cortés killing three Mexica, allowing enough time for Cortes' men to come to his defense. **Lerma, Lepe de**—considered fearless. After being reprimanded by Cortés he deserted and went to live with the Indians. No record of him thereafter."

14. Nor are contemporary intellectual leaders immune from such charms. To choose just one instance: Cornell President Hunter Rawlings in his October 2000 state of the university address makes a strong appeal to the board of trustees for a renewed commitment to the humanities on precisely those grounds: the value of the traditional course of humanities studies for "the development of moral knowledge" (Crawford 7).

15. Bird uses untranslated Spanish at various points in his texts. The rendition of this title would be: "A chronicle of the conquest of Mexico and especially of those gentlemen whom ancient writers neglected to celebrate."

16. A rendition of the reference to Cervantes's *Don Quixote:* "This is unimportant to our story: it is enough that the narration does not distance itself at any point from truth."

17. We might note, however, that this appeal to the Republic may well have had a different valence in the 1820–35 period than contemporary scholars might suspect. Martin Bernal, for example, reminds us that while most pre-1970 modern readers were trained in what he calls the "Aryan model" (which affirms the direct line between Greece and white Europe), the prevalent understanding until the middle of the nineteenth century was what Bernal calls the "Ancient model" (which gave considerable credence to Phoenician and Egyptian influences, among others). Bernal in numerous books has upheld the "Revised Ancient" model, and he eloquently and succinctly defines the stakes of these two versions of classical influence: "We should turn from the image of a civilization springing, like the conventional image of Athena from the head of Zeus, white, virgin, fully formed, to an image of a new civilization growing up at the intersection of Europe and the Middle East as a thoroughly mixed and eclectic culture. The greatness and extraordinary brilliance of Greek civilization in Antiquity, and the central role it played in the formation of all later European cultures, was not the result of isolation and cultural purity but of frequent contact and stimulus from the many surrounding peoples with the already heterogeneous natives of the Aegean" (2–5 passim, 11).

CHAPTER 3. CROSSING

1. The information in this paragraph comes from Stanley Williams' article.

2. Stanley Williams alludes to a later translation done by Mexican *modernista* poet Gutiérrez Nájera titled "Rip-Rip": in this adaptation of the story, the protagonist is a woodsman "who, after a severe day's work in the woods, falls asleep for the stereotyped period. Rip-Rip returns, according to this writer, the incarnation of the vanity of all things, and finds, as he did in the Catskills, all changed, but in addition, '¡su mujer había cambiado, y estaba en brazos de otro hombre que no conocía, satisfecha de su nuevo carino! ¡Le había olvidado!' " [His wife had changed and was in the arms of another man who he did not know, satisfied with her new love! She had forgotten him!] ("First Version" 197).

3. "¡Cuál sería el asombro de Andrés al descubrir repentinamente en este sitio una lucidísima comparsa de caballeros moriscos bizarramente vestidos! . . . Quería ya el temeroso labrador volver sobre sus pasos para retirarse, é incontinenti los moriscos le rodean, le detienen, y le saludan á la usanza mora, cruzando las manos sobre el pecho y haciéndole profundas zalemas. En seguida le depojan de la rústica zamarra, la montera y las albarcas, y le visten un magnífico Caftan forrado de pieles de marta, y bordado de oro con franjas de lo mismo" [Imagine the shock of Andrés when he suddenly discovered in this place a very clear retinue of Moorish gentlemen bizarrely dressed! . . . The fearful workman now wanted to backtrack over his path to withdraw, and suddenly the Moors surround him, they hold him back, and they greet him in Moorish style, crossing their hands on their chests and making deep bows. Immediately they take away his rustic jacket, his cap, and his sandals, and they dress him in a magnificent caftan lined with marten fur and embroidered and fringed with gold] (cited in Williams, "First Version" 199).

4. All quotations from "Rip Van Winkle" come from the unpaginated Web site.

5. A typical nineteenth-century genre focusing on everyday life and customs, somewhere between folktale and proto-ethnographies.

6. Among Irving's "Spanish" texts are: *Columbus, The Conquest of Granada, The Alhambra, The Voyages of the Companions of Columbus, The Crayon Miscellany* (about one third of the stories), *Mahomet and His Successors*, and the posthumous *Spanish Papers*.

7. To be more accurate, from another perspective, people like Hopenhayn and Castro-Gómez—along with other scholars such as Ernesto Laclau, Enrique Dussel, Gayatri Spivak, or Homi Bhabha, to name just a few—represent courtesy members of the first-world "us," always marked by (and often celebrated for) a putative or real aura of otherness, that in turn and paradoxically makes them "other" to the intellectual institutions of their home countries as well as, obviously, other to the subalternized citizens inhabiting those local realities.

8. Loose rendition: stuffed him with speed and loaded him with acid and pills up to the eyeballs.

9. Heavy-duty trip that made him think that right there the bus of life was going to drop him off.

10. Playing something like the U.S. national anthem to a merengue beat.

11. The fucking café was closed. And the restaurant next door too. And the Chinese place. And even the Cuban joint, man, that didn't even close for Muñoz's funeral.

12. All sailed off to NYC looking for the bucks.

13. An old woman who sniveled disconsolately.

14. When he realized he was falling hopelessly. Yuniol was grabbing him by the neck, and he was two seconds away from the time bomb between his ears blowing his brain into a thousand fucking pieces.

15. And everything quieter than . . . for the last chapter of Cristina Bazan.

16. You have to forgive me for bringing you down from your TGIF high, but I'm here to let you know how it went down with me: streetwise, order to go.

17. Fuentes's transnational experience is such that noted Chicana thinker and culture critic María Herrera-Sobek has argued forcefully that he should be considered a Chicano writer.

18. This vignette in chapter 9 is homage to Ricardo Aguilar Melantzón, prolific scholar and author from El Paso/Juárez (Cayuela Gally 4). Aguilar is well known for his anthologies of Chicano literature in Spanish and is famous for his daily crossings between those two cities on his Suzuki 450-T motorcycle. In addition, "Cumplir mi justa condena" in his *Madreselvas* features a character named Edumenio who travels between the countries on motorcycle, and José Manuel García further argues that Fuentes was clearly inspired by "Puente Negro" in Aguilar's *Aurelia* (247). In his *A barlovento* Aguilar somewhat sardonically refers to "Charlie Fountains" who "también menciona a tu servilleta y el capítulo nueve refunde el último de mi *Madreselvas* y otros de mi *Aurelia*" [mentions me and in chapter 9 recasts the end of my *Madreselvas* and other bits of my *Aurelia*] (41).

CHAPTER 4. ARRIVAL

1. New York City seems to be a particularly privileged site for such immigration stories. Not only is it the location of the earliest known novel of immigration (Colombian Alirio Díaz Guerra's *Lucas Guevara* (1914), it is also the site of many other later fictions: Guillermo Cotto-Thorner's *Trópico en Manhattan*, Ivan Acosta's *El super*, Roberto Quesada's *Nunca entres por Miami*, Jaime Manrique's *Latin Moon over Manhattan*, among the most notable. See Nicolás Kanellos and Imara Liz Hernández, "Introducción," for more on this point.

2. I am thinking here of his notorious early work in collaboration with Mattelart, *How to Read Donald Duck* (1971), as well as his more recent (post–*Heading South)* fictional narratives like *The Nanny and the Iceberg* (1999), about the Chilean iceberg exhibit in the Sevilla World's Fair, and *Blake's Therapy* (2001), first published in an earlier version in Portuguese before appearing in either Spanish or English.

3. The Spanish here struggles to give a sense of the U.S. children's culture alluded to, but has to sacrifice the poetic echoes of the verb "to fall" common in all three children's rhymes: "lo que descendía en mi vida era el London

Bridge de las canciones infantiles y el Humpty Dumpty, ese personaje-huevo que se había caído de su muralla, la única caída que me importaba era mi deseo perpetuo de echarme en la tierra y revolcarme" (89).

4. Lupe Vélez worked extensively in Hollywood from the 1920s until her death by suicide on December 14, 1944. She is probably best known for her "Mexican Spitfire" series of movies in the late 1930s to mid-1940s.

5. These observations follow directly upon Sainz's 1995 commentary about the reflexive structure of *A la salud de la serpiente.* Sainz writes, "es evidente que mis libros son realistas, incómodamente realistas, o realistas en el más posmoderno sentido del término. . . ." He divides realist narrators into two large categories: (1) "unos que creen que pueden ordenar la desordenada realidad de acuerdo a valores burgueses muy bien establecidos desde la época de Balzac" and on the other hand, (2) "escritores que no intentan mostrar la realidad, o que aceptan como la única realidad posible la de la lengua." Finally, "El tema del joven escritor en busca de su identidad es . . . una tema común . . . en toda mi producción" ("Búsqueda" 157–58, 159, 160).

6. The standard for this rapidly evolving subgenre was set by the crossover success of Nan McCarthy's trilogy of e-novels, *Chat, Connect,* and *Crash* from their self-published format (1995) and online distribution through McCarthy's Rainwater Press Web site (www.rainwater.com), prior to mainstream publication in the Simon and Schuster Pocketbook imprint (October 1998). The novels follow the e-mail communications of Max and Beverly. The series ends when Max, who is flying across country to meet Beverly, dies in a plane crash (*Crash* 117).

7. Literally: "his found America, Newland, kingdom populated only by him."

8. Note also the sequence of prepositions in the subtitle of Sainz's novel that echo Donne's line exactly, though in different order ("atrás, arriba, adelante, debajo y entre"):

> License my roving hands, and let them go
> Before, behind, between, above, below.
> O my America! my new-found-land,
> My kingdom, safeliest when with one man manned (55).

9. A series of word plays based on the name, followed by the query "but how to think about Camila if he lacked images?"

10. A special prize category for literature by U.S. Latino/as; the committee for this prize was composed of well-known Chicano scholar José David Saldívar, U.S.-Cuban writer Emilio Bejel, and Cuban poet Pablo Armando Fernández.

11. The English edition of this book includes an eighth story after the translation of "La más prohibida." This story, "The Fifth River," the least successful of the volume, pulls together references to all the characters in the collection and thus serves as an epilogue to as well as compendium of the rest.

CHAPTER 5. LANGUAGE GAMES

1. In the earlier part of this analysis, Trilling explores the breakdown of the concept of sincerity under pressure from the emerging capitalist system.

See also Regenia Gagnier and Rachel Bowlby for other important discussions of this issue.

2. An analysis of this essay would have to take into account that Lugones's playful practice is only partly successful insofar as it largely reproduces stereotypical understandings of the relations of the two languages and cultures. English is the language of philosophical argument, critical distance, and academic authority; Spanish is the language of poetry, emotion, and the feminine domestic space. Her essay is in the middle of the generational break described by Gómez Peña: "in the 1970s and 1980s, the combination of Spanish and English in a text was very formulaic: Spanish was reserved for the private realms of home, intimacy, the family, and memory; English was meant for the public realm, for politics, for the streets. What my generation did in the late 1980s, early 1990s, was to create a new formula: Spanish and Spanglish would be languages of occultation and complicity, partially forbidden zones, so to speak, and only those fully bilingual would have access, temporary access, to these zones" (550).

3. I am aware that Spivak is making a very different point in this interview response, as her commentary lauds Beckett for stepping out of English and into French, rather than encouraging a bifocal perspective. Nevertheless, her phrasing is apt and applicable.

4. The English version is divided into three parts with a separate prologue: (1) Jehú's letters, (2) Galindo's "soundings and findings," and (3) conclusions. The Spanish text has two parts: (1) "Malilla platicada" (Galindo's prologue plus the letters) and (2) "Sondas y ciertos hallazgos de P. Galindo" (including twenty-three commentaries from townspeople as well as Galindo's conclusions). The numbering of letters and commentaries is similar in the two versions, with the exception of letter 11 in Spanish, which is divided into two letters in the English text (11 and 12).

CHAPTER 6. CONCLUSION

1. Along similar lines, Mark Shell comments: "Among American literary scholars a distinct focus on anglophone literature written by 'ethnic' groups with all-too-familiarly racialist hyphenated names seems generally to have displaced most literature written in America in languages other than English" (5).

2 Werner Sollers reminds us that this provincialism of American studies was not always the case: "originally, an 'Americanist' was a person who studied American Indian languages. Later, writing about 'American literature' meant describing, analyzing, and criticizing works that were written or published in the many different languages in the various colonies and in the United States" (*Multilingual America* 5).

Works Cited

Aguilar Melantzón, Ricardo. *A barlovento.* Torreón: Ed. del norte mexicano, 1999.

———. *Madreselvas en flor.* Xalapa: Universidad Veracruzana, 1987.

Alarcón, Norma, Caren Kaplan, and Minoo Moallem. "Introduction: Between Woman and Nation." Ed. Kaplan, Alarcón, and Moallem.

Alborg, Concha. *Beyond Jet-Lag: Other Stories.* New Jersey: Ediciones Nuevo Espacio, 2000.

Alonso, Carlos. "Where Were We?" *PMLA* 117.5 (2002): 1137–41.

Anderson, Benedict. *Imagined Communities: Reflections on the Origin and Spread of Nationalism.* Rev. ed. London: Verso, 1991.

Anzaldúa, Gloria. *Borderlands/La Frontera: The New Mestiza.* San Francisco: Spinsters/Aunt Lute, 1987.

Aparicio, Frances, and Suzanne Chávez Silverman, eds. *Tropicalizations: Transcultural Representations of Latinidad.* Hanover, NH: UP of New England, 1997.

Appiah, Kwame Anthony. "Cosmopolitan Patriots." *Cosmopolitics: Thinking Beyond the Nation.* Eds. Pheng Cheah and Bruce Robbins. Minneapolis: U of Minnesota P, 1998. 91–114.

Apter, Emily. "Étienne Balibar: Introduction." *PMLA* 117.1 (2002): 68–71.

Armas, Genaro. "Fifth of Kids Speak Two Languages." AP report. *Ithaca Journal* August 6, 2001: 1B.

Armijo, Ricardo. "La vocación de la rabia." Rev. of *Se habla español.* Unpublished ms. 2001.

Arteaga, Alfred, ed. *An Other Tongue: Nation and Ethnicity in the Linguistic Borderlands.* Durham: Duke UP, 1994.

———. "An Other Tongue." Arteaga 8–33.

Balibar, Étienne, and Immanuel Wallerstein. *Race, nation, classe: Les identités ambiguës.* Paris: Éditions la Découverte, 1988.

Barradas, Efraín. "La necesaria innovación de Ana Lydia Vega: Preámbulo para lectores vírgenes." *Revista Iberoamericana* 51. 132–33 (1985): 547–56.

Barrio, Raymond. *The Plum Plum Pickers.* Binghamton: Bilingual Press, 1969.

Barthes, Roland. *Roland Barthes.* Trans. Richard Howard. New York: Hill and Wang, 1977.

Bartholomae, David. "Literacy and Departments of Language and Literature." *PMLA* 117.5 (2002): 1272–79.

Baucom, Ian. "Globalit, Inc.; or, the Cultural Logic of Global Literary Studies." *PMLA* 116.1 (2001): 158–72.

Bécquer, Gustavo Adolfo. *Rimas.* Ed. José Carlos de Torres. Madrid: Castalia, 1982.

Bernal, Martin. *Black Athena Writes Back: Martin Bernal Responds to His Critics.* Ed. David Chioni Moore. Durham: Duke UP, 2001.

Berríos, Nelsón Gabriel. "Ana Lydia rehúsa ser la redentora" (interview). *El mundo* (San Juan, PR) December 23, 1984: 10B.

Beverley, John. *Subalternity and Representation: Arguments in Cultural Theory.* Durham: Duke UP, 1999.

Beverley, John, José Oviedo, and Michael Aronna, eds. *The Postmodernism Debate in Latin America.* Durham: Duke UP, 1995.

Bhabha, Homi. "The World and the Home." *Social Text* 10 (1992): 141–53.

Bird, Robert Montgomery. *Calavar; or The Knight of the Conquest: A Romance of Mexico* (1834). 2 vols. Leipzig: Alphons Dürr, 1856.

———. *The Infidel; or The Fall of Mexico. A Romance.* 2 vols. Philadelphia: Carey, Lea, and Blanchard, 1835.

———. *Nick of the Woods; or The Jibbenainosay.* 2 vols. Philadelphia: Carey, Lea, and Blanchard, 1837.

Blanco, José Joaquín. *La paja en el ojo: Ensayos de crítica.* Puebla: Editorial U Autónoma de Puebla, 1980.

Bowlby, Rachel. *Shopping with Freud.* London: Routledge, 1993.

Braham, Persephone. Review of *Yo Yo Boing!* <http://www.americas-society.org/as/literature/br60braschi.html>.

Braschi, Giannina. "Blow Up" in Paz-Soldán, Edmundo and Alberto Fuguet, eds. *Se habla español: Voces latinas en USA.* Miami: Alfaguara, 2000: 365–76.

Braschi, Giannina. "Pelos en la lengua." *Hopscotch* 2.2 (2000): 50.

———. *Yo-Yo Boing!* Pittsburgh: Latin America Literary Review P, 1998.

Bruce-Novoa, [Juan]. *Retrospace: Collected Essays on Chicano Literature.* Houston: Arte Público, 1990.

———. "Dialogical Strategies, Monological Goals: Chicano Literature." Arteaga, 225–45.

———. "Righting the Oral Tradition." *Denver Quarterly* 16.3 (1981): 78–86.

Brushwood, John. "Sobre el referente y la transformación narrativa en las novelas de Carlos Fuentes y Gustavo Sainz." *Revista iberoamericana* 47 (1981): 49–54.

Bryant, William Cullen. Review of *Jicotencal. United States Review and Literary Gazette* 1.5 (1826): 336–46.

Calderón, Héctor. "The Novel and the Community of Readers." *Criticism in the Borderlands.* Héctor Calderón and José David Saldívar, eds. Durham: Duke UP, 1991. 97–113.

Callahan, Laura. "Metalinguistic References in a Spanish/English Corpus." *Hispania* 84.3 (2001): 417–27.

Campos, Javier. "Escritores latinos en los Estados Unidos." Rev. of *Se habla español. Ventana abierta* 3.10 (2001): 81–85.

Cañizares-Esguerra, Jorge. Renaissance Mess(tizaje): What Mexican Indians Did to Titian and Ovid." *The New Centennial Review* 2.1 (2002): 267–76.

Carrión, María Mercedes. "Geographies, (M)Other Tongues and the Role of Translation in Giannina Braschi's *El imperio de los sueños.*" *Studies in Twentieth Century Literature* 20 (1996): 167–91.

Castañeda, Quetzil E. *In the Museum of Maya Culture: Touring Chichén Itzá.* Minneapolis: U of Minnesota P, 1996.

Castro-Gómez, Santiago. "La filosofía latinoamericana como ontología crítica del presente: Temas y motivas para una 'Crítica de la razón latinoamericana.' " Unpublished ms., 2000.

Cayuela Gally, Ricardo. "Nuevo tiempo mexicano: Entrevista con Carlos Fuentes." *La jornada semanal* April 21, 1996: <http//www.jornada.unam.mx/1996/abr96/960421/sem-cayuela.html>, 10 pp.

Cheah, Pheng, and Bruce Robbins, eds. *Cosmopolitics: Thinking and Feeling Beyond the Nation.* Minneapolis: U of Minnesota P, 1998.

Chow, Rey. "How (the) Inscrutable Chinese Led to Globalized Theory." *PMLA* 116.1 (2001): 69–74.

Clifford, James. "Traveling Cultures." *Cultural Studies.* Lawrence Grossberg, Cary Nelson, and Paula Treichler, eds. New York: Routledge, 1992. 96–116.

Crawford, Franklin. "Cornell Embodies a Long, Vital Tradition in Humanities Studies." *Cornell Chronicle* 33.112 (2001): 1, 7–8.

Dahl, Curtis. *Robert Montgomery Bird.* New York: Twayne, 1963.

Davis, Mike. *Magical Urbanism: Latinos Reinvent the US City.* New York: Verso, 2000.

de Certeau, Michel. *Heterologies: Discourse on the Other.* Trans. Brian Massumi. Minneapolis: U of Minnesota P, 1986.

Díaz, Nancy Gray. "Performing *Soledad*: The Demythification of Identity in Giannina Braschi's *El imperio de los sueños.*" *Romance Notes* 37 (1997): 331–37.

Díaz, Roberto Ignacio. *Unhomely Rooms: Foreign Tongues and Spanish American Literature.* Lewisburg: Bucknell UP, 2002.

Díaz Guerra, Alirio. *Lucas Guevara.* 1914. Houston: Arte Público, 2001.

Domínguez, Christopher. Review of *Peregrinos de Aztlán. Vuelta* August 1989: 88.

Donne, John. *John Donne's Poetry.* Ed. A. L. Clements. New York: Norton, 1966.

Dorfman, Ariel. *Blake's Therapy.* New York: Seven Stories, 2001.

———. *Heading South, Looking North: A Bilingual Journey.* New York: Penguin, 1998.

———. *The Nanny and the Iceberg.* New York: Farrar, Straus, Giroux, 1999.

———. *Rumbo al sur, deseando el norte: Un romance en dos lenguas.* New York: Siete cuentos, 1998.

Dorfman, Ariel, and Armand Mattelart. *How to Read Donald Duck: Imperialist Ideology in Disney Comics.* Trans. David Kunzle. New York: International General, 1991.

Escanlar, Gustavo. "Pequeño diccionario Spanglish ilustrado" in Paz-Soldán, Edmundo and Alberto Fuguet, eds. *Se habla español: Voces latinas en USA.* Miami: Alfaguara, 2000: 35–50.

Farred, Grant. "Victorian with a Rebel Seed: C. L. R. James, Postcolonial Intellectual." *Social Text* 38 (Spring 1994): 21–38.

Faverón Patriau, Gustavo. Review of *Se habla español.* Mss cited with permission.

Feliciano, Wilma. " 'I am a Hyphenated American': Interview with Dolores Prida." *Latin American Theatre Review* 29.1 (1995): 113–18.

Flores, Juan, and María Milagros López. "Dossier Puerto Rico: Introduction." *Social Text* 38 (Spring 1994): 93–95.

Follari, Roberto, and Rigoberto Lanz, eds. *Enfoques sobre la posmodernidad en América Latina.* Caracas: Editorial Sentido, 1998.

Foster, Thomas. "Cyber-Aztecs and Cholo-Punks: Guillermo Gómez-Peña's Five-Worlds Theory." *PMLA* 117.1 (2002): 43–67.

Foucault, Michel. "Of Other Spaces." Trans. Jay Miskowiec. *Diacritics* 16.1 (1986): 22–27.

Foust, Clement E. *The Life and Dramatic Works of Robert Montgomery Bird.* New York: Knickerbocker P, 1919.

Fregoso, Rosa Linda. "*Born in East L.A.* and the Politics of Representation." *Culture Studies* 4.3 (1990): 264–80.

Fuentes, Carlos. *Crystal Frontier.* Trans. Alfred Mac Adam. New York: Farrar, Straus and Giroux, 1997.

———. *El espejo enterrado.* México: Fondo de cultura económica, 1992.

———. *La frontera de cristal: Una novela en nueve cuentos.* México: Alfaguara, 1995.

———. "Land of Jekyll and Hyde." *The Nation* March 22, 1986: 334.

———. *Nuevo tiempo mexicano.* México: Aguilar (Alfaguara), 1994.

Gagnier, Regenia. *Idylls of the Marketplace.* London: Scholar P, 1987.

García, José Manuel. "Los juarenses qeu todavía somos, el Juárez que ya no es." Aguilar, *A barlovento.* 229–51.

García Canclini, Néstor. "Comunidades de consumidores: Nuevos escenarios de lo público y la ciudadanía." *Cultura y tercer mundo 2: Nuevas identidades y ciudadanias.* Ed. Beatriz González Stephan. Caracas: Nueva Sociedad, 1996. 1–16.

———. *Culturas híbridas: Estrategias para entrar y salir de la modernidad.* México: Grijalbo, 1989.

———. *Latinoamericanos buscando lugar en este siglo.* Buenos Aires: Paidos, 2002.

García Riera, Emilio. *México visto por el cine extranjero.* 6 vols. Guadalajara: U de Guadalajara, 1990.

Gelpí, Juan G. *Literatura y paternalismo en Puerto Rico.* San Juan: Editorial de la U de Puerto Rico, 1993.

"Genealogy of Mexico: Those who served with Cortés." *<http://members.tripod.com/~GaryFelix/index2.htm#Lerma>.*

Gómez Peña, Guillermo, and Eduardo Mendieta. "A Latino Philosopher Interviews a Chicano Performance Artist." *Nepantla* 2 (2001): 539–54.

González, Aníbal. "Ana Lydia Pluravega: Unidad y multiplicidad caribeñas en la obra de Ana Lydia Vega." *Revista Iberoamericana* 59 (1993): 289–300.

Gonzalez, Juan. *Harvest of Empire: A History of Latinos in the United States.* New York: Penguin, 2000.

González Acosta, Alejandro. *El enigma de Jicotencal: Estudio de dos novelas sobre el héroe de Tlaxcala.* Mexico: UNAM, 1997.

González Viaña, Eduardo. *Los sueños de América.* Lima: Alfaguara, 2000.

Greene, Roland. "The Post-English English." *PMLA* 117.5 (2002): 1241–44.

Griffin, Eric. "From Ethos to Ethnos: Hispanizing 'the Spaniard' in the Old World and the New." *The New Centennial Review* 2.1 (2002): 69–116.

Grosfoguel, Ramón, Frances Negrón-Muntaner, and Chloé S. Georas. "Introduction: Beyond Nationalist and Colonialist Discourses: The *Jaiba* Politics of the Puerto Rican Ethno-Nation." *Puerto Rican Jam: Essays on Culture and Politics.* Eds. Grosfoguel and Negrón-Muntaner. Minneapolis: U of Minnesota P, 1997. 1–36.

Gruesz, Kirsten Silva. *Ambassadors of Culture: The Transamerican Origins of Latino Writing.* Princeton: Princeton UP, 2002.

Gunn, Dewey Wayne. *American and British Writers in Mexico, 1556–1973.* Austin: Texas UP, 1974.

Gunn, Giles. "Introduction: Globalizing Literary Studies." *PMLA* 116.1 (2001): 16–31.

Hancock, Joel. "Re-Defining Autobiography: Gustavo Sainz's *A la salud de la serpiente.*" *Revista de estudios hispánicos* 29 (1995): 139–52.

Helman, Edith F. "Early Interest in Spanish in New England (1815–1835)." *Hispania* 29 (1946): 339–51.

Hernández, Carmen Dolores. "A Sense of Space, a Sense of Speech: A Conversation with Ana Lydia Vega." *Hopscotch* 2.2 (2000): 52–59.

Hinojosa-Smith, Rolando. "The Baroque in the Life and Literature of the Hispano-American." *Points of Contact* 3.3 (1993): 22–27.

———. *Dear Rafe.* Houston: Arte Público, 1985.

———. *Mi querido Rafa.* Houston: Arte Público, 1984.

———. "The Sense of Place." In *The Rolando Hinojosa Reader.* Ed. José David Saldívar. Houston: Arte Público, 1985. 18–24.

Hopenhayn, Martín. "Tribu y metrópoli en la postmodernidad latinoamericana." Follari and Lanz, 19–35.

Horn, Maja. "National Desires/Desiring the Nation: Discourses of Place and Pleasure in the Stories of Mayra Santos-Febres and Sonia Rivera-Valdés." Unpublished ms., December 2002.

Horno-Delgado, Asunción, et al. *Breaking Boundaries: Latina Writing and Critical Readings.* Amherst: U of Massachusetts P, 1989.

Hutner, Gordon. "In the Middle: Fictions, Borders, and Class." *The New Centenntial Review* 1.2 (2001): 89–108.

Irving, Washington. "Rip Van Winkle." *The Sketch Book* (1819–20). *<http://www.cwrl.utexas.edu/~daniel/amlit/rvwrvwtext.html>.*

Jameson, Fredric. "Notes on Globalization as a Philosophical Issue." Jameson and Miyoshi, 54–77.

———. "Preface." Jameson and Miyoshi, xi–xvii.

Jameson, Fredric, and Masao Miyoshi, eds. *The Cultures of Globalization.* Durham: Duke UP, 1999.

Johnson, David E. "The Time of Translation: The Border of American Literature." *Border Theory: The Limits of Cultural Politics.* Ed. Scott Michaelson, and David E. Johnson. Minneapolis: U of Minnesota P, 1997. 129–65.

Johnson, David E. and Scott Michaelson. "Border Secrets: An Introduction." In Michaelson and Johnson: 1–39.

Jones-Correa, Michael. *Between Two Nations: The Political Predicament of Latinos in New York City.* Ithaca: Cornell UP, 1998.

Kanellos, Nicolás, and Imara Liz Hernández. "Introducción." Díaz Guerra, *Lucas Guevara.* iii–xix.

Kaplan, Caren, Norma Alarcón, and Minoo Moallem, eds. *Between Woman and Nation: Nationalisms, Transnational Feminisms, and the State.* Durham: Duke UP, 1999.

Kaplan, Caren, and Inderpal Grewal. "Transnational Feminist Cultural Studies: Beyond the Marxism/Poststructuralism/Feminism Divides." Kaplan, Alarcón, and Moallem 349–63.

Karem, Jeff. "On the Advantages and Disadvantages of Postcolonial Theory for Pan-American Study." *The New Centennial Review* 1.3 (2001): 87–116.

Khatibi, Abdelkebir. "The Colonial Labyrinth." Trans. Catherine Dana. *Yale French Studies* 83 (1993): 5–11.

———. *Figures de l'étranger dans la littérature française.* Paris: Denoël, 1987.

Kroker, Arthur, and David Cook. *The Postmodern Scene: Excremental Culture and Hyper-Aesthetics.* New York: St. Martin's, 1986.

Kutzinski, Vera M. "Borders and Bodies: The United States, America, and the Caribbean." *The New Centennial Review* 1.2 (2001): 55–88.

LaCapra, Dominick. "Experience, Identity, Objectivity." Unpublished ms., October 2001.

Lafaye, Jacques. *Quetzalcóatl and Guadalupe: The Formation of Mexican National Consciousness 1531–1813.* Trans. Benjamin Keen. Chicago: U of Chicago P, 1976.

"La literature de latinos conquista Estados Unidos." <http://www.ambitoweb.com/seccionesespeciales/suplementos/libros/actual/Index_Libros.asp>.

Laviera, Tato. *AmeRícan.* Houston: Arte Público, 1985.

Lee, Rachel. "Notes from the (Non) Field: Teaching and Theorizing Women of Color." *Meridians* 1.1 (2000): 85–109.

Lipski, John M. "Rethinking the Place of Spanish." *PMLA* 117.5 (2002): 1247–51.

López, María Milagros. "Post-Work Selves and Entitlement 'Attitudes' in Peripheral Postindustrial Puerto Rico." *Social Text* 38 (Spring 1994): 111–33.

Lugones, María. "Hablando cara a cara/Speaking Face to Face: An Exploration of Ethnocentric Racism." *Making Face, Making Soul/Haciendo caras: Creative and Critical Perspectives by Women of Color.* Ed. Gloria Anzaldúa. San Francisco: Aunt Lute. 1990. 46–54.

Mansilla, Margarita. *Karenina Express.* Mexico: UNAM, 1995.

Martín-Barbero, Jesús. "Hegemonía comunicacional y des-centramiento cultural." Follari and Lanz 37–71.

McCarthy, Cormac. *All the Pretty Horses.* New York: Vintage, 1992.

———. *The Crossing.* New York: Vintage, 1994.

McCarthy, Nan. *Crash.* New York: Pocketbooks, 1998.

Méndez M., Miguel. *Peregrinos de Aztlán.* Tuscon: Editorial Peregrinos, 1974. Trans. David William Foster as *Pilgrims in Aztlán.* Tempe: Bilingual Press, 1992.

Mendieta, Eduardo. "What Can Latinas/os Learn from Cornel West: The Latino Postcolonial Intellectual in the Age of the Exhaustion of Public Spheres." *Nepantla* 4.2 (2003): 213–33.

Michaelson, Scott, and David E. Johnson, eds. *Border Theory: The Limits of Cultural Politics.* Minneapolis: U of Minnesota P, 1997.

Mignolo, Walter. *Local Histories/Global Designs: Coloniality, Subaltern Knowledges, and Border Thinking.* Princeton: Princeton UP, 2000.

Miller, J. Hillis. "Literary Study among the Ruins." *Diacritics* 31.3 (2001): 57–66.

Miyoshi, Masao. "In Place of a Conclusion." Jameson and Miyoshi, 371–83.

Monsiváis, Carlos. "De la cultura mexicana en vísperas del TLC." *La educación y la cultura ante el Tratado de Libre Comercio.* Ed. Julio López et al. Mexico: Nueva Imagen, 1992. 189–209.

Mora, Pat. *Borders.* Houston: Arte Público, 1986.

Morris, Meaghan. *Too Soon Too Late: History in Popular Culture.* Bloomington: Indiana UP, 1998.

Moya, Paula. "With Us or Without Us: The Development of a Latino Public Sphere." *Nepantla* 4.2 (2003): 245–52.

Moya, Paula, and Ramón Saldívar. "Fictions of the Transamerican Imaginary." *Modern Fiction Studies* 49.1 (2003): 1–18.

Murrell, Mary. "Is Literary Studies Becoming Unpublishable?" *PMLA* 116.2 (2001): 394–96.

Nabokov, Vladimir. *Lolita.* 1955. New York: Berkley, 1977.

Navarrete, Ruben, Jr. "Straddling Separate Worlds." *The Latino Condition: A Critical Reader.* Ed. Richard Delgado and Jean Setancic. New York: New York UP, 1998. 442–43.

Navarro, Mireya. "The Tricky Business of Cross-Cultural Theater." *New York Times* February 27, 2001. *<http://www.puertorico-herald.org>*.

Negrón-Muntaner, Frances, and Ramón Grosfoguel, eds. *Puerto Rican Jam: Essays on Culture and Politics.* Minneapolis: U of Minnesota P, 1997.

Nethersole, Reingard. "The Priceless Interval: Theory in the Global Interstice." *Diacritics* 31.3 (2001): 30–56.

Olalquiaga, Celeste. *Megalopolis: Contemporary Cultural Sensibilities.* Minneapolis: U of Minnesota P, 1992.

Olea, Raquel. "Feminism: Modern or Postmodern?" Beverley, Ovieda, and Aronna, 192–200.

Oropeza, Margarita. *Después de la montaña.* Hermosillo, Sonora: Instituto sonorense de cultura y gobierno, 1992.

Ortega, Julio. "El español, una lengua diversa." *El país* October 13, 2001. <http://www.elpais.es/suplementos/babelia/images1/1gris.gif>.

———. "Tres notas mexicanas." *Cuadernos hispanoamericanos* 381 (1982): 667–78.

Palumbo-Liu, David. *Asian/American: Historical Crossings of a Racial Frontier.* Stanford: Stanford UP, 1999.

Paz, Octavio. "Foreword: The Flight of Quetzalcóatl and the Quest for Legitimacy." Lafaye ix–xxii.

———. "Literatura hispana de y en los Estados Unidos." *Vuelta* 124 (March 1987): 54–56.

Paz-Soldán, Edmundo, and Alberto Fuguet. "Prólogo: El monstruo come (y baila) salsa." *Se habla español: Voces latinas en USA.* Miami: Alfaguara, 2000. 13–22.

Peña, Isaías. *José Eustasio Rivera.* Bogotá: Procultura, 1989.

Perea, Juan F. "Death by English." *The Latino Condition: A Critical Reader.* Ed. Richard Delgado and Jean Setancic. New York: New York UP, 1998: 583–95.

Poe, Edgar Allan. Review of *The Infidel. Southern Literary Messenger* June 1835: 582–85. <http://www.eapoe.org/works/criticsm/slm35b03.htm>.

Pratt, Mary Louise. "Daring to Dream: Re-Visioning Culture and Citizenship." *Critical Theory and the Teaching of Literature: Politics, Curriculum, Pedagogy.* Ed. James S. Slevin and Art Young. Urbana: National Council of Teachers of English, 1996. 3–20.

———. "What's Foreign and What's Familiar?" *PMLA* 117.5 (2002): 1283–87.

Prescott, William H. *History of the conquest of Mexico: with a preliminary view of the ancient Mexican civilization, and the life of the conqueror, Hernando Cortés.* New York: Harper & brothers, 1846.

Prida, Dolores. *Beautiful Señoritas and Other Plays.* Houston: Arte Público, 1991.

———. "The Show Does Go On." Horno-Delgado et al. 181–88.

———. "Coser y Cantar" in *Beautiful Señoritas and Other Plays.* Houston: Arte público, 1991. 47–67.

Quiroga, José. *Tropics of Desire: Interventions from Queer Latino America.* New York: New York UP, 2000.

Rangel Gómez, María Gudelia. Untitled ms., cited with permission, 1996.

Richardson, Edgar P. "The Athens of America: 1800–1825." Weigley 208–57.

Rivera-Valdés, Sonia. *The Forbidden Stories of Marta Veneranda.* Trans. Dick Cluster, et al. New York: Seven Stories, 2001.

———. *Las historias prohibidas de Marta Veneranda.* La Habana: Casa de las Americas, 1997.

Robbins, Bruce. "Introduction Part I: Actually Existing Cosmopolitanism." Cheah and Robbins 1–19.

———. "Comparative Cosmopolitanisms." Cheah and Robbins 246–64.

Rodriguez, Richard. *Days of Obligation: An Argument with my Mexican Father.* New York: Viking, 1992.

Rodríguez del Pino, Salvador. *La novela chicana escrita en español: Cinco autores comprometidos.* Ypsilanti: Bilingual Press, 1982.

Rodowick, D. N. "Introduction: Mobile Citizens, Media States." *PMLA* 117.1 (2002): 13–23.

Said, Edward. "Globalizing Literary Study." *PMLA* 116.1 (2001): 64–68.

Sainz, Gustavo. "A la búsqueda de un yo reflexivo." *Revista de estudios hispánicos* 29 (1995): 153–65.

———. *La novela virtual (atrás, arriba, adelante, debajo y entre).* Mexico: Joaquín Mortiz, 1998.

———. "A la búsqueda de un yo reflexivo." *Revista de estudios hispánicos.* 29 (1995): 153–165.

Salazar Trujillo, Boris. *La otra selva.* Bogotá: Tercer mundo, 1991.

Saldívar, José David, ed. *The Dialectics of Our America: Genealogy, Cultural Critique, and Literary History.* Durham: Duke UP, 1991.

———. *The Rolando Hinojosa Reader.* Houston: Arte Público, 1985.

Saldívar, Ramón. *Chicano Narrative: The Dialectics of Difference.* Madison: U of Wisconsin P, 1990.

Sandoval (Sánchez), Alberto. "Dolores Prida's *Coser y cantar*: Mapping the Dialectics of Ethnic Identity and Assimilation." Horno-Delgado et al. 201–20.

———. "Puerto Rican Identity Up in the Air: Air Migration, Its Cultural Representations, and Me 'Cruzando el Charco.' " Negrón-Muntaner and Grosfoguel 189–208.

Shaw, Donald L. "Three Post-Boom Writers and the Boom." *Latin American Literary Review* 24.47 (1996): 5–22.

Shell, Mark. "Language Wars." *The New Centennial Review* 1.2 (2001): 1–17.

Sollers, Werner. "Introduction." *Multilingual America: Transnationalism, Ethnicity, and the Languages of American Literature.* New York: New York UP, 1998. 1–13.

———. "Introduction." *The Multilingual Anthology of American Literature.* New York: New York UP, 2000. 1–11.

Sommer, Doris. "Choose and Lose." In *Multilingual America: Translation, Ethnicity, and the Languages of American Literature.* Ed. Werner Sollers. New York: New York UP, 1998. 297–309.

Sommer, Doris, and Alexandra Vega-Merino. "Introduction: Either/And." Braschi, *Yo-Yo Boing!*

———. "Introduction: Either/And." In *Yo-Yo Boing!* Giannina Braschi. Pittsburgh: Latin American Literary Review Press, 1998: 11–18.

Spivak, Gayatri Chakravorty. "Bonding in Difference." 273–85.

———."Cultural Talks in the Hot Peace: Revisiting the 'Global Village.' " Cheah and Robbins 329–48.

————. *The Post-Colonial Critic: Interviews, Strategies, Dialogues.* Ed. Sarah Harasym. New York: Routledge, 1990.

Stanton, Domna. "From Imperialism to Collaboration: How Do We Get There?" *PMLA* 117.5 (2002): 1266–71.

Stavans, Ilan. "The Gringo's Tongue: A Conversation with Ariel Dorfman." *Michigan Quarterly Review* 34.3 (1995): 303–12.

Stoler, Ann Laura. "Making Empire Respectable: The Politics of Race and Sexual Morality in Twentieth-Century Colonial Cultures." *Dangerous Liaisons: Gender, Nation, and Postcolonial Perspectives.* Ed. Anne McClintock, Aamir Mufti, and Ella Shohat. Minneapolis: U of Minnesota P, 1997. 344–73.

Sugg, Katherine. "Multicultural Masculinities and the Border Romance in John Sayles' *Lone Star* and Cormac McCarthy's Border Trilogy." *New Centennial Review* 1.3 (2001): 117–54.

Tabuenca Córdoba, María Socorro. "Border Perspectives desde las Fronteras: A Reading of Rosario Sanmiguel's 'El reflejo de la luna.' " *Living Chicana Theory*. Ed. Carla Trujillo. Berkeley: Third Woman P, 1998. 232–62.

Tarica, Estelle. "Creolité and French Caribbean Identity." Unpublished ms., cited with permission, 1999.

Tittler, Jonathan. "Neo-Colombian Literature: For a Loose Canon." *Dispositio* 16.41 (1991): 1221–32.

Todorov, Tzvetan. "Dialogism and Schizophrenia." Trans. Michael B. Smith. Arteaga 203–14.

Trilling, Lionel. *Sincerity and Authenticity*. Cambridge: Harvard UP, 1973.

United States Government, "2000 Census Report." <http://www.census.gov>.

Van Delden, Maarten, *Carlos Fuentes: Mexico and modernity*. Nashville: Vanderbilt University Press, 1998.

Varela, Félix. *Jicoténcal*. (1826) Ed. Luis Leal and Rodolfo J. Cortina. Houston: Arte Público, 1995.

———. *Xicontencatl*. Trans. Guillermo I. Castillo-Feliú. Austin: U of Texas P, 1999.

Vega, Ana Lydia. "De bípeda desplumada a escritora puertorriqueña con E y P machúsculas: Textimonios autocensurados." *La torre del viejo* 1.2 (1984): 44–48.

————. "Cloud-Cover Caribbean." Trans. Mark McCaffrey. *Her True True Name: An Anthology of Women's Writing from the Caribben*. Ed. Pamela Mordecai and Betty Wilson. London: Heinemann, 1989. 106–11.

———. *Encancaranublado y otros cuentos de naufragio*. Puerto Rico: Antillana, 1982.

———. "Pollito Chicken." *Vírgenes y mártires*. 73–79.

Vega, Ana Lydia, and Carmen Lugo Filippi. "Cuatro selecciones por una peseta." *Vírgenes y mártires*. Puerto Rico: Antillana, 1983: 127–37.

Villanueva, Tino. "A Brief History of Bilingualism in Poetry." *The Multilingual Anthology of American Literature*. New York: New York UP, 2000. 693–744.

Virilio, Paul. *The Information Bomb*. Trans. Chris Turner. New York: Verso, 2000.

———. *A Landscape of Events*. Trans. Julie Rose. Cambridge: MIT, 2000.

Visweswaran, Kamala. "Betrayal: An Analysis in Three Acts." *Scattered Hegemonies: Postmodernity and Transnational Feminist Practices*. Ed. Inderpal Grewal and Caren Kaplan. Minneapolis: U of Minnesota P, 1994. 90–109.

Wainwright, Nicholas B. "The Age of Nicholas Biddle: 1825–1841." Weigley 258–306.

Weber, Samuel. “Globality, Organization, Class.” *Diacritics* 31.3 (2001): 15–29.

Weigley, Russell, ed. *Philadelphia: A 300-Year History.* New York: Norton, 1982.

Welchman, John C. “The Philosophical Brothel.” *Rethinking Borders.* Ed. John C. Welchman. Minneapolis: U of Minnesota P, 1996. 160–86.

Williams, Stanley T. “The First Version of the Writings of Washington Irving in Spanish.” *Modern Philology* 28 (1930): 185–201.

———. *The Spanish Background of American Literature.* 2 vols. New Haven: Yale UP, 1955.

Index